HISTORY OF COMMUNISM IN BRITAIN

ESSAYS ON THE HISTORY OF COMMUNISM IN BRITAIN

BY

Michael Woodhouse

AND

Brian Pearce

NEW PARK PUBLICATIONS

Published by New Park Publications Ltd.,
186a Clapham High Street, London SW4 7UG

Set up, Printed and Bound
by Trade Union Labour

Distributed in the United States by:
Labor Publications Inc.,
135 West 14 Street, New York
New York 10011

ISBN 0 902030 77 9

Printed in Great Britain by
Grafton Litho Ltd. (TU)
150 Stonhouse Street, London SW4

Contents

CONTENTS

Publishers' Note

Marxism and Stalinism in Britain 1920-1926, by Michael Woodhouse.
Originally published in *Fourth International* vol. 4 no. 2 (July 1967)., vol. 5 no. 1 (February 1968), vol. 5 no. 2 (August 1968) and vol. 6 no. 1 (Summer 1969).

Some Past Rank and File Movements, by Brian Pearce.
Originally published in *Labour Review* vol. 4 no. 1 (April-May 1959), and reprinted as a separate pamphlet in November 1959.

British Communist History, by Brian Pearce.
Originally published in *Labour Review* vol. 2 no. 4 (July-August 1957), and reprinted in *Early History of the Communist Party of Great Britain* in August 1966.

Early Years of the Communist Party of Great Britain, by Brian Pearce.
Originally published in *Labour Review* vol. 3 no. 1 (January-February 1958), and reprinted in *Early History of the Communist Party of Great Britain* in August 1966.

The Communist Party and the Labour Left 1925-1929, by Brian Pearce.
Originally published in April 1957 as 'Reasoner' Pamphlet number one.

From 'Social-Fascism' to 'People's Front', by Brian Pearce.
Originally published in *Labour Review* vol. 2 no. 5 (September-October 1957).

The British Stalinists and the Moscow Trials, by Brian Pearce.
Originally published in *Labour Review* vol. 3 no. 2 (March-April 1958) and reprinted in *The Moscow Trials – An Anthology* published by New Park Publications in November 1967.

Introduction

This book brings together a series of articles dealing with the early struggles to establish the Marxist movement in Britain in the period after 1880, the historical problems this movement encountered and its later degeneration under the impact of Stalinism in the 1920s and 1930s. Originally published in the theoretical journals *Labour Review* and *Fourth International* between 1957 and 1969, they represent the first attempts within the British Trotskyist movement to develop a serious study of these questions.

The study of this history is now vital for a new generation of workers coming forward into revolutionary struggles at the onset of the severest slump in the history of capitalism. For the working class can never escape from its history. All its present great strengths and weaknesses are a reflection of the historical development of the class struggle, internationally and in Britain. Only now, by starting from the great tasks facing the working class in preparing for the social revolution, is it possible to grasp the real significance of the long-drawn-out struggle for Marxism in Britain.

This struggle has centred on the fight against sectarianism and opportunism within the British working class movement. By opportunism Marxists mean the tendency to substitute the immediate, short-term interests of sections of the class for its overall historical interests. The roots of this tendency are to be found in the peculiar course which the emergence of British capitalism took in the last centrry. By the middle of the nineteenth century British capital had established itself as the workshop of the world, the leading industrial, commercial and financial power. It was on this basis that a labour aristocracy was to emerge consisting of the most privileged and often conservative workers. But by the end of the nineteenth century this monopoly position was under increasing attack from Germany, America and later Japan. It was these changes in the relationship of British capitalism to world economy which were reflected in the changes in the labour movement of the period — notably the emergence of the 'New Unionism' of the unskilled in the 1880s and 1890s and later the great 'Labour unrest' in the years immediately preceding the First World War.

These changes in turn brought out the serious weakness which marked the early Marxist movement from the founding of the Social Democratic Federation in 1884. Its reaction tended to be impressionistic and empirical, either standing aside from the new forces which the class struggle was bringing forward, or tending to capitulate to the spontaneous movement of the working class and abandon the fight for revolutionary leadership. The idealist methods expressed in these responses fostered the emergence of a strong syndicalist tendency in the period before 1914. This was a tendency which opposed the fight for revolutionary politics in the working class, just as it opposed the building of a leadership independently of the reformist bureaucracy.

The First World War marked a decisive turning point in the history of the British working class movement. For it was after 1914 that the state increasingly intervened to regulate wages, working conditions and the movement of labour. What previously had been economic struggles now tended to become political issues, involving the capitalist state. During the war, and particularly towards its end, increasing layers of workers were thrust into a political fight against the government which provided valuable experiences, despite the continuing weaknesses of the left-wing groups and the betrayal of the labour leaders. But the most decisive event of all in the development of the Marxist movement in Britain was of course the Russian Revolution. It was to this revolution that all the most class conscious workers in Britain rallied, laying the basis for the creation of the single united Communist Party in 1920-21.

It was inevitable that this young Communist Party should inherit many of the weaknesses from the groups out of which it was formed. It was in any case only after considerable, protracted negotiations and concerted pressure from the Communist International that the various Marxist groups were able to come together to form the Communist Party of Great Britain. This was a measure of the deepseated sectarianism which remained.

In the early years after its foundation, the British Party, like all others, received considerable assistance from Lenin, Trotsky and the leadership of the Communist International. Lenin patiently explained the need to turn to the mass movement as the only way in which the propagandism of the past could be overcome. There was considerable discussion on these problems with Gallagher and the leaders of the Party. By 1923-24, on this basis, the Party was beginning to make significant progress. It strengthened considerably its trade union work and began to influence important elements within the Labour Party. Here the Reorganization Report of 1922-23 was of great value in that it began to establish a degree of centralism in a Party which had carried over many aspects of the federalist structure characterizing the pre-1920 groups.

This promising beginning was however to be cut short by the growth of Stalinism within the Soviet Union and the Communist International. This cannot be the place to deal with this development in detail. But it was the product of a series of defeats for the international working class in the early 1920s which left an economically and culturally backward Russia in temporary isolation. This was the material basis for the emergence of a conservative and parasitic bureaucracy inside Russia led by Stalin. The theoretical cornerstone for this bureaucracy became the 'theory' of socialism in one country, first advocated by Stalin in 1924, the year of Lenin's death. This theory rested on the quite false assumption that it would be possible to establish socialism in backward Russia; but until this was completed the Soviet bureaucracy would have to engage in a foreign policy of 'peaceful coexistence' with the capitalist world. Such was the theory of Stalinism as it emerged in the 1920s.

It was under the impact of these developments that the Communist International was transformed from an instrument to prepare the world socialist revolution into an appendage of the Soviet bureaucracy. The articles in this book indicate the implications which the growth of Stalinism had for the British Communist Party which, as its record in the 1926 General Strike exposed, was rapidly destroyed as a revolutionary instrument.

It is however important to stress the *international* nature of these developments. In centrist circles it has long been the fashionable view that Bolshevism is in some way 'alien' to the British working class movement. This is the standpoint of anti-Marxist theoreticians such as Kendall and Laski. They perpetrate the myth that the pre-1920

Marxist movement was fine — until it became contaminated with the disease of Bolshevism which ultimately destroyed it.

This is essentially the position taken up by the revisionists of the Thornett-Clinton school today. In their attacks on the Workers Revolutionary Party they try to equate centralism with Stalinism. Leninism for them is equal to Stalinism; the circle is squared, and Thornett's position is revealed for what it is: Menshevik hostility to the October Revolution.

This is exposed quite clearly in Thornett's document referring to the period covered by this book, where Thornett-Clinton claim that the degeneration of the CPGB resulted not from class forces but from a 'top-heavy' structure fostered by the Comintern's Reorganization Report. Here the contribution of the first four congresses of the Communist International is deliberately distorted into its opposite; the Leninist measures to strengthen the young Communist Parties are represented as the source of bureaucratization. (See *Whither Thornett?*, by Michael Banda, published by Workers Revolutionary Party 1975, especially pp. 37-44.)

In fact there is no possibility of building the revolutionary party without assimilating the lessons of the first four congresses. The formation of the Third International was a powerful blow against the petty-bourgeois idealism which expressed itself in opportunism and sectarianism in the British movement. It was only the defeats of the international working class during the 1920s which gave these tendencies the opportunity to reassert themselves. It is a measure of the degeneration of the Thornett group that they now openly reject these lessons and set out to strengthen the tendencies against which the Third International fought in the early years.

The revisionists of today above all seek to belittle the consistent and successful fight against Stalinism within the international and British working class movement. Throughout every turn and zig-zag of Stalinist policy in the 1920s and 1930s, Trotsky and the Left Opposition fought for a return to Lenin's revolutionary internationalism. And this fight found its reflection in Britain, albeit in small numbers of people who were often isolated from the working class. But these small numbers did reject Stalin's 'Third Period' policy in which the social democrats were designated social fascists, with such tragic consequences for the working class in Germany especially, as well as the Popular Front policy which followed it. On this basis a Trotskyist movement was established in Britain. Despite its many difficulties it grew and developed in struggle against Stalinism and revisionism, and now exists as the Workers Revolutionary Party, British section of the International Committee of the Fourth International.

The task of building this party is posed under vastly changed conditions from those described and analysed in this book. Today the working class is on the offensive all over the world, an offensive which is creating an ever greater crisis within the Stalinist movement. Revisionism seeks to deny this and to tie the working class to the bureaucracy at the very moment when it has no choice but to make an independent fight. As a part of this Thornett and the modern revisionists consciously distort the history of the struggle to build a communist party in Britain.

But for our movement the revolutionary crisis makes the lessons of this history vital. That is why every comrade who comes into the party must study the following pages, as the first attempts by British Trotskyism to analyse the early years of the Communist Party, and to take up the struggle waged by the Comintern under Lenin to build revolutionary parties to lead the working class to power.

Marxism and Stalinism in Britain 1920-1926

by M. Woodhouse

L. J. Macfarlane, in his work on the Communist Party of Great Britain (*The British Communist Party – Its Origin and Development until 1929*), has performed a valuable task for British Marxists in that he has brought together in one book the great bulk of material relevant to the history of Communism in Britain in the 1920s. What is debatable, however, is whether he has written a history of the CPGB that in itself elucidates this vital period in British working-class history when, for a few years, there was a real attempt to create a revolutionary party, and whether lessons can be drawn from the book as it stands that will enable the failures of the CPGB to be understood and help in the reconstruction of a revolutionary party in the present epoch.

The central point of interest in Macfarlane's book lies in his account of the role of the CPGB in the General Strike. The history of the party up to 1926 is the history of its preparation for such a development (which had been foreshadowed in the strike movements of 1919-21 and in the growing working-class confidence which attended the election of the first Labour Government, and led on to Red Friday); yet in this struggle, which was crucial for the emergence of the party as a mass revolutionary organization, capable of assuming leadership in opposition to the right-wing and centrist tendencies, the party appeared virtually *en bloc* with the General Council of the TUC and of account only as a militant and industrious 'ginger group' at local level.

It is a wasted labour to look to Macfarlane for an explanation of why the CPGB failed in its first decisive test as a revolutionary organization, for the whole of his book is permeated with the assumption that the CPGB could be no more than a 'ginger group', a militant and valuable addition to the post-1920 Labour movement but essentially unable to break the leadership of the Labour Party and TUC bureaucracies. This assumption is based very largely on Macfarlane's statement, for which he offers no substantiation, that 'The history of the

Communist Party of Great Britain in the nineteen-twenties is the story of the struggle to forge a revolutionary party in a non-revolutionary situation'.[1] This being the case, the struggles of the British working class in the 1920s to defend wages and conditions against the employers' attacks, the latter often backed by the power of the state, did not involve the question of political power and so defensive struggles only were possible. In these circumstances the role of the CPGB could only be that of agitating among the rank and file to hold the leadership of the Labour movement to its defensive policies, above all at the time of the General Strike. Essentially this is the meaning of Macfarlane's statement: 'Stalin's policy of working for a united Trade Union International through a concerted joint British-Russian trade union campaign was one which fitted in well with the British party's conception of trade union work. It also assisted the growth of the British party. This happy period ended with the General Strike'.[2] (i.e. when the right-wing ruptured the united front).

This statement, and the analysis on which it is based, wholly ignore the fact that the CPGB's position in 1926 represented a complete reversal of its policy towards the official leadership of the Labour movement up to 1925, and it can be shown (see below, Part 3) that Macfarlane ignores important material in arguing his case. Equally important, his analysis ignores the real development of the British working class up to 1926 and the relationship of this to the sharp changes in post-war British capitalism. From the end of the post-war boom it became clear that British capitalism could support itself, with its out-dated industries and weakened position as world financier, only by severe deflation, a level of unemployment that never fell below one million, a whole series of wage cuts, particularly in the 'unsheltered trades' — mining, engineering, etc. — and rationalization programmes which worsened conditions further. Initially British capitalism could stabilize itself in this way, heading off direct confrontation in 1919 by making judicious concessions, and then by choosing its time to decontrol the mines, relying on the leaders of the Triple Alliance to make no challenge to the state. Black Friday and the defeat of the miners in the lock-out of 1921 destroyed any hope of joint working-class resistance, and in the mood of demoralization after 1921 the working class turned to parliamentary action and the hope of reform via a Labour Government. Behind the disappointment of

---

[1] Macfarlane, p.275. [2] Macfarlane, p. 277

these hopes during the first Labour government lay the fact that the Conservatives, under Baldwin, had used the Labour interlude as a breathing space in which to consolidate their forces, in particular to deal with the disruptive efforts of the Liberals which threatened to distract attention from the need for a further, united capitalist offensive against the working class. During the period of the Labour government it became clear that a whole series of further attacks on working-class conditions and wages were required to 'stabilize' British capitalism, particularly after the implementation of the Dawes Plan.[3] Associated with this was the growing demand for the recapture of Britain's pre-eminence in international finance by a return to the gold standard, which required deflating at home and further downward pressure on wages to counteract the fact that at the pre-war parity sterling was over-valued, thus handicapping exports.

At the same time the mood of the working class was quite different from the 1922-23 period. Disillusionment with the Labour government prompted a move back to direct industrial action, but at a higher level of consciousness because of the experience of Black Friday. Amongst important sections of the working class the conviction developed of the inevitability of an all-out struggle against the Baldwin government and a determination that no retreats by the leadership, as in 1921, would be tolerated. Citrine, the acting secretary of the TUC General Council, who was at the centre of the activities of the TUC during Red Friday and the developments that led up to the General Strike, recorded how anxiety at the mood of the rank and file forced the General Council to act. 'We had visions of Black Friday, 1921, in our minds. On the present occasion the miners had expressly handed their powers over to the General Council, but it would not do to force a decision upon them.'[4] It was because of the experience of the working class over the previous six years that there was enthusiasm for the General Strike and a readiness to fight it through to a decisive

[3] The Dawes Plan was imposed on Germany after the French occupation of the Ruhr and the failure of the attempted revolution in Germany in the autumn of 1923. Designed to ensure the regular payment of reparations, it involved a severe attack on the wages and conditions of German workers and consequently, in the conditions of severe international competition in the 1920s, led to similar attacks elsewhere, notably in Britain, to restore competitiveness. Thus the Dawes Plan, which 'stabilized' the German economy, helped lay the basis for major conflicts in Britain.

[4] Lord Citrine, *Men and Work*, p. 167. Citrine here refers to the attempt of the General Council on the eve of the General Strike to get the MFGB to accept the proposals of the Samuel Commission, involving wage cuts, as a basis for negotiations.

conclusion. Far from their being in a non-revolutionary situation, the working class looked for a leadership that would give conscious expression to their objectively revolutionary aspirations. It was with this sort of development in mind — a sharp change in consciousness in relation to the permanent crisis in the economic basis — that Trotsky wrote:

> Today . . . every new sharp change in the political situation to the left places the decision in the hands of the revolutionary party. Should it miss the critical situation, the latter veers round to its opposite. Under these circumstances, the role of the party leadership acquires exceptional importance. . . .[5]

Given Macfarlane's premise, however, that the CPGB was operating in a non-revolutionary situation, he is not concerned to study the party's history from the point of view of a revolutionary leadership for the working class in the process of development. Nowhere does he examine the party's role in the various struggles of the working class between 1920 and 1926 and indicate how far the party assimilated the lessons of these struggles and corrected its mistakes in its effort to develop a revolutionary leadership. Similarly, Macfarlane never really considers to what degree the party's campaigns changed working-class consciousness and prepared the way for mass revolutionary action. Consequently, the party's history is presented almost wholly in organizational terms and its activities as a series of discrete events bearing little relationship to each other or to the overall development of the party. It follows from this that little attempt is made to understand the nature of the tendencies which gave birth to the CPGB or to appreciate the struggle of the CPGB to escape from its sectarian and syndicalist inheritance whilst at the same time differentiating itself from centrist tendencies in the Labour movement in the 1920s. In conformity with his presentation of the CPGB as a mere agitational group within the British Labour movement, moreover, Macfarlane is very little interested in the party's relationship to the Communist International except in the crucial period at the end of the twenties during the struggle for the ultra-left line. But what is of vital importance is to understand the process whereby the CPGB became 'Stalinized' by the mid-1920s and a willing tool of Stalin's policy of rapprochement with imperialism in this period, from which flowed the failure to prepare for revolutionary struggle in the General Strike.

[5] Trotsky, *The Third International After Lenin*, New Park Publications 1974, p. 63.

This is a question, along with others of equal importance, that Macfarlane totally fails to consider. Some of them will be taken up in the course of this review.

Part 1: The British Labour movement before 1914

Essential in understanding the early history of the CPGB is an appreciation of the radical changes in British capitalism in the two to three decades preceding the formation of the party and the revolutionary tendencies to which these changes gave birth. In fact, the twenty years before the CPGB came into existence had seen successive attempts to establish revolutionary groups and parties, and in the process strong tendencies were created which both formed the basis for the later CPGB, yet, at the same time, passed on to the CPGB an inheritance of sectarian, syndicalist and propagandist methods of work derived from a one-sided analysis of the needs of a revolutionary party and an adaptation to particular features of capitalism in this period. The first part of Macfarlane's book concerns itself with these groupings — the British Socialist Party (BSP), the Socialist Labour Party (SLP) and the Syndicalist movement — but only in an organizational sense and with no real attempt to characterize the tendencies they represented and their relationship to the specific conditions of British capitalism in the period before 1920.

The period up to 1914 represented the peak of the expansion of British imperialism; it was followed by the full employment of the war period and the brief inflationary post-war boom. This, then, was a period in which the working class was in an increasingly powerful bargaining position, a period when the objective conditions for extracting reforms were ripe. Yet the history of the period revealed that such reforms could be achieved only through the medium of an increasingly class-conscious and organized working class. Following a brief attempt by the Liberals after the 1906 election to check the move to independent working-class politics by posing as a rejuvenated and adequate vehicle for social reform, the antagonism of the propertied basis of the Liberal party towards the growing militancy of Labour (both in Parliament and in the constitituencies) put an end to effective concessions to the Parliamentary Labour Party from around 1909. The Miners' Minimum Wage Act of 1912 was scarcely an exception to this; conceding the principle rather than the substance it was received with indignation by wide sections of the rank and file, and even Enoch Edwards, President of the Miners' Federation of Great Britain and prominent Lib-Lab MP, was forced to bemoan the fact that the Liberal Government had given nothing away '. . . because we did expect at any rate that a Liberal Government would have taken their courage in their hands and accepted the 5s. and 2s. . . .' (i.e. the minima demanded by the MFGB). The fact was, of course, that even the limited recognition given by the Liberal government to the concept of the minimum wage had been made only as the result of struggles outside Parliament, beginning with the Cambrian Combine strike and proceeding through to the national miners' strike of 1912. To a considerable extent the 1912 strike, a major factor in which had been the syndicalist-inspired South Wales rank-and-file movement, exemplified the mood of advanced, well-organized sections of workers in the pre-war period. Among them was to be found a growing rejection of the amicable relations of the older generation of trade union officials with the employers and the state and of the parliamentary collaboration of the Labour Party with the Liberals. It was in relation to these developments, in a period when a determined struggle to link immediate demands for reform to socialist politics could have created a general socialist consciousness among wide sections of workers, that the revolutionary tendencies which came together to form the CPGB crystallized.

The upsurge in working class activity and organization from around 1900 was derived from two interrelated processes: accelerating changes in the structure of British capitalism and a continuation of the struggles of the 1880s — for independent working-class politics and industrial unionism — at a higher level. In 1885 Engels had drawn attention to the implications of the 'Great Depression' and the loss of Britain's economic predominance for the development of socialism in Britain:

> . . . during the period of England's industrial monopoly the English working class have, to a certain extent, shared in the benefits of the monopoly . . . With the breakdown of that monopoly the English working class will lose that privileged position; it will find itself generally — *the privileged and leading minority not excepted* — on a level with its fellow workers abroad. And that is the reason why there will be socialism again in England. [My emphasis — M. W.][6]

[6] Engels, quoting from his article in *The Commonweal*, March 1, 1885, in the Preface to the English edition of *The Condition of the Working Class in England* (1892).

The implication of Engels' statement, particularly the emphasized section, became increasingly clear in the ensuing decades. To meet the loss of its privileged position in world markets and the growth of modern technology in Germany and the USA, British industry was forced, despite its entrenched conservatism, to undertake a series of technological and structural changes whose tempo accelerated with the turn of the century. The drive towards the concentration of ownership and the rationalization of production techniques meant that important sections of the working class, not least the skilled 'aristocrats' of the metal-working trades, came under increasing attack as traditionally established working conditions were eroded and swept away. These changes can be most clearly illustrated from two industries, engineering and mining; in the first there were considerable technological changes, in the other there were few. In both industries there was a marked move, from the 1890s, towards concentration of ownership. In engineering this provided the basis for the introduction of mass production techniques which hit directly at the established craft position of the engineer, based as it was on limited techniques, high levels of personal skill and considerable control over job and workshop practice by the engineer. As the experience of the erosion of privileged status became general, it produced, in less than two decades, a reversal, generally speaking, of the trade union outlook of the engineers. For important sections of the engineers the methods of the 'model' trade unionism of the Amalgamated Society of Engineers, established in the boom years of mid-Victorian capitalism, appeared out-dated; pressure developed from the early 1890s for a centralized union based on class, not craft, interests. This pressure was greatly increased after the experience of the 1898 lock-out of the engineers, when it became clear that employers were determined to break the established practices on which craft unionism rested. A series of powerful unofficial strikes coupled with a mounting reform agitation produced the rules revision of 1912 and the decision to bring unskilled workers into the ASE.[7]

This was a most significant development. What had been a relatively conservative section of the working class had moved towards a realization of the need for a direct confrontation with the powerful national organization of the employers. Moreover, sections of the engineers, particularly the generation coming into the industry from

[7] J. B. Jeffreys, *The Story of the Engineers*, chapter 7, passim.

the turn of the century, looked for forms of revolutionary organization which would permit a direct struggle to be waged against capitalism. For many, the Labour Party appeared irrelevant to the immediate, serious questions on the shop floor, which could only be solved by powerful trade union organization. Thus, at the same time as the Labour Party became increasingly subservient to Liberalism in Parliament, the complementary idea developed of the use of industrial organization for direct political action. A member of the ASE summed up this growing idea when he stated, in 1909: 'The most charitable thing that can be said about political action (i.e. the Parliamentary Labour Party) is that it is slow, so slow that it breaks men's hearts.'[8]

For a number of the younger generation of engineers the campaign against the employers' offensive and for the reform of the ASE on industrial unionist lines was seen in revolutionary terms, as a struggle that could lead on by a natural progression to the establishment of workers' control. It was in such terms that the Amalgamation Committee Movement (an offshoot of Tom Mann's Syndicalist movement) was established in the engineering industry in England in 1912 to work for industrial unionism, and this was one of the organizations from which the Shop Stewards' Movement crystallized during the war. In Scotland the SLP, through its campaigns to establish alternative revolutionary trade unions (the Industrial Workers of Great Britain) attracted a number of the younger generation of engineers who initially organized the Singer works and later became prominent in the Clyde Workers' Committee.[9] Yet this development was essentially contradictory. While the changes in the engineering industry created the conditions for the emergence of revolutionary tendencies, the preoccupation of most advanced engineers was not really with the question of working-class power, except in a very formal sense, but with preservation of their own power within the engineering workshops. In so far as the Syndicalist movement in engineering reflected this particular preoccupation alone it remained a limited and, in some senses, retrogressive movement. On the eve of the war J. T. Murphy recorded that this was very much the situation in the Amalgamation Committee Movement. In Sheffield he noted that:

> . . . the questions under discussion were very practical — the encroachment of unskilled workers on to skilled workers' jobs; the new machine processes and the division of labour that was going on apace in the

[8] Ibid, p.161.

[9] Tom Bell, *Pioneering Days*, pp.72-75 & 99.

workshops; the wages question; the hours of labour, overtime and the speed-ups and our organizational weaknesses.[10]

Despite the greater influence and revolutionary potential of the Shop Stewards' Movement during the war, much the same could be said of this organization, and it was only under the stimulus of the Russian Revolution that the interests of the shop stewards began to embrace the question of revolutionary action as well as the defence of their immediate workshop conditions.

In the mining industry a similar process of radicalization occurred among the generation coming into mining from the turn of the century. Unlike engineering the mining industry experienced no significant technological change before the first world war. In the face of intense conservatism, lack of capital and the difficulties of introducing mechanization, the industry remained technologically stagnant. Yet this same period witnessed a drive towards centralization of ownership, particularly in the exporting areas (notably South Wales) which felt the sharpest effects of world competition. In South Wales, for example, the Powell Duffryn Combine or the Cambrian Combine of D. A. Thomas typified the methods of advanced coalowners, to concentrate productive units to allow the full exploitation of existing techniques and to extend vertically at the same time into by-products, docks, railways and shipping. In an industry where the labour costs represented around 70 per cent of the whole, rationalization without technological innovation meant a drive to cut wages and speed up production at the expense of greater physical exertion. This was marked throughout the coalfields from the turn of the century, particularly after the introduction of the Eight Hours Act in 1909. Against the disinclination of the local and national leadership of the Miners' Federation to put up any effective resistance to this process, which involved widespread attacks on customarily established conditions, notably payment for 'dead work', powerful rank-and-file opposition developed which was canalized by the campaigns of the South Wales Unofficial Reform Committee into the demand for the minimum wage. Under the pressure of this campaign the 1912 strike was fought and the minimum partially won.

Here, as in engineering, the response of numbers of young miners to changing conditions in the industry and the attendant sharpening of class antagonisms had been to see the struggle against the coalowners in revolutionary terms and to look for a direct form of

[10] J. T. Murphy, *New Horizons*, p.35.

revolutionary struggle through 'direct action'. For the Syndicalists of the South Wales Unofficial Reform Committee the campaign for the minimum had been coupled with a repudiation of parliamentary action, and for many miners the mutilation of their demands in the 1912 Minimum Wage Act convinced them of the futility of the Labour Party as a reformist annexe of Liberalism.

The examples of engineering and mining indicate that the change in consciousness of the working class that produced the 'labour unrest' of the pre-1914 period was a reaction not merely to the decline in real wages, as argued by historians of this period, but to deep-going changes in the organization of capitalism, particularly to the increasingly powerful organizations of employers and their growing reliance on the state power. This was the experience of wide sections of workers from the 1890s, skilled and unskilled alike. The newly organized general unions, the engineers and the miners all came into conflict with nationally organized, powerful employers' federations from the 1890s; at the same time the state, through the medium of the law courts and repressive agencies, police and military, fully backed the moves of the employers to break the new unions and humble the miners and engineers.[11] In fact, even before the Taff Vale judgment workers had evidence of a whole series of court rulings directed against the power of the trade unions, and exploiting the ambiguities of the trade union legislation of the 1870s.

The impetus these developments gave to independent working-class politics and the formation of the Labour Representation Committee was only one of the results of the experiences of the 1890s. As the 'Great Depression' passed away and the bargaining power of the working class increased there was a rapid growth of the understanding of the need for a movement outside Parliament to meet the employers on their own terms. The second wave of new unionism developed on this basis and from the earlier experiences of this form of organization in the 1880s and '90s. The new upsurge was marked by more definite and developed aims and a tenacity and determination to win that often went far beyond the union leadership, a fact that applied as much to the London dock strike of 1911, where Tillett represented 'advanced' trade union leadership, as it did to the rail strike of the same year.[12]

---

[11] See J. Saville, 'The Trade Unions and Free Labour: the Background to the Taff Vale Decision', in A. Briggs and J. Saville, *Essays in Labour History*.

[12] See Sires, 'Labour Unrest in England', 1910-1914, *Journal of Economic History*, 1955.

The recurring strikes which preceded the First World War were not in themselves revolutionary; they arose from immediate aims — wages, better trade union organization, the enforcement of collective bargaining — yet they led to direct clashes with the state power (e.g. in the Cambrian Combine strike, 1910, and the rail strike and Liverpool dock strike of 1911) and revealed that even in a peak period of prosperity for British imperialism reforms could be obtained only through powerful and determined working-class organization. This in itself represented a marked change in the decade since 1900. The propaganda work for working-class political independence, the campaign for working-class representation on local government bodies, School Boards, Boards of Guardians, etc., the formation of the Labour Representation Committee itself, had all helped to create, through molecular processes within the working class, a sense of class identity and the growth of political understanding. Superficially, this appeared to be a slow, hesitating process in the period up to the election of the 1906 Liberal Government, yet within the course of a few years it was revealed that this preparatory work had evoked a readiness to fight which went far beyond the Lib-Lab pressure-group politics of the Parliamentary Labour Party. These struggles indicated the emergence of an objective basis for revolutionary politics in Britain, though in themselves they did not, of course, represent any form of spontaneous revolutionary activity. The highest form of organization to emerge from them was the Triple Alliance (negotiations for the formation of which began in 1913) and this, as the negotiations to form it revealed, was seen by the leaders of the unions involved largely as a pressure group for obtaining better trade union legislation, a glorified form of TUC Parliamentary Committee.[13]

An important factor in the development towards the assertion of independent working-class power was the role assumed by young workers. Writing of the widespread strikes of 1910, most of them carried out in opposition to the trade union leaders, Askwith, head of the Labour Department of the Board of Trade, recorded that they were 'largely due to the action of young men'.[14] In a whole number of industries undergoing radical change in this period the new generation of workers was confronted with major changes in industrial

---

[13] As revealed in the statements of trade union leaders, particularly Robert Smillie, at the joint conferences of the MFGB, NUR and TWF, April 23, 1914, and December 9, 1915.

[14] Sir G. Askwith, *Industrial Problems and Disputes*, p.134.

organization and, largely free from the past ingrained traditions of working-class organization, eagerly sought new forms of organization that would allow a direct struggle against the employers and their state. Marxism supplied them with an explanation of the basic reason for the class war with which they were so starkly confronted, and on the main tenets of Marxism they sought to establish a movement which would contend with the bourgeoisie for power. The youth were forced to this position by the logic of events from the turn of the century. The period up to 1914 saw the relatively widespread and rapid attack in key industries on the established customs and privileges built up during the boom years of Victorian capitalism. These attacks rendered the old forms of organization increasingly obsolete and rendered ineffective the established methods of defence. It was the younger generation of workers who were forced to take up the fight for new methods of working-class organization, and in conditions when the movement for working-class political independence was accelerating, the tendency was to turn to aggressive forms of organization transcending the defensive mentality associated with earlier forms of trade union organization. Such a movement was clear among the new generation of workers in engineering, the railways and transport industries who played such a key role in the strike movements after 1900. It was particularly clear among the miners, above all in South Wales.

In South Wales the struggles which culminated in the Cambrian Combine strike were led for the most part by young miners who were in revolt against the dominance of the chapel and the permeation of the leadership of the South Wales Miners Federation with the philosophy of religious non-conformity, with its emphasis on industrial peace and conciliation. The chapel itself, which hitherto had embraced a large section of miners, local tradesmen, coalowners and their officials, was increasingly split on class lines in this period as the drive of the South Wales owners to rationalize production intensified after the 1898 lockout. Inevitably in these circumstances nonconformity, especially Methodism, was forced to reveal the nature of its allegiance to capitalism, to whose interests in South Wales it gave ideological expression. To the young miner, groping his way towards a materialist explanation of the world and towards an effective form of organization against the attacks of the local coalowners, the chapel appeared increasingly as a barrier to social progress. Based fundamentally on the vested interests of property, the chapel denounced militant trade unionism; as the organizational expression of the Liberal Party in South Wales it denounced movements towards independent working-class politics. For the new generation of miners it was therefore seen as a hostile force, a survival of the past history of the miners when the chapel had served to help in the adjustment to industrial life and had played a limited part in developing trade unionism but now was rendered obsolete by the new problems facing the miners.

The movement of the new generation towards a materialist outlook was not straightforward, however. Rejection of the chapel did not necessarily mean the rejection of religion. The great religious revival of 1904-5, started by a young ex-miner, was a last desperate attempt to find a solution, in religious terms and within its past ideological traditions, to the increasing insecurity in the mining community. The revival, significantly, took place outside the chapel and quite spontaneously. The nonconformist establishment had little to do with it and it attracted a considerable number of young miners who were looking for a new social philosophy. Ablett, later the most prominent of the South Wales Syndicalists, took up training for the chapel as a result of the revival, as did Horner, who became a Baptist preacher during the war when he was, at the same time, a member of the Unofficial Reform Committee.[15] The effect of the revival was necessarily ephemeral. It could provide no answers to the problems which gave birth to it and a substantial number of miners attracted by it went on to seek a direct solution to their problems through political action. The Independent Labour Party (ILP) expanded in South Wales with the passing of the revival (taking over, incidentally, a large part of the religious outlook of non-conformity) while a significant number went beyond this to Marxism. Ablett abandoned his chapel training to become the leader of this tendency, which found its expression in the Plebs League, established in 1909. For the Plebs members in South Wales the main question was the creation of a revolutionary trade union which would be able to check the owners' attacks and eventually be able to seize control of the mines. A major part of their propaganda was for 'militant materialism' against the chapel and its ideological hold over the Welsh miners.

The developments sketched above provided the basis for the emergence of revolutionary tendencies in the period before 1914. The attempts in this period to establish revolutionary leaderships were

---

[15] A. Horner, *Incorrigible Rebel.*

characterized, however, by a one-sided reaction to the mounting class struggle in industry and the growing propensity for independent working-class action via the Labour Party. In many ways these one-sided reactions were the immediate response of young workers to the developments sketched above, and the generation of young militants who came to the fore in the working-class movement after 1900 were to provide the leadership for the CPGB which emerged in 1920. The tendencies they represented were carried over into the CPGB and their inter-relationship must be understood if the forces shaping the party at its birth are to be appreciated. Although he describes the main phases in the development of these tendencies — the BSP, the SLP, the Syndicalist movements — Macfarlane makes no real attempt to relate them to the specific developments in the working class which gave rise to them or to understand their political significance in relation to the later practice of the CPGB.

Part 2: Tendencies in the early Communist movement

The Marxist tendencies which existed in the period immediately prior to the formation of the CPGB stemmed from the Social Democratic Federation (SDF), the only Marxist party which existed in 1900. The Marxism of the SDF was an extreme form of the essentially arid and dogmatic Marxism of the main parties of the Second International in this period, most notably the German Social Democrats and their ideologue, Kautsky. In Britain the adherence of the SDF to formal aspects of Marxism, rather than to its use as a method for understanding society in order to actively intervene in its transformation, was more clearly revealed than in Germany, where the SPD had a mass following. In Britain the SDF was able, to a limited extent, to play the role of awakening the class consciousness of sections of the working class and of helping to develop the understanding of the need for independent political action, but this was hampered by the sectarianism of the SDF leadership. Work was undertaken by the party rank-and-file often quite spontaneously at local level and irrespective of the attitude of the party leadership. Such work was often carried out in close co-operation with non-Marxist 'reformist' organizations, e.g. the ILP and the Clarion Scouts, and in many areas the SDF, in organization and political outlook, closely resembled the ILP.

Activities of this sort could be very fruitful in creating the conditions for the emergence of independent political consciousness among workers; the actions of SDF branches in relation to the London County Council and parliamentary constituencies in the East End of London were very significant in this respect.[16] But such activities were undertaken largely intuitively in response to the growing feeling of the need for an independent working-class party. In the absence of any guidance from the leadership of the SDF the party's local branches were not acting upon a political estimation of the role Marxists could play in the formation of a mass working-class party that would initially be purely reformist and 'labourite' in consciousness. Such a party, as Engels clearly realized, was a necessary first step for the development of revolutionary consciousness, but to transcend this stage a creative application of Marxist theory to the question of changing reformist to revolutionary practice was required. The work of the local SDF branches met the first of these requirements but to meet the second the dogmas of the SDF leadership and the sectarian methods flowing from them had to be overcome; as Engels noted, writing in the early 1890s on the position of the SDF and Fabian Society:

> . . . both in the SDF and in the Fabian Society the provincial members were better than the central body. But that is of no avail as long as the attitude of the central body determines that of the Society.[17]

To a large extent, the leadership of the SDF was drawn from a section of the bourgeoisie and upper reaches of the petty bourgeoisie who were disorientated by the collapse of the mid-Victorian boom, the 'Great Depression' and the relative economic decline of Britain, and who derived from Marxism a series of formulae which predicted the imminent collapse of capitalism and indicated salvation through the revolutionary action of the working class, suitably led by these converts to Socialism from the privileged classes. For a number of advanced workers, particularly in London, who were moving under the impact of the depression from Liberal-Radicalism to Socialism, the theories of Hyndman, with their emphasis on the need for a revolutionary party for the working class, completely separate from the two established bourgeois parties, were distinctly attractive. For some of these workers (Harry Quelch is the best example) the strategy

---

[16] See P. Thompson, 'Liberals, Radicals and Labour in London', *Past and Present*, 1964.

[17] Marx and Engels, *On Britain*, p. 576.

established by Hyndman for the SDF in the 1880s became almost a religion, an immutable expression of the absolute truths of Marxism; as Engels expressed it, writing to Sorge in America:

> The Social Democratic Federation here shares with your German-American Socialists the distinction of being the only parties who have contrived to reduce the Marxist theory of development to a rigid orthodoxy. This theory is to be forced down the throats of the workers at once and without development as articles of faith, instead of making the workers raise themselves to its level by dint of their own class instinct. That is why both remain mere sects ...[18]

Holding that the collapse of capitalism was an inevitable and automatic process, the leaders of the SDF adopted for themselves the role of the ultimate inheritors of state power when the collapse occurred. To play its revolutionary role correctly, therefore, it had to remain doctrinally 'pure' and free from compromise with reformist tendencies in the Labour movement.

In a period when significant sections of the working class were beginning to move towards political action independent of the two bourgeois parties as well as towards a major extension of trade unionism, the leadership of the SDF stood aside from such developments. Work in the trade unions was at best self-defeating, if not irrelevant; they could play no part in the transition to Socialism in that, by bargaining for better wages, they supported the wages system and thus capitalism. Partly under pressure from the membership of the SDF and partly in the hope of playing the chief role in the formation of a united Socialist party, Hyndman and the leaders of the SDF participated in the negotiations leading to the establishment of the Labour Representation Committee (LRC), but within a year, when it was found impossible to convert the trade union-dominated LRC to a specifically Socialist programme, the SDF withdrew from the LRC. There was much to justify Engels' assertion, as far as the leaders were concerned, that '... the SDF is purely a sect. It has ossified Marxism into a dogma and, by rejecting *every* labour movement which is not orthodox Marxism ...it renders itself incapable of ever becoming anything else but a sect ...'[19]

The chief responsibility for the sectarianism of the SDF devolved upon the small clique of founder members who dominated the executive by the turn of the century; Hyndman, Belfort Bax, Burrows and

[18] *Ibid.* p. 582.

[19] *Ibid.*, p. 574.

Quelch. The maintenance of their hegemony depended not only on their operation of a fairly tight bureaucracy but also on the fact that no alternative to their political theories was seriously advanced within the SDF. The period after 1900 was to see increasing opposition to the leading clique, from those who broke away to form the Socialist Labour Party (SLP) and the Socialist Party of Great Britain (1903-4) and from those who wanted a return to 'ginger group' activities within the Labour Party, but there was never any theoretical understanding of the political significance of the 'Marxism' of Hyndman; the approach to Marxism which the opposition groups adopted was very much of the type evolved by the SDF over the previous period.

The political manifestations of the 'Marxism' of Hyndman and his colleagues in fact produced among their opponents in the SDF membership reactions that were wholly empirical in character. Hyndman's theories 'did not work'; better ways had to be found. Such attitudes derived very largely from the practical experience of the SDF's sectarianism. Treating Marxism as a set of dogmas, the leadership were unable to apply Marxism as a method to the day-to-day needs of the party in its work among the working class. The SDF consequently tended to vacillate between ultra-revolutionary and purely reformist policies and appeared thoroughly opportunist in practice. After the disappearance of the expectation of cataclysmic revolutionary upheavals in the 1880s, the SDF's revolutionary strategy rested wholly upon the concept of a peaceful, parliamentary transition to Socialism. The work of the SDF came to be based almost wholly upon parliamentary and local electioneering. Vital though this was as part of a general strategy for awakening working-class political consciousness, so far as the SDF leadership was concerned it represented the totality of their activities. In its day-to-day practice, therefore, the SDF appeared as reformist as the ILP, but, because of its sectarian approach to the unions, far less influential. Moreover, in the absence of any theoretical understanding of the connection between participation in local government (where the SDF did obtain successes) and the creation of working-class political consciousness, the SDF members elected to public positions tended to become wholly involved in the routine of local government, trapped within its limitations, and their political outlook increasingly moulded by this limiting experience.

The Socialist Labour Party was formed as a breakaway of several Scottish branches of the SDF (with a few in Southern England) in opposition to the growing opportunism of the SDF leadership. The break was of significance not only in that it represented the outcome of mounting opposition to the Bax-Hyndman group by young working-class militants, but in its association with the current struggle within the Second International against revisionist and opportunist tendencies. The issues involved in the debate at the International's 1900 Congress on the entry of Millerand, the French Socialist, into the French government at the height of the Dreyfus crisis were brought directly into the struggle within the SDF which culminated in the formation of the SLP in 1903. The support given by the SDF delegation at the Paris Congress to Kautsky's resolution allowing participation in bourgeois governments in specific circumstances (the 'india-rubber' resolution) was strongly attacked by militants at the 1901 Annual Conference of the SDF, particularly by the Scottish delegates soon to take the lead in forming the SLP. The support of the SDF leadership for Kautsky's resolution was clearly considered support for opportunism, and was coupled with the growing evidence of the opportunist practice of the SDF in Britain.[20] Opposition to revisionism, therefore, or, more accurately, to its practical aspects, was an integral part of the movement of working-class militants in the SDF to a revolutionary position.

However, the reaction against the SDF was purely empirical. It was attended by none of the theoretical investigation of the roots and nature of revisionism currently being carried out by Rosa Luxemburg. The SLP looked instead for a form of organization which would permit more direct access to the working class, which would lead to a more direct confrontation with capitalism than the 'parliamentarianism' of the SDF and which would permit the preservation of the revolutionary purity that had attended the struggles of the SDF in its early years. In its policies the SLP carried over from the SDF an adherence to Marxism as a set of formulae, not a guide to action, to be safeguarded from reformist corruption by a rejection of all forms of tactical alliance with reformist organizations within the Labour movement, trade unions and political parties alike. The SLP thus represented what was really an intuitive reaction against that process whereby organized sections of the working class were being adapted to capitalism via the medium of trade union and political bureaucracies, and with its ideas of revolutionary action through the establishment of industrial unions the SLP sought to by-pass this growing

[20] For details of the formation of the SLP, see Tsuzuki, 'The Impossibilist Revolt in Britain', *International Review of Social History*, 1956.

bureaucracy. At the same time, the reaction against bureaucracy in the Labour movement was accompanied by a hostility to the permeation of the movement by Fabian ideas, particularly to the ultimate goal of Fabianism, collectivist bureaucratic capitalism. Against the 'state socialist' ideas of the leaders of the ILP and Labour Party, which the SLP saw as the vehicle for this form of collectivism, was posed the conception of a Socialist system based upon the direct control of production by the working class through their industrial unions. Connolly (who was intimately connected with the formation and early development of the SLP) clearly characterized this system and the process whereby it would be created:

> . . .In the light of this principle of Industrial Unionism every fresh shop or factory organized under its banner is a fort wrenched from the capitalist class and manned with the soldiers of the revolution to be held by them for the workers.
>
> On the day that the political and economic forces of labour finally break with capitalist society and proclaim the Workers' Republic these shops and factories so manned by Industrial Unionists will be taken charge of by the workers there employed and force and effectiveness given to that proclamation . . .[21]

The concept of Socialist revolution set out by Connolly, as J. T. Murphy noted,[22] powerfully influenced every revolutionary movement in Britain up to the formation of the CPGB, and Connolly's schema was very characteristic of the Marxism of these movements. Such Marxism was permeated with positivist and idealist assumptions. It saw in Marx's writings the best description of the capitalist system and drew from this description the clear fact of the class struggle between workers and employers, based on industrial exploitation. The state, government and political parties were mere reflexes of this basic fact of the industrial class war, and although both Connolly and the SLP stressed the need for political (i.e. parliamentary) action in order to awaken working-class political consciousness, the emphasis was placed on the primacy of industrial organization for both immediate and eventual revolutionary ends. As a general perspective for working-class action there was nothing here with which a Marxist could disagree, but in the practice of the SLP this perspective was reduced to an ideal scheme which was inextricably linked to the mechanical approach of the SLP to Marxism. The movement of the

---

21 Connolly, *Socialism Made Easy*

22 J. T. Murphy, *Preparing for Power*, p. 90.

working class towards a revolutionary position was seen as an automatic reflex to the development of capitalism from an individualistic to a monopoly form. As ownership became concentrated and employers nationally organized, so the working class would see the need for the establishment of industrial unions, embracing all the workers in an industry, in place of the old, narrow, craft unions. As the quotation from Connolly indicates, the very process of constructing such unions would lead the working class towards the conquest of power; the process was automatic, and the transition to Socialism would occur, through an undefined cataclysmic upheaval, when the working class was fully organized in industrial unions. The role of the party in this process was necessarily limited and essentially propagandist. It existed to make clear to the working class the nature of capitalism and the need for class, not craft, industrial organization to confront the bourgeoisie. The SLP existed, in fact, like the SDF, not to give leadership on day-to-day issues as an expression of a fully considered Marxist position on current problems, but to awaken in the minds of workers the idea of revolutionary socialism and the idea of how to organize to achieve it.

The expectation was that, if instructed sufficiently well, the working class would spontaneously move towards a revolutionary position through the adoption of the ideal organization, the industrial union. The description given by T. A. Jackson of the working of an SDF branch in this period equally well applied, with a few minor changes, to that of an SLP branch and indicated the purely propaganda role of the party:

> The normal SDF branch numbered something between a score and fifty — the regular attenders at a branch meeting being somewhat better than a dozen. The customary routine was, after the minutes and correspondence, to fix arrangements for the Sunday propaganda meetings, and for any weekday meetings there might be. The life activity of the branch centred around these propaganda meetings. . . .The speeches at these open air meetings usually took the form of a general statement of socialist aspirations, a general criticism of capitalism and its evils, and a special application to current happenings — particularly the doings of the local Borough or Town Council . . .[23]

Inevitably, so brief a characterization of the theory of the SLP is over-rigid, but essentially it was this theory that the SLP developed in

---

[23] T. A. Jackson, *Solo Trumpet*, pp. 54-55.

the years before 1914 in its attempt to find a direct, revolutionary road to the working class. Moreover, the importance of the contribution of the SLP to the theory and practice of the revolutionary movement in Britain should not be underestimated. Despite the miniscule size of the party itself, the propaganda of the SLP had considerable influence in shaping the outlook of the leaders of the industrial ferment of the immediate pre-war period. In a period of deepening class struggle, when young militants were looking for new forms of organization, the theories of the SLP, widely circulated in a series of excellently produced pamphlets by the Socialist Labour Press, had considerable attraction and played no small part in the shaping of the amorphous body of ideas that became known as Syndicalism around 1910. At the time when Tom Mann began interpreting French anarcho-syndicalist methods in terms of the British working-class experience in 1910, SLP ideas were already influential among advanced workers. Among the railworkers, miners and engineers of the pre-1914 period particularly SLP ideas took root; the theories of the SLP, developed in opposition to the growing bureaucracy in the Labour movement, were a major factor in the Ruskin strike in 1909 which led to the establishment of the Plebs League and the Labour College movement. Students from the mining and railway unions were prominent in this development, and the *Miners' Next Step,* produced by members of the Plebs League, displayed definite signs of the influence of SLP ideas.

The significant fact about the theories of the SLP however, was that although they became an integral part of the theoretical equipment of advanced workers in this period, they did not lay the basis for the construction of a mass revolutionary party. The fact was that in reducing Marxism to a few basic postulates on the nature of capitalism and presenting the movement of the working class towards Socialism as an automatic process, the SLP had obscured both the role of the party and the need for the working class to destroy the existing bourgeois state in order to effect the Socialist revolution. In the last analysis the SLP's theories could be reduced to the purely practical premise of the need for effective trade union organization, and it was in this sense that the SLP prepared the way theoretically for the growth of syndicalism in Britain.

The development of the SLP was not the only reaction to the growing bureaucratic control and sterile formulae of the SDF leadership. From the turn of the century there was a parallel movement to the SLP within the SDF, in this case to turn the SDF away from its sectarianism and towards affiliation with the Labour Party. This tendency was, in effect, the obverse of that represented in the SLP; it originated from the same reaction against the SDF leadership but sought to orientate the SDF towards the mass Labour movement via the LRC and, later, the Labour Party. Thus while the SLP looked for a direct revolutionary route to the working class through its theories of industrial unionism, the opposition that remained inside the SDF looked for a similar route to the working-class masses through the LRC which, it held, could be converted by the SDF to Socialism. Objectively, these two tendencies represented in a fragmented way an important reaction against the methods established by the SDF by the turn of the century. Both were an intuitive recognition of the need for mass work at a time when the working class was only beginning to develop an awareness of its separate class interests, but because the two tendencies were completely separated, the one in the SLP, the other in what became the BSP by 1911, the two aspects of mass work, in the Labour Party and trade unions, were not to be united in an overall revolutionary perspective until the formation of the CPGB. As a result of this, both tendencies suffered from the weaknesses attendant upon their one-sided reaction to the leadership of the SDF and the particular stage reached by the British working class in the 1900s.

The major question before Marxists in Britain from the 1880s was the creation of an independent working-class party in conditions where the working class as a whole were only beginning to awake to their antagonism to capital. The immediate issues raised in this process were the extension of the trade unions and the mounting demand for social reform; as Engels appreciated, a movement for working-class political independence would have to concentrate on these immediate issues and through the process of agitating on them develop a Socialist consciousness among the working class.[24] The relevance of Engels' suggestions for British Marxists was increasingly appreciated by rank-and-file members of the SDF. In the 1890s there was a significant degree of local co-operation between the members of the SDF and the ILP over immediate issues, while from 1901, when the SDF decided to withdraw from the non-Socialist, trade union-dominated LRC, this experience of the 1890s produced, in areas where the SDF had a significant working-class membership (as in

[24] See Engel's articles in the *Labour Standard* for 1881, reprinted in *The British Labour Movement*.

Lancashire) a growing demand for the repudiation of the sectarian SDF leadership and re-affiliation with the LRC. It was only in this way, the supporters of this tendency agreed, that the SDF could play an effective role in converting the working class to socialism; to reject affiliation meant isolating the LRC from Marxism and leaving its supporters at the mercy of the vague, petty-bourgeois ideology of the ILP. 'Are we', asked a Lancashire delegate at the 1905 Annual Conference of the SDF, 'going to leave the moulding of the working-class movement to the leaders of the ILP?' and it was the Lancashire delegate at this conference who stressed in a principled way the need for affiliation to the LRC — A. Greenwood of Blackburn, speaking on the Lancashire resolution for affiliation, stated the position held by this tendency up to the founding of the BSP, and beyond, to the affiliation to the Labour Party in 1916:

> The LRC represents the beginning of the last and greatest struggle for the political machinery of the country by the most intelligent and best organized of the workers. This does not seem to be appreciated by the SDF . . .the LRC movement is a semi-conscious recognition of the conflict of interests between the proletariat and the master class; it is better in character than its leaders in the House of Commons. . . .We want to make it a Socialist movement, and must establish sympathetic relations with it.

Harry Quelch's reply for the Executive made clear the rigidity of thought of the SDF leaders against which the supporters of the Lancashire resolution struggled:

> Not a single new reason has been placed before us for adopting the course recommended. . . .If we rejoin the LRC we shall have no voice in the selection of candidates but will be called on to support them no matter whom they are. . . .We cannot have Socialist unity under the LRC, which contains anti-Socialists.

The movement against the positions represented by Quelch gathered impetus during the course of the 1906 Liberal Government and led eventually to the formation of the BSP in 1911 (a merger of the SDF with a number of ILP branches and Clarion Scout groups), and to the decision to affiliate to the Labour Party in 1914. This development was, however, very much an empirical reaction to the previous sectarianism of the SDF. In the same way that the SLP made no overall analysis and Marxist evaluation of the SDF and its defects, so the tendency which pressed for affiliation to the Labour Party did so not from the standpoint of a developed theoretical position but from a purely practical standpoint. The specific role of a revolutionary party in relation to the Labour Party and to the overall development of the Labour movement was never considered and the 'conversion' of the Labour Party to Socialism was throughout conceived in the very general terms set out by Greenwood in 1905, and wholly in the context of 'parliamentary Socialism'.

The processes that led to the formation of the BSP and its affiliation to the Labour Party were, in fact, not only the product of a long-drawn-out struggle in the SDF but a reaction to the 'labour unrest' of the immediate pre-war period which served to crystallize dissatisfaction with the Lib-Lab policies of the Parliamentary Labour Party and awaken the feeling in the ILP and SDF of the need for a more determined struggle for Socialist objectives. There was, consequently, the growth of a significant centrist tendency in the Labour Party and ILP at the very time when the BSP decided to affiliate to the former, and, in fact, the actual formation of the BSP and the terms in which it anticipated affiliation made it clear that it was part of this centrist current. The BSP entered the Labour Party essentially as a 'ginger group' whose role could be considered analogous to that of the ILP. On the question of the war it displayed, along with a large section of the ILP, an opposition that was, in the last analysis, pacifist;[25] practical action against the war was seen in terms of exerting pressure on the wartime coalition to conclude a 'democratic peace' in line with the majority at the Zimmerwald conference, and there was no evidence that the BSP considered intervening in the industrial struggles during the war in an attempt to give them an anti-war character. Again, the immediate effect of the Russian Revolution on the BSP was similar to the effect on the ILP; there was enthusiasm for the Revolution, a large amount of activity in opposition to Allied intervention in Russia and a general desire to emulate the success of the Bolsheviks. Yet all this did not essentially change the character of the BSP; given its Marxist commitment it took up, from 1919, the idea of forming a Communist Party in Britain, but the nature of the party that was envisaged was an enlarged and more effective version of the BSP. The methods of work associated with the party's 'ginger group' activities within the Labour Party had become deeply ingrained, and while it moved towards the creation of a Communist Party, the BSP essentially anticipated a continuation of its role on the extreme left wing of social democracy. This attitude towards the formation of the CP and its relations with the Labour Party was reinforced by the strong vested

[25] I.e. after the small chauvinist group led by Hyndman had left the BSP in 1916.

interest built up by sections of the BSP in the local government and parliamentary work of the Labour Party, whence a strong opportunist current emanated. This was to remain influential in the CP during its early years, a point strongly stressed by Tom Bell in his autobiography.[26]

Because of its revolutionary traditions, extending back to the 1880s, and because it was the largest of the Marxist groups in Britain, the BSP inevitably played a major part in the formation of the CPGB. But Macfarlane is incorrect in his implicit suggestion that the BSP was in some ways an embryo Communist Party. The fact that it began to consider industrial action in addition to parliamentary agitation before the First World War did not in any way anticipate the relationship between industrial and political activity which the CPGB was later to attempt to establish, as Macfarlane seems to argue.[27] The consideration of industrial agitation by the BSP was a direct response to the syndicalist upsurge after 1910, but although the BSP had a correct appreciation of the weaknesses of syndicalism its leaders made no attempt to establish the relationship which industrial could have to political action. The nature of the imperialist state was ignored and the significance of direct revolutionary struggle in the factories for the establishment of alternative working-class power was wholly neglected. Thus Fred Knee, a leading BSP militant on the London Trades Council, wrote very correctly of syndicalism that:

> You cannot get very far by mere 'industrial action'. So long as the Capitalist state remains, with its army, navy, and police, and its hand on the machine of administration, so long will it be possible for this capitalist state, when thoroughly awake to any danger, to throttle any strike, however big. . . .[28]

But the policy offered by Knee and the BSP generally was parliamentary action to take over the existing state as a vehicle for socialist legislation. The role of trade unionism, in this context, was limited to the fight for immediate improvements in wages etc. To this end the BSP adopted an 'industrial policy' that had for its aim the support of such trade union actions and the development of strong trade union organization, but this differed very clearly from the later trade union work of the CPGB, which was conceived in a wholly revolutionary context.

---

26 Tom Bell, op. cit., pp. 190-191.

27 Macfarlane, op. cit., pp. 18-19.

28 *British Socialist,* June 1912.

The taking up of industrial organization by the BSP leadership before 1914 was, moreover, largely an attempt to head off the growing opposition in the party to pure parliamentary activity, and the growing support for syndicalism. But the fact that the BSP (like the ILP, where similar developments occurred) was unable to provide a revolutionary political lead in the trade unions, as part of a general attempt to take up the class struggle on all fronts, left the field wide open for syndicalism. This did not apply just to the 1910-1914 years of 'labour unrest'. The feeling among rank-and-file members of both the BSP and the ILP that the struggle against capitalism on the industrial front was somehow primary, and parliamentary struggle secondary, deepened during the war and under the impact of the Russian Revolution. Indication of the mood was provided by the resolution adopted by the ILP Divisional Conference in South Wales in 1918 that:

> The time is ripe for the ILP to extend its activities to the Economic, in addition to the Political Field, seeing that it is in the field, factory, workshop, and mine that the real issue with the capitalist class is met, and that only by the workers organizing industrially as well as politically will the overthrow of Capitalism be brought about.[29]

It was because neither the BSP nor the ILP were capable of conducting their political work in the manner suggested by this resolution that many of the rank-and-file of both parties, before, during, and immediately after the war were swept into the syndicalist movement in its various forms. On the whole they remained members of their respective parties, but as industrial militants they sought expression for their conviction of the need for revolutionary struggle outside Parliament, which, in the absence of a lead from their parties, could only be provided by syndicalism. In treating all the revolutionary groups of the pre-1920 period in clinical isolation, Macfarlane is guilty of excessive formalism. He describes the evolution of organizations, not the way these groups were related to the real problems and aims of workers. The fact was, that in the 1919-1920 period members of the revolutionary groupings, including sections of the ILP, came to share a basically syndicalist outlook despite the formal policy difference of the groups and parties to which they belonged, and because they could not connect theoretically and politically these syndicalist tendencies, the BSP and SLP in particular played an essentially syndicalist role in the industrial field up to the founding of the CPGB.

---

[29] *Merthyr Pioneer,* January 19, 1918.

Syndicalism as a consciously organized force existed for a relatively brief period in the British labour movement, from 1910 to 1914; but in the absence of any viable alternative linking revolutionary activity in the trade unions to that in Parliament and elsewhere it exerted a powerful influence on young militants, and established methods of organization and revolutionary action which persisted among advanced workers up to and beyond the formation of the CPGB. Two ideological influences were at work in the creation of British syndicalism; the theories and methods of French anarcho-syndicalism, which represented the past petty-bourgeois anarchism of the French artisans carried over into the modern factory-based working class of France, and the theories of the SLP on industrial unionism, discussed above. The former were brought to Britain by Tom Mann, and with their emphasis on violent, direct struggle against the industrial bourgeoisie they found a response in a working class which was entering a period of unprecedented industrial struggles. The latter were even more influential, in that they offered an elaborated scheme for revolutionary action which proceeded from the immediate aims of the working class for strong trade unionism and showed how this could be associated with the eventual revolutionary overthrow of capitalism. These ideas of the SLP were taken over and incorporated into the general philosophy of syndicalism, while the SLP itself tended to remain uninvolved in the syndicalist struggles of the period. Its sectarianism and unwillingness to work with any tendency that did not completely accept its policies meant that the SLP did not effectively participate in the industrial struggles of the pre-1914 period or attempt to bring theoretical clarity to their leadership. When SLP-ers did begin to participate in such struggles, notably during the war in the Shop Stewards' Movement, it was on a wholly 'practical' trade union basis. For a while the SLP's sectarianism succumbed to purely syndicalist practice.

Syndicalism provided an organized expression for the revolt of rank-and-file militants, particularly in the rail, mining and engineering unions, against the domination of the union by the old Lib-Lab leaderships, the expression of whose industrial outlook was found in the industrial relations established since the 1890s. Close relations with the employers and, increasingly, the state had been built up via conciliation machinery, the Board of Trade, etc. Such leaders looked to the state, particularly after 1906 when it was administered by a Liberal government, to intervene in and adjust industrial disputes, notably in industries which were nationally organized, or in which unions were struggling for nationally-organized collective bargaining — mining, railways, engineering, etc. The period after 1906 in particular saw this developing relationship between the state and unions expanded and institutionalized by the movement of the trade union officials into full or part-time posts in government departments to administer the embryonic welfare services of the Liberal Government, the Labour Exchanges, the Trade Board Acts, and to act as Labour Advisers to the Board of Trade. By 1913, 117 places had been provided at the Board of Trade for trade union officials, 124 in the National Insurance Department, 48 at the Home Office (where, for example, Tom Richards, secretary of the South Wales miners, was an assistant official) and 85 in other departments.[30] In quantitative terms this development represented only a small beginning compared with developments during and after the First World War, but in qualitative terms it represented an important advance from the position hitherto occupied by Lib-Lab trade unionists in their relations with the state and served to consolidate and give an institutional form to the previous disposition of such trade unionists to class peace. In rebelling against the domination of such officials in the mining, railway and engineering unions in particular, young militants were rebelling, in part at least, against a significant new stage in the evolution of the imperialist state and its relation with the working class; the need of the state in a period of mass trade unionism to bring the leaders of the unions into an institutionalized relationship with it and to subject them more effectively to the requirements of capitalism as a whole. Thus the pattern was established that was to become of particular significance after the war. The unions and employers were brought into organized contact with the state for the purpose of settling crucial disputes in key industries and the result of their joint effort imposed upon rank-and-file trade unionists. In the event of resistance from below to the terms so concluded, the repressive powers of the state were deployed to coerce the rank and file into acquiescence. Even before the war this sort of development became apparent in the great industrial disputes between 1910 and 1914. In South Wales, for example, the Cambrian Combine strikers had to struggle not only against the employers but against the efforts of the SWMF and Board of Trade officials to impose a compromise settlement on the one hand,

---

30 Halévy, *History of the English People*, vol. 6, pp. 446-7.

and the massive detachments of police and troops dispatched by Churchill on the other. After the war, the dual procedure of coupling repression by the state with reliance on the trade union bureaucracy to come to terms became most marked, notably in the 1921 struggle and the General Strike. The syndicalism of the 1910-1914 period, and indeed the syndicalist manifestations of the whole period up to the General Strike, were an intuitive and empirical reaction to these developments, but, lacking an overall understanding of them, produced no permanent revolutionary opposition, only a propensity among advanced workers towards specific forms of militant but essentially limited rank-and-file activism.

As a way round the growing bureaucracy in the unions and the conciliation machinery, etc., on which this was based, Syndicalists proposed the building of mass industrial unions controlled by rank-and-file executives who would be wholly responsible in the most direct manner to the membership. The abolition of sectional craft unions which such a development would bring would allow effective industry-wide action against the employers (who in this period were grouping themselves in trade federations) and would pave the way for the eventual seizure of industry by the unions. *The Miners' Next Step*, dealing with the new problems posed by the growing centralization of ownership in the mines, set out clearly the attitude held by advanced rank-and-file militants:

> A rapidity of industrial development is forcing the (Miners') Federation to take action along lines for which there exists no machinery to properly carry out.
>
> The control of the organization by the rank and file is far too indirect. The system of long agreements, with their elaborate precautions against direct action, cramp the free expression of the might of the workmen and prevent the securing of improved conditions, often when the mere exhibition of their strength would allow of it. The sectional character of the organization in the mining industry renders concerted action almost impossible, and thus every section helps to hinder and often defeat the other ...[31]

The answer lay in the construction of a revolutionary industrial union the very logic of whose militancy would lead to the eventual seizure of power: as a policy for such a union the authors of *The Miners' Next Step* proposed:

> ... that a continual agitation be carried on in favour of increasing the minimum wage and shortening the hours of work until we have extracted

[31] *The Miners' Next Step*, pp. 16-17.

> the whole of the employers' profits. . . .That our objective be, to build up an organization that will ultimately take over the mining industry and carry it on in the interests of the workers.[32]

It is readily apparent that the real concern of such a policy was with the immediate, day-to-day issues confronting rank-and-file miners. Certainly, it expressed in a general way the growing feeling of the need for revolutionary change, but by totally ignoring the state and the political questions raised by revolutionary trade union action, the syndicalism of *The Miners' Next Step* could offer no more, and no less, than a series of proposals for fighting the mine owners on the industrial front on something like an equal footing.

An essential part of the syndicalist philosophy, moreover, was its rejection of leadership and its development of something approaching a mystique from the concept of rank-and-file spontaneity. The rejection of the need for an alternative leadership within the trade unions stemmed originally, at least in the practical form which it took from 1910, from the South Wales syndicalist movement, and was enshrined in the proposals of *The Miners' Next Step:* but the rejection of leadership characterized the movement generally, both before and during the war. The failures of the Trade Union and Labour Party leaderships were blamed not merely on misleadership and wrong policies but on the institution of leadership itself.

> Leadership implies power held by the Leader. Without power the leader is inept. The possession of power inevitably leads to corruption. All leaders become corrupt, in spite of their own good intentions. No man was ever good enough, brave enough or strong enough, to have such power at his disposal, as real leadership implies.[33]

So wrote the authors of *The Miners' Next Step*, who described their movement as a 'no leader movement'. Essentially, the aim of such a movement was to encourage the rank and file to assert control over the apparatus of the union and direct it to their own ends. The official leaders would become subordinate to an 'unofficial executive' of rank-and-file members from whom the policies of the union would flow in accord with the wishes of the membership, expressed at regularly held conferences. In practice, this form of syndicalism was, in the last analysis, the purest 'rank-and-filism'; it confined its attention to agitation among the rank and file, on a 'ginger group' basis, on immediate issues, with the aim of pressurizing the existing union

---

[32] *Ibid*, p. 26.

[33] *The Miners' Next Step*, p. 13.

leaders into the adoption of specific policies. A number of supporters of the unofficial movement in South Wales clearly expressed such an aim when they wrote that:

> ... we ought to be a 'ginger group' constantly attempting to galvanize the executive committee into life and focussing their efforts in the direction of our programme ...[34]

Because of this, the syndicalist movement, in South Wales and elsewhere, was marked by its weak organization and diffuse character, its ability to unite a wide range of tendencies around immediate objectives (as in South Wales over the minimum wage issue or during the war over dilution in the engineering industry) and its failure to develop any permanent revolutionary tendency out of such agitations.

In a sense, this neglect of leadership was bound up with the syndicalist theory of the automatic movement of workers towards the seizure of industry. The very spontaneity of the movement made powerful organization unnecessary; all that was needed was a loose association of propagandists to stimulate the thinking of the rank and file along the right lines. This became very apparent in the proposals brought forward shortly before the war for the development of a national syndicalist movement:

> The ISEL [Industrial Syndicalist Education League] consists at present of a small number of loosely organized groups and a large number of individuals scattered all over the country. The time is now ripe for the formation of strong Syndicalist organization, on national lines, whose function shall be the spread of Syndicalism throughout the length and breadth of the land. This could be done by means of autonomous local groups of Syndicalists federated into a national body, without, if possible, an Executive Committee, for Executives are always caucuses.[35]

This was written in 1913 by the Northern Organizer of the ISEL, and although his proposals never came into operation as far as the ISEL was concerned, as the League was in a state of disintegration by the end of 1913, they indicated the general lines of syndicalist thinking on organization and accurately reflected the outlook of leading elements in the South Wales unofficial movement, the Amalgamation Committees in the engineering industry and the Vigilance Committees on the railways, and anticipated the weak, decentralized form that the Shop Stewards' Movement was to assume during the war.

The antipathy to leadership and the predilection for pressure group

---

[34] *Merthyr Pioneer*, July 13, 1918. [35] *The Syndicalist*, January 1913.

tactics from below were thus given theoretical form in the years of 'labour unrest' before 1914 and became deeply ingrained in the consciousness of leading militants. The experiences of this period were to be of major importance in shaping the outlook of the Shop Stewards' and Workers' Control Movement (SS & WCM) in particular, from which emerged the industrial basis of the CPGB in 1920-21. Despite its militancy and strength under the peculiar wartime conditions in the engineering industry, the SS & WCM was never much more than the federation of autonomous groups of militants envisaged by *The Syndicalist*. Its National Administrative Committee (NAC) had no executive powers and it could not direct national campaigns. This was to make for the loss of initiative by the SS & WCM in crucial struggles, most notably that for the 40-hour week on the Clyde in 1919. The lack of power of the NAC was a concrete expression of the strong feeling against leadership that found expression equally in the failure of the SS & WCM to make any effort to win leading positions in the engineering unions. As J. T. Murphy commented:

> It is quite certain that had the leading shop stewards of that period, when the workers were supporting them, really made a planful effort to win the leadership of the engineering unions, they could have succeeded in the course of a few years.[36]

A similar state of affairs prevailed in the unofficial movement in South Wales, which was, as Macfarlane notes, to become an important basis of support for the CPGB in 1920-21. Here there was no dogmatic opposition to the election of supporters of the movement to official positions, but such elections were never conceived in relation to the overall strategy of the movement. Supporters were elected to the EC of the SWMF as individuals, not representatives of the unofficial movement, and in no sense under the discipline of the latter. Indeed, such a movement could have no disciplined expression and those of its supporters who did become union officials tended to reveal themselves as quite orthodox trade unionists within a very short time. On the eve of the war, some of the leaders of the unofficial movement were attacking their 'spokesmen' on the union EC, notably the former protagonist of the movement, Noah Ablett:

> They were pledged to abstain from supporting reactionary policies, [wrote C.L.Gibbons, one of the authors of *The Miners' Next Step*], . . . they were to keep revolutionary policies and militant policies to the fore; they were to

[36] J. T. Murphy, *New Horizons*, p. 81.

> force the EC to take action along lines laid down by the militant section in the coalfield. Have they done this? Unhesitatingly we answer 'No'. They have ceased to be revolutionary except in words. In the matter of deeds they are not to be distinguished from members of the openly reactionary majority on the EC. . . .[37]

The lesson drawn from this, however, was not the need to elaborate a form of organization that could work as a disciplined body against the 'reactionary majority on the EC', but the futility of contesting the leadership of the union at all. What was needed was more effective 'rank and filism', more pressure from below, and in the subsequent period, culminating in the lock-out of 1921, the unofficial movement concentrated on the development of 'ginger groups' at local level. The question of supplanting the leaders of the SWMF by an alternative was ignored, with disastrous consequences in 1921.

It is important to note that the syndicalism characterized above did not arise solely from the purely practical problems confronting rank-and-file trade unionists before and during the war. Syndicalism arose from specific theoretical premises that were closely associated with the level of understanding of Marxism that existed in this period, not only among Syndicalists but among members of the BSP and SLP. It was the theoretical postulates of Syndicalism that gave the very specific and necessarily transitory rank-and-file struggles of the period a definite revolutionary orientation and won from such struggles numbers of advanced militants whose syndicalist inclinations were to persist after the immediate struggles had died away and who continued to represent a definite tendency in the areas where they worked, ready to give syndicalist leadership to whatever new struggle developed. A degree of permanency was given to the syndicalist tendencies established before the war by the Central Labour College and its classes in the localities. The College evolved from the students who broke away from Ruskin College in 1909 in opposition to the indoctrination of the potential trade union leaders at the College with bourgeois theory and values. The 1909 strike and the subsequent establishment of the CLC were an integral part of the reaction of young militants to the growing bureaucratization of the unions and their development of organized ties with the employers and the state. Ruskin was understood by these militants, many of whom were from

---

[37] *South Wales Worker*, June 13, 1914.

unions like the SWMF and the ASRS (the most important of the rail unions) where rank-and-file unrest was strongest, as an institution for the training of trade unionists in their new role as associates of the employers and state in the development of peaceful industrial relations. In opposition to this, the Ruskin strikers wanted training in Marxist theory to prepare trade unionists for a revolutionary role. Not only would the CLC train trade unionists to confront the employers as educated militants, it would create, in the person of every trade unionist who attended the College, a potential local revolutionary leader who would return to his locality to organize classes in Marxism and thus help develop an informed rank and file who could consciously assert their control over union affairs and direct the course of the unions towards the seizure of industry. The Plebs League was the embodiment of this concept. Its branches acted as the local units of the CLC, organizing classes in Marxist economics and industrial history, and drawing around them advanced rank-and-file militants who opposed the conciliatory policies of their union leaders. The role of such branches and class leaders was clearly expressed by Ablett, who suggested that:

> In the present loose democracy of the trade unions individuals count for much. Such a body of men, scientifically trained to adapt themselves to the needs of the workers, with a knowledge of the economics of Labour, coupled with the ability of speech and pen would naturally be expected to wield a great influence in their respective localities . . .[38]

His prognosis proved very apt in relation to the Cambrian Combine strike where the Rhondda Plebs played a major role in canalizing the struggle into a general movement for the minimum wage; in fact, the Plebs League and CLC were to be very closely connected with the South Wales unofficial movement up to and beyond the formation of the CPGB. Elsewhere, too, the Plebs and CLC played an important part in developing rank-and-file consciousness. Indicative of their influence among the miners and railworkers was the agreement in 1914 by the SWMF and the NUR to assume joint sponsorship of the CLC.[39] Elsewhere the ties with the unions were less close, but there is little doubt, from an examination of the reports in *Plebs Magazine* over the period 1910-1920, that the movement established itself

[38] *Plebs Magazine*, February 1909.

[39] This sponsorship was, it might be noted, indicative of the fact that the 'Marxism' of the CLC did not fundamentally conflict with the outlook of the orthodox trade union leaders on the ECs of the NUR and SWMF.

firmly in a number of important industrial areas, London, Lancashire, North-East England and West of Scotland included, and exercised considerable influence in forming the outlook of some thousands of militants.[40]

The widespread influence of the Labour College movement is worth emphasizing, for it meant that, more than the BSP and SLP, it acted as the main institution for the propagation of Marxism among advanced workers.[41] The Marxism of this movement was highly abstract and formal in character. Marxism was presented by the CLC and Plebs as the best means of explaining the world and attention was confined to education in Marxism in the purest sense. Marxist method was employed to explain the working of the economic system and the evolution of class society; the *fact* of the class struggle was made clear but no attempt made to relate such education to the immediate and long-term ends of the workers' movement, except in the most general and formal sense. Such Marxism was very much under the influence of positivism and ideas of mechanical evolution inherited from the later decades of the nineteenth century. It explained the necessary evolution of capitalism from an individualistic to a monopoly stage and held that the development of the class struggle to a consequently higher stage was an automatic reflex of this process. Once workers had been taught the elementary facts of the class struggle and had learnt the nature of their exploitation, they would automatically develop strong organization to confront the employers and eventually contend with them for power. Such an approach to Marxism was clearly related to the propagandist character of the revolutionary movement of the period. More important, it essentially denied the need for any organized party and placed the emphasis merely on the propaganda work of small groups of activists, as in the Plebs League. As such, it was quite in line with the current ideas and methods of the BSP and SLP, as set out above. J. T. Murphy pointed to these characteristics of the CLC movement when formulating a critique of it in the early 1920s:

> What 'certain fundamental elementary principles' do you propose to get across? [he asked the CLC, referring to a recent statement of aims], merely the fact of the class struggle and never a single suggestion as to *how* the workers are to wage the struggle? No mention of what are the fundamental

[40] E.g. in South Wales by 1917 the CLC classes were attended by 500 miners.

[41] Of course, a large number of CLC local organizers and Plebs members were also members of the BSP, SLP or ILP. They all tended to share a common approach to Marxist theory.

> and elementary requirements of victory in the struggle? Shall we spend months unravelling the Theory of Value and never mention the elementary fact that the workers must have a revolutionary workers' party — lest we be accused of party politics?[42]

Murphy was correct in his characterization of the education activities of the movement; he was wrong, however, in suggesting that no practical, political activity flowed from them. The presentation of Marxism in mechanical terms provided the theoretical basis for the advocacy of spontaneity and the opposition to leadership in the practice of the Syndicalist movement, which was so closely linked to the CLC. At its worst, this educational movement provided the training for left opportunists in the trade unions, men who could address correctly formulated rhetoric to the rank and file but who had no lead to offer except within the context of orthodox trade unionism. When such trade unionism was fundamentally challenged in the post-war period of political-industrial struggles such leaders were reduced to impotence, like Robert Williams, or moved very rapidly to the right, like Frank Hodges. At its best, the CLC took advanced militants part of the way towards an understanding of the class struggle but because it could establish little connection between Marxist theory and the day-do-day problems of the Labour movement the CLC left such militants leaderless and prone to purely localized forms of struggle on immediate trade union objects.[43] The experiences of 1919-1921 were to be of fundamental importance in revealing to such militants the inadequacies of this form of Marxism. J. T. Murphy's critique, quoted above, was one example of the reaction of a leading militant to his experience of the Marxism of the CLC. At the same time, the CLC and Plebs had formed very close links with organized workers in a number of areas, and in these cases the reaction against the theory of the movement and its practical expression in Syndicalism came only as a result of the bitter experiences of 1921, when the inadequacy of syndicalist forms of organization was experienced in practice. This was particularly so in South Wales where the CLC had become very firmly entrenched in the indigenous Syndicalist movement. It was here that Syndicalist organization achieved its full expression in the months before the lockout in 1921 and there was the clearest evidence that the loose, highly parochial organization that existed was felt to be

---

42 *Plebs Magazine,* April 1923.

43 A. J. Cook, an active member of the Plebs League and lecturer at numerous CLC classes, represented one of the best products of this movement.

entirely adequate to provide leadership for the rank and file. Towards the end of 1920 Will Hewlett, a leading member of the unofficial movement, expressed this feeling in an article explaining how the South Wales rank and file were organized; it is worth quoting at some length for the evidence it provides of Syndicalism in its most advanced form on the eve of the massive industrial struggles of the 1920s:

> I know there is an idea abroad that South Wales is covered by a network of Unofficial Committees. This is not so. In fact there is no permanent unofficial organization in the coalfield. What does happen when it is necessary is that the advanced or rebel element does meet and discuss matters . . .then go back to their respective Pit Committees and Lodges, put their views forward . . .and if their opinions are accepted the delegates to the Councils and Conferences are instructed to act accordingly. Thus we are enabled to carry out our advanced policy in a constitutional manner. It is fair to claim that the major portion, if not the whole of the advanced reforms in the coalfield is attributable to the unofficial or rebel element. This element is generated and developed through the 'Central Labour College Evening Classes' owned and controlled by the NUR and the SWMF. This again is provided for in the constitution. . . .

Hewlett then went on to advise the emulation of this movement; correct organization would flow from education on CLC lines. He urged:

> Comrades . . .to form up their evening classes for the study of Industrial History and Economics (Marxian) this winter, develop them to their fullest capacity, impart to the rank and file all the knowledge possible, then I do not fear the result . . .[44]

To a very large extent, the attachment to spontaneity, the opposition to strong leadership, the avoidance of questions of political action and the role of the state, and the purely mechanical approach to Marxism were inextricably bound up with the character of British capitalism in the period up to 1921. In a period of expansion, with booming profits and full employment, capitalism could afford to meet the demands of organized workers, if pressed in a sufficiently firm and militant manner. In these conditions, it seemed to rank-and-file militants that they did not need to look beyond the forms of trade union activity advocated by syndicalism, nor question the Marxism that gave theoretical justification to this syndicalism. The methods of 'direct action', the theories of the CLC, were all acceptable to

[44] *The Worker*, September 4, 1920.

advanced militants because in the specific conditions up to 1921 they were empirically viable; they worked. There was no apparent need to look for higher forms of organization or policy. This was borne out by the successes achieved by 'direct action' before the war, by the partial successes of the SS & WCM in controlling workshop conditions during the war and by the South Wales miners' successful resistance to the Government's attempted imposition of the Munitions Act in 1915. But, militant as these struggles were, they remained, it must be emphasized, wholly concerned with trade union issues, and while they were political in that they had the effect of prompting the intervention of the state and limiting the scope of governmental action to some extent, they had no consciously political aim, even during the war. Murphy stressed that none of the actions of the SS & WCM during the war had any anti-war intention:

> None of the strikes that took place during the course of the war were anti-war strikes. They were frequently led by men such as myself who wanted to stop the war, but that was not the actual motive. Had the question of stopping the war been put to any strikers' meeting it would have been overwhelmingly defeated. The stoppages had a different origin and a different motive. They arose out of a growing conviction that the workers at home were the custodians of the conditions of labour for those in the armed forces, as well as themselves . . .[45]

Implicit in Murphy's estimate of the movement during the war was an acceptance of its purely syndicalist, non-political character. Murphy, a member of the SLP, along with other leading shop stewards, members of the BSP, ILP or SLP, submerged themselves in syndicalist activity during the war and made no real attempt to give the SS & WCM any definite revolutionary purpose until the post-war years. Indeed, in certain critical periods, notably during the ferment on the Clyde early in the war, the movement was a definite block to the development of political understanding. The Clyde Workers' Committee (CWC) was wholly concerned with defending workshop conditions and laying the basis for a new industrial union for the metal-working trades. Despite the prominence of people like Gallacher (BSP), Macmanus (SLP) and Kirkwood (ILP) in its leadership, the CWC failed, in fact refused, to link its workshop activities to a struggle against the war, despite the objectively favourable conditions. This came out most clearly over the deportation from Glasgow

[45] J. T. Murphy, *New Horizons*, p. 44.

of Macmanus, Kirkwood and four other leading shop stewards early in 1916. Opposition to the Government's action was intense throughout the Clyde and there was a wave of demands from the workshops for a strike, but a report of a meeting of the CWC to consider this demand indicated how steeped the leaders of the Committee were in their syndicalist theories:

> At this meeting it was quite evident that the members were very indignant against the action of the Government. So keen was the indignation that a motion was submitted that the CWC should declare a strike in the Clyde District. The chairman, William Gallacher, ruled this motion out of order as it was against the accepted aims of the CWC. This aim was the building of one industrial organization in the engineering industry. The members of the committee could inform their fellow workers in the shop where they worked as to what happened at the Forge (i.e. Parkhead Forge) but beyond that the CWC had no jurisdiction . . .[46]

Concomitant with the syndicalist attitudes of the leaders of the SS & WCM (whatever their formal political affiliations) was the organizational weakness of the movement, noted above, which prevented effective concerted action and produced dismal failure in the possibly revolutionary situation at the end of the war. In brief, the war saw a strengthening of syndicalism because of the singularly favourable bargaining position of workers, the abnegation of leadership by the trade union signatories of the Treasury Agreements and the desperate need of the Government to keep the war effort in top gear.

Developments similar to those among the Shop Stewards occurred in South Wales, although there was no organized contact. South Wales saw a high level of industrial militancy during the war, notably in the 1915 strike in defiance of the Munitions Act. Like engineering, the coal industry was absolutely essential to the war effort and the bargaining position of the miners was consequently enhanced, despite the firm support for the war given by the leaders of the Miners' Federation. In these circumstances the syndicalism that had developed in the area before the war was reinforced even though the formal organizational structure of the unofficial movement disappeared with the outbreak of the war. The success of the miners in 1915 seemed to provide a complete vindication for the methods of syndicalism and greatly increased the propensity to this type of action in the period up to 1921. The full effect of the 1915 struggle on leading

---

[46] Quoted by J. T. Murphy, *Preparing for Power*, p. 123.

South Wales syndicalists was indicated in a controversy in the *Plebs Magazine* on the question of the nature and role of the state and the need for a working-class revolutionary party to oppose the bourgeois state. The contribution of the protagonist of a revolutionary party, Will Craik, is worth quoting in some detail in order to bring out the full significance of the opposition to it from syndicalist sources:

> Since Imperialism set in, the State has come to acquire a new significance. It becomes the driving force for the expansion of national capital over the face of the earth. . . . The organs and operations of the State are changed and augmented to meet the needs of this Imperialist phase of capitalism and especially to meet the need for war which henceforth becomes *the* means for capitalist expansion. . . The State that requires war without needs peace within. It has, therefore, to adapt itself to maintaining the latter as well as for the conduct of the former. It must become, directly, an economic power. Less than ever, then, can the industrial organization (of the working class) expand and the area of its activities extend without political consequences, without State intervention. The working class cannot attack the economic power of capitalism without attacking the political organization of that power . . .[47]

This argument of Craik's was, in a formal way, an anticipation of the understanding that was to grow amongst advanced workers after the war of the need for a revolutionary party. However, the counter-arguments of Ablett to Craik in the *Plebs Magazine* showed a complete inability to comprehend the theoretical objections raised by the latter to syndicalism. Ablett's arguments were, in fact, an indication of the way syndicalism was deeply rooted in the empiricist traditions of the Labour movement, to which Marxism was adapted; they indicated also the degree to which syndicalism was intensified by the specific conditions of British capitalism in the years before the post-war depression. It was only when this new economic phase began and the state intervened to support the coalowners in making the savage wage reductions of 1921 that the failings of Ablett and his co-thinkers were revealed. In opposing Craik, Ablett based his arguments on the specific, limited experiences in South Wales between 1910 and 1915:

> The economic power of the working class grows apace, and Mr. Craik may rest assured that there is already sufficient economic power to deal with any more political or even the more serious juridical obstacles without in any way frittering away our energy by creating a political organization. During that period the miners, particularly the South Wales miners, have

[47] *Plebs Magazine*, March, 1917.

> been through several crises in which the Government has had to intervene. The Government was compelled to meet us directly. If at any period the negotiations were transferred to the 'House' then our business would have to be dealt with by men who could not understand as fully as we could our contentions. In the end the whole matter ...would be decided by our economic power. ...It is easy to deduce from this that the larger the industrial organization the less need is there for any political organization. If the Triple Alliance decided to strike, of what use would a political organization be to them? ...

The struggles of the post-war years, however, and the profound influence of the Bolshevik Revolution broke down the narrow, trade union outlook of people like Ablett. The question of revolutionary action in Britain became inextricably bound up with the international struggles of the working class and the Bolshevik experience in Russia. The period 1919-1921 was to see the struggle to form a revolutionary party, the value of which had been denied by Ablett, but in conditions where the influence of Ablett's syndicalism remained strong and where the propensity towards the methods of the South Wales syndicalists or the Shop Stewards' Movement remained unchallenged. It was only through the decisive experiences of 1919-1921 that these traditional methods were broken down and the basis laid for a revolutionary party with the potential to intervene decisively in the struggles that were to culminate in the General Strike.

Part 3: The formation of the CPGB

The theme of the initial sections of this article has been the failure of L. J. Macfarlane, in tracing the history of the Communist movement in Britain from the 1900s through to the late 1920s, to relate the development of the revolutionary tendencies that emerged across this period to the specific stages of development of the working class, its consciousness and the organizational forms through which this was expressed, and the changing character of British capitalism; the relatively rapid change from the booming imperialist economy of the immediate pre-war years to the stagnant, crisis-ridden economy of the 1920s, and the impact this had on wide sections of the working class, is completely ignored by Macfarlane. Without such analysis, however, it is really impossible to explain in any satisfactory manner how the weak revolutionary sects that came together to form the CPGB in

1920-1921 were in a position, at least potentially and in a fair degree actually, to play an extremely influential role in the major developments that took place in the Labour movement around 'Red Friday' and the General Strike.

In the earlier sections of this article an attempt has been made to indicate the main phases of development of British capitalism across the period dealt with by Macfarlane's book and to delineate the main revolutionary tendencies that established themselves in the Labour movement by the end of the First World War. It has been argued, against Macfarlane's purely descriptive approach to these tendencies, that it is crucial to understand theoretically the political significance of the tendencies, syndicalist and centrist, which were to be so influential at the time of the formation of the CPGB and which were to determine its character and general political role in its early years. In fact, it was only by a conscious struggle to overcome the legacy of these tendencies that the CPGB was able to create the conditions for its emergence as a party of the Bolshevik type and in studying the early years of the party's history it is this process that one is studying. Inevitably, therefore, Macfarlane's book provides much information on this process; the theoretical significance of the process, however, and the degree to which the CPGB had established, by 1924-1926, the pre-conditions for effective communist work, he largely ignores.

It is because he ignores these factors that the section of Macfarlane's book with which this part of the review deals, the years from the formation of the party up to the General Strike, is so unsatisfactory and, as a historical evaluation of the significance of the party in the most crucial period of its development, misleading and confused. For those who are concerned with understanding why the CPGB failed dismally in its first serious test as a revolutionary organization during the General Strike of 1926 a clear estimation of the tendencies operating in the party during its early years is essential. The failure of the CPGB to develop the undoubtedly revolutionary potential of the General Strike, its failure to learn from its weaknesses in this period and its inability to resist the pressures working for the Stalinization of the international Communist movement in these years, resulted in the consummation of the process, operating from 1925 at least, whereby the CPGB became utterly subordinate to and dependent on the bureaucratized apparatus of the Comintern. After 1926 the CPGB was never again to be in a position to play any revolutionary role in the British labour movement. The struggles in the party at the end of the

1920s were not in any real sense connected with an attempt to reverse the rightward tendencies displayed by the majority of the leadership from the time of the General Strike but were, essentially, struggles between two contradictory phases of Stalinism. Significantly enough, it is in this section of his book, where Macfarlane is not concerned with the crucial relationship of the party's theory and policy to the working class in a period of revolutionary development, that one finds least to complain of. What is of the greatest concern is Macfarlane's apparent inability to explain why the CPGB was unable to develop the revolutionary potential of the General Strike and at least win from this sturggle the basis for its emergence as a mass revolutionary party. As was pointed out in the first section of this article, an explanation of the party's failure entails examining the degree to which it overcame the weaknesses apparent at its origin, the degree to which it was emerging as a really effective alternative leadership in the Labour movement in the period before the General Strike, and to what extent the pressures of Stalinism on the party checked its exploitation of the very favourable conditions that existed for communist work in the period around and after 'Red Friday'. It has been suggested that because Macfarlane never really examines the CPGB as a revolutionary party in the process of development and never in the context of developments in the international Communist movement, except very formally, he portrays the history of the party in static terms and argues, implicitly and from an idealist and superficial standpoint, that the party could play only a limited role in relation to the Labour movement as a whole. In what follows it is suggested that a very different interpretation, based on material from Macfarlane's book and a study of the original sources, can be advanced for the history of the CPGB between 1920 and 1926.

Within the scope of a review of this character it is impossible to deal in any adequate manner with the crucial movement amongst the working class from the latter stages of the war through to the miners' struggle in 1921 which formed the background against which the negotiations to form a united Communist Party took place. Some understanding of these movements is clearly needed, however, for an understanding of the factors which made for the formation of the CPGB by January 1921. Macfarlane recounts at great length the details of the tortuous process whereby the CPGB was formed, but by treating this process in clinical isolation from the potentially revolutionary developments in the Labour movement he negates much of the value of his account and reveals his deep attachment to the technique of bourgeois formalism endemic amongst students of 'political institutions'.

The factors making for potentially revolutionary action by the British working class in the period 1917-1921 cannot be separated out in any clear-cut way; they interacted and reinforced each other. The Russian Revolution aroused tremendous sympathy among wide sections of the working class and a great readiness to defend the revolution from attack by the Coalition Government in 1919 and 1920. At the same time there is plenty of evidence from 1917 of intense war-weariness and a growing determination to demand and fight for major improvements in wages and conditions as some compensation for the intense sacrifices the working class had made in the workshops and on the battle front. The example of the Russian Revolution was of major importance in strengthening the determination of British workers to fight their own bourgeoisie, and while it would be a-historical to argue that the Russian example encouraged direct revolutionary emulation, except among the revolutionary sects that came together to form the CPGB, the very fact that the revolution encouraged the militancy of British workers, and led important sections of them (e.g. the miners) to identify themselves in a general sense with the Bolshevik success, strengthened the consciousness in the bourgeoisie of the need to retain a united front against Labour in the anticipated 'difficult situation' in the post-war period. Moreover, the fact that this united front was maintained in the form of the Coalition Government, which had confirmed itself in power by the most blatant use of political chicanery in the 1918 election, strengthened the consciousness of wide sections of rank-and-file workers of the need to fight the bourgeoisie as a class. That the Labour Party had made few gains in the 1918 election and was an insignificant group in Parliament dominated by some of the most conservative representatives of the bureaucracy of the Miners' Federation meant that in the post-war situation there could be no question of seeking parliamentary channels into which to divert working class struggles. The fight for improved post-war conditions and for the defence of the Russian Revolution inevitably had to be a fight between the organized working class in the trade unions and the Coalition Government. In these conditions, particularly in the crucial year 1919, the very real possibility existed of a general political struggle by the unions against the Government which would inevitably have had revolutionary implications.

The fact that the possibility never became reality in 1919 and the fact that the events of 1920 (Councils of Action against intervention in the Russian-Polish war) and 1921 (the miners' lock-out) never developed their full potential for revolutionary opposition to the Government was due to the interaction of two opposed tendencies: the opposition of the trade union leadership, both left and right wings, to any form of action against the Government which raised the question of political power, and the inability, both organizational and theoretical, of the revolutionary groupings at the time of the formation of the CPGB to develop the very real revolutionary potential amongst the trade union rank and file which was so clearly held back by their leadership. As noted above, 1919 was the crucial year. The claims of the rank and file, held up during the war by the trade union leadership in the interests of the war effort, could no longer be postponed. The three most important unions, the miners, the railworkers and transport workers, the constituents of the Triple Alliance, were advancing demands for major improvements in wages and conditions. The Triple Alliance had, in fact, concluded an agreement for mutual support in the furthering of their post-war programmes with a stipulation that none of the constituent unions was to come to terms until the demands of all three unions had been realized. This agreement, coming into force at the time when the struggle for the 40-hour week, with its insurrectionary overtones, was being fought on the Clyde, had very clear political implications. If carried out, it inevitably meant taking on the Coalition Government and being prepared to undertake a general strike. All the evidence, however, indicates that the leadership of the Triple Alliance concluded its agreement very much under the pressure of rank-and-file militancy. None of the leaders of the Alliance, and this included the left-wingers, Smillie and Hodges of the miners, were prepared to make their unions' demands a political, revolutionary issue, i.e. one which raised in a clear way the question of which class held power. After all, while Robert Smillie was a pioneer of the ILP in the Miners' Federation, his political beliefs had become very much shaped by the strait-jacket of orthodox trade unionism, particularly after he became president of the MFGB in 1912, and while he supported in words the pacifist section of the ILP during the war, in practice he lent his services very fully to the Government's war-time schemes for coal production with all that they involved in increased exploitation and the maintenance of the slaughter on the Western front. Neither he, nor his colleague Hodges, one-time supporter of the South Wales unofficial movement, now MFGB Secretary and convert to the specious theories of Guild Socialism, was prepared to envisage a struggle against the Government if it could be avoided. Both wanted the nationalization of the mines not as a step in the process of winning working-class power but as a co-operative enterprise between miners, Government and consumers (i.e. private industry) to increase the efficiency of the industry with higher wages and shorter hours as a quid pro quo. Any strike against the Government, in the conditions of 1919, would sacrifice what they regarded as a practical proposition; moreover, to impose the miners' claims on 'the community' by strike action would be unethical. This viewpoint was summed up by Smillie at the crucial conference of the MFGB which met to consider whether to participate in the Sankey Commission or whether to strike for the union's demands:

> ... we had no right to force conditions on the nation because of our strength if the claims we put forward were not just [he argued] in favour of participating in the Commission. Moreover: If we get into a fight it must be to secure improvements for our people, and if we can get these improvements for our people with a fight, then in God's name, do we want a fight if we can secure them without . . .[48]

What lay behind these pleadings was a clear understanding that, with the mood of the rank and file, not only in the MFGB but the Triple Alliance as a whole, a strike would soon pass from a limited economic to a general political affair. The Webbs, who acted as go-betweens for Lloyd George and the MFGB leaders, realized exactly what a miners' strike implied:

> If the Government, confident of their power to beat the miners, go into battle — theirs is the responsibility . . .[wrote Beatrice Webb] 'Blockading the miners' will be a difficult and dangerous task: the railwaymen and transport workers might be drawn in, the army might refuse to act. And then? . . .[49]

In the event, the Webbs, as Beatrice Webb's diaries show, were largely responsible, in consultation with Lloyd George and Smillie and Hodges, for working out the idea of the Coal Commission and thus offering the miners' leaders a possible way out of the apparent impasse.

The success of the leaders of the MFGB in inducing the union to participate in the Commission, together with the concessions that

[48] MFGB conference, February 28, 1919.

[49] *Beatrice Webb's Diaries*, 1919-1924, p. 150.

came from the first stage of the Commission (the 'Sankey wage' and the 7-hour day), sufficed to blunt rank-and-file pressure for immediate action on the question of nationalization, with the result that Lloyd George was relatively safe in rejecting the Commission's recommendation for nationalization later in 1919. The long-term reaction of the miners' leaders to this rejection was of the greatest significance in the context of the general trends within the unions in the inter-war years. After the formalities of the 'Mines for the Nation' campaign and the predictable rejection by the TUC of an appeal for general strike action in support of the miners in March 1920, the leadership of the MFGB moved steadily towards the evolution of some permanent system of wage regulation in the industry which would take over from the system of Government control of the mines which survived from the war period. The ideas that were crystallizing in the minds of the leaders of the MFGB, notably Hodges, and the leaders of the Mineowners' Association from the time of the 'datum line' strike in October 1920 through to the eve of the 1921 lock-out involved co-partnership, with the miners being tied in by their leadership to a long-term productivity deal in which wages were related directly to the profitability of the industry. The owners in the various districts guaranteed a definite level of profits which had to be met before wages could rise. It was a scheme on these lines that came into force after the defeat of the miners in 1921; its essentials had been worked out by the bureaucracy of the MFGB well before this struggle broke out, and had been clearly understood and rejected by the majority of the rank and file at the time of the 'datum line' strike. What had been envisaged in October 1920 was the relation of wage increases to the achievement of higher levels of output by the rank-and-file miner; what came into force in 1921 was a more developed form of this basic idea and the practical results of this system were clearly explained by a representative of the South Wales left-wing:

> If our Executive Council would take into consideration what the establishment of a datum line means they would realize that they are playing the same game as the coal-owners . . . to exploit the men to produce coal for the mining industry. To establish a datum line, we have for the first time admitted that the miners are to blame for the shortage of output today.[50]

---

[50] MFGB Conference, September 20 and October 1, 1920. This same speaker, Ted Williams, miners' agent in the Garw, gave a dramatic illustration of what the tendencies in the MFGB leadership towards an exploitative form of co-partnership meant. 'I have here on my left,' he said, referring to a delegate at the conference, 'a man of 40 years of

These developments among the miners have been noted at some length because they displayed in a very clear way the pressures acting upon the trade union bureaucracies, even where these had an established 'left-wing' content, to come to terms with post-war capitalism once the alternative, the objective need to fight the state and undertake revolutionary action, had been faced and rejected. Amongst the right-wing leaders of the unions, in both the TUC and the Triple Alliance, there was never the slightest hesitation over their role in the critical situation of 1919. During the crucial period in February and March 1919, when the miners were poised on the brink of action which might have precipitated a general strike, the leaders of the MFGB studiously avoided any appeal for joint action to their allies in the Triple Alliance, although both the Transport Workers' Federation and the NUR were pressing their own programmes at this time and the NUR was being held back with the greatest difficulty by J. H. Thomas from strike action. Similarly, in September 1919 when the rail strike did take place the role of the NUR's allies, along with members of the TUC Parliamentary Committee, was to deputize the Government in the hope of obtaining a compromise solution which would end the strike. There was no consideration of sympathetic action in support of the railworkers. These developments, furthermore, negated threats by the Triple Alliance in the latter part of 1919 to undertake industrial action to force the Government to drop its interventionist activities in support of the White Guards in Russia. Under the pressure of rank-and-file opinion the leaders of the Alliance talked in militant terms, but when they failed to get the TUC to take up the question they neglected to consider unilateral action despite the fact that they formed the most effective industrial bloc within the TUC.

What was at stake in all these developments, it must be emphasized, was the fear of the trade union leaders that once strike action was unleashed on any of the issues noted above the potentially revolutionary tendencies working amongst the rank and file would come to the surface and destroy all chance of control of the strike movement from above. As Clynes warned at the special conference of

---

age who is absolutely finished as a producer of coal. . . .He is finished because he has been all his life on the piecework system. He has put into every single tram of coal every ounce of energy he possibly could and as a consequence he is old at 40. . . .This is what happens to thousands of men in the mining industry today owing to this speeding up system. ...'

the TUC in March 1920, which met to consider sympathetic action in support of the miners' demand for nationalization:

> It is far easier to get your men out than to get them back, and all the time your government and the other remaining parts of the community, you imagine, will be doing nothing. . . .Surely all experience is against such lame and impotent conclusions as that. You cannot bring millions of men out to begin a great struggle like this without anticipating a condition of civil war.[51]

Clynes was, of course, completely correct. The Government, during 1919-1921, had fully prepared itself to deal with strike movements which, it considered, might very well develop along the lines envisaged by Clynes. During 1919, particularly at the time of the rail strike, the Government had elaborated plans for an emergency system of communications, maintenance of essential services and the use of the army for strike breaking; in fact, the plans produced by the Government at this time almost directly anticipated those put into effect during the 1926 strike. In addition, the Government had, under the wartime Defence of the Realm Act, unlimited and implicitly dictatorial powers which it hastened to renew via the Emergency Powers Act introduced during the miners' strike in October 1920.[52] All the preconditions for the 1926 General Strike were thus established in this period of near revolutionary ferment in the immediate post-war years. The essential difference between the two periods was that in 1919-1921 the trade union bureaucracy was, to a considerable extent, able to maintain control. This it did by blocking potentially dangerous working-class movements as far as possible, and where it was impossible to avoid action, as in the 1919 rail strike or the movement against the likelihood of British intervention in the Russian-Polish war in 1920, leading these movements in order to confine them within safe channels. The militant, even revolutionary, demagogy of the right-wing Labour Party and trade union leaders at the time of the 1920 Council of Action was employed in exactly this context. In 1919 J. H. Thomas had stated that he had led the rail strike to maintain control over the rank and file and avert the dangers of revolution: the country, he claimed, had never been nearer to civil war.[53] In 1920 the actions of Thomas and his colleagues were construed in the same terms; at the 1920 TUC, a month after his famous militant speech at the Council

[51] Quoted by W. H. Crook, *General Strike.*

[52] For details, cf. W. H. Crook, op. cit.

[53] *The Times,* October, 1919.

of Action, Thomas warned, in connection with developing industrial struggles:

> We are far too near the precipice to allow dignity or pride on either side to prevent a peaceful settlement. Let the motto for the workers of the country be, 'Settle Down'.[54]

It would be wrong, however, to imagine that the Labour bureaucracy was in any material sense more powerful than in 1926. Its work of assisting the Coalition Government to overcome the dangers of the post-war period was greatly assisted by the high political consciousness of Lloyd George and his acute perception of the character of the Labour leaders, of how to manoeuvre with them and when to make judicious concessions to assist them in their task of controlling the rank and file (as his handling of the miners and railworkers in 1919 demonstrated). Even more important, in fact crucial in this context, was the inability of the revolutionary groups and the unofficial movements in the unions to which they were related to develop among the rank and file of the trade unions and Labour Party a level of political consciousness which would have enabled them to exploit the real revolutionary possibilities which existed in the postwar period. It would be too simple, indeed fallacious, to argue that because the revolutionary groups were involved in the negotiations surrounding the formation of the CPGB they were too pre-occupied to play any significant part in the working-class struggles of this period. Basically it was because these groups were so imbued with syndicalist, propagandist and sectarian tendencies that they were unable to give conscious, political expression to the objectively revolutionary currents that became apparent in the struggles of 1919-1921. Even in 1921, when the work of unification of the revolutionary rendencies had been completed, the CPGB was to show that, at this stage, it was little more than a better organized form of what had existed before in the revolutionary movement in Britain. Given the deep-rooted nature of the pre-1920 tendencies, outlined in the earlier sections of this article, this was inevitable. The CPGB was involved from the moment of its inception in a potentially revolutionary situation with which it had neither the theoretical nor organizational equipment to deal. The working-class struggles of 1919-1921 provided the essential preconditions for the unification of the previously diffuse revolutionary tendencies and, despite the considerable weaknesses shown by the

---

[54] Quoted by Blaxland, *A Life for Unity* (Biography of J. H. Thomas).

newly-formed CPGB in coming to terms with these struggles, the experiences of this period were to provide invaluable lessons for the party in its period of consolidation and development in the years after 1921. In short, it took this experience, particularly of the miners' lock-out of 1921, to reveal to the party in a very concrete way the failings of its syndicalist and propagandist methods; without this experience and the assimilation of its lessons the conditions for the establishment of a potentially effective revolutionary party could not have been realized by 1924-1925.

The most distinctive feature of the CPGB as it emerged from the final round of unity negotiations in January 1921 was the extremely formal character of its adherence to the decisions of the Communist International (notably its Second Congress) on the organizational forms and methods of work of Communist Parties. What the vital Second Congress of the CI had attempted to instil in the consciousness of the delegations attending the Congress was an understanding of the character of the Bolshevik form of political organization and its relationship to the successful seizure of power in 1917. In short, what the leadership of the CI was attempting was to generalize upon the Bolshevik experience and educate the participants in the Congress in those principles of Bolshevism which were of general application to Communist work outside Russia. To the British delegates the idea of a disciplined, centralized party, working in a planned, organized way in the trade unions and Labour Party was something completely new and outside their previous experience, as was the emphasis of the CI upon the need for a theoretically-trained membership educated to use Marxism not in the sterile, formal manner of the Second International but creatively, as a method to evaluate the political perspectives before the party and for relating to this, the day-to-day work of the party in its various forms. The revolutionary groups that had come together to form the CPGB had been attracted by the success of the 1917 Revolution and had been attracted to the *ideal* of a Communist Party, but it took the Second Congress and then the experience of the working-class struggles in Britain in 1921 to produce any real understanding of the major departure from previous political practices required in the formation of a Communist Party affiliated to the CI. J. T. Murphy, a delegate at the Second Congress, described very graphically the shock which the Congress administered to his previous political conceptions which, it may be noted, were those of the British revolutionary groups in general:

> I had left England as a young provincial skilled workman with a clear-cut theory of how society could be reorganized under the control of the workers . . .I was quite sure that capitalism was breaking down everywhere and in the process helping the workers to see their way to Socialism through industrial organization and the General Strike. . . .My experience in Russia . . .had shown me the real meaning of the struggle for political power. Instead of thinking that a Socialist Party was merely a propaganda organization for the dissemination of Socialist views, I now saw that a real Socialist Party would consist of revolutionary Socialists who regarded the Party as a means whereby they would lead the working class in the fight for political power.[55]

The leadership of the newly-formed CPGB in 1921 had undergone the same process of political re-orientation as Murphy but the attachment to the new political concepts and methods of work was inevitably formal; when the crisis of the miners' lock-out arose the party reverted quite instinctively to the predominantly sectarian and syndicalist traditions of its constituent groups. The formal character of the party's acceptance of the directives of the CI for an orientation of party activity towards serious mass work came out initially over relations with the Labour Party. As Brian Pearce notes, the application for affiliation to the Labour Party in 1920 was presented in terms designed to invite rejection and there was clearly general relief in the party, particularly among the tendencies emanating from the SLP and syndicalist groups, at the escape from the possible compromise with reformism.[56] In fact, this sectarian attitude to the mass political organization of Labour, in a period when the Labour Party was beginning to establish an increasingly strong appeal to the working-class electorate, was to arrest the CPGB's own development as an influential force within the Labour movement; until the sectarianism of the early period was overcome, by 1923, much of the potential goodwill among left-wingers in both the Labour Party and ILP was left unrealized, a fact which may well have helped consolidate the ascendancy of the centrist currents around MacDonald and Clifford Allen in the 1922-1923 period.

More important, however, in the context of the events of 1919-1921 was the continuing predominance, indeed strengthening, of the syndicalist element of the revolutionary movement. As noted above, the very weakness of the Labour Party in Parliament meant that the

---

[56] Brian Pearce, 'The Early Years of the CPGB'

[55] J. T. Murphy, *New Horizons*, pp. 189-190.

Labour struggles of the period had to be fought out very largely on the industrial front with the intervention of the Coalition Government giving these struggles an inevitably political character. The weakness and ineptitude of the Parliamentary Labour Party together with the existence, up to the end of 1920, of boom conditions in the economy provided the pre-conditions for the resurgence of syndicalist tendencies amongst wide sections of the working class particularly at a time when, under pressure, employers and the Government, in its role as controller of the mines and railways, could make economic concessions. This background is essential for understanding the continuation of syndicalist tendencies in the groups that formed the CPGB for, up to the end of the boom, it seemed to provide the conditions for continuing and extending the established methods of work: while powerful trade union action, 'direct action', could yield results there was no great pressure to think in political terms about the significance of these trade union struggles. This factor was to be of the greatest importance for what might be termed the 'industrial wing' of the CPGB. It was noted, in the second part of this review, that despite the formal policy differences amongst the revolutionary groupings that formed the CPGB there was a general tendency to share a common syndicalist outlook in relation to work in the trade unions. Effective industrial unionism, the steady encroachment on the power of the employers and the eventual take-over of industry through the general strike, these were the commonplaces of the BSP, the SLP, the WSF of Sylvia Pankhurst, and the Shop Stewards' and Workers' Committee Movement (SS & WCM), in which representatives of the revolutionary groups and 'non-party' syndicalists were active. The SS & WCM did in fact become the industrial basis of the CPGB by March 1921 following discussions between its representatives and the leadership of the CPGB after the Second Congress of the CI and, although the SS & WCM formally agreed to the subordination of its industrial activities to the political direction of the party, there were many indications that leading members of the Movement regarded the party's industrial wing as being of prime importance, a fact which pointed to the likelihood of the continuation of its syndicalist methods.

During the period 1920-1921, when the CPGB was being formed and the SS & WCM was being brought into an organizational relationship with it, there was considerable evidence that, despite the work of the Second Congress of the CI, the tendency was to regard the CPGB as a more highly developed form of the syndicalist movement that had existed, in various forms, from the early 1900s. At the Second Congress Jack Tanner, the official delegate of the SS & WCM, explicitly denied the need for any separate party; in his speech he indicated that the SS & WCM now accepted the need for a revolutionary seizure of power, as carried out by the Bolsheviks, but held that this task could be accomplished by the SS & WCM:

> We understand and realize that the dictatorship of the proletariat must be wielded by a minority — the revolutionary minority of the proletariat as expressed through the Shop Stewards' Committee Movement . . .[but he added that] . . . a number of those who are active in the shop stewards' movement are not greatly concerned about the formation of the party because they have been convinced by their experience in other parties that it was a loss of time to share in the work of such parties. . .[57]

Other members of the SS & WCM who were actively involved in the political revolutionary groups might have disagreed with Tanner on the question of the party but at the same time indicated that, essentially, they saw the same role for the SS & WCM as Tanner; such a movement would carry out the practical tasks of the revolution, the party would provide the propaganda and the organizational apparatus for bringing the various unofficial, syndicalist groups in the unions into effective contact with each other. It was this sort of attitude to which MacManus, a prominent figure in the formation of the CPGB, gave expression when he stated to a conference of the SS & WCM that:

> They (the Bolsheviks) have got to the roots and have found a way out, and what is of even greater interest is that they have found the way out to be by means of just such committees as we are building up in this country. They call them Soviets, we call them Workers' Councils.[58]

It is of significance that the movement of the SS & WCM towards this position marked a very definite shift away from its war-time attitudes. Then it had existed purely as a co-ordinating organization for the local, autonomous unofficial movements in the engineering industry. Now it was adopting a specifically centralized form in connection with its development into a definite revolutionary tendency. As MacManus' remarks indicated, this had come about very much through the influence of the Russian Revolution; at the same time, the passing of the special war-time conditions which had provided the SS

---

[57] Cf. *Proceedings of the Second Congress of the CI*, July-August 1920.

[58] SS & WCM conference, January 10-11, 1920.

& WCM with its original strength forced the movement to reconsider its position. As the unions asserted control over the Shop Stewards during 1919-1920 and effectively limited their role through agreements with the engineering employers, and as employers were increasingly able, particularly outside Scotland, to break up the workshop committees, so the SS & WCM was forced to move, quite empirically, to realize the weakness of localized, autonomous forms of unofficial movement, particularly at a time when the trade union bureaucracies were holding back the rank and file as far as possible and when there consequently existed the chance of rebuilding the unofficial movement on a much higher level.

The SS & WCM was made painfully aware from the immediate post-war period of its considerable weaknesses and the need to evolve some more effective form of organization. The action of the Clyde Workers' Committee in January 1919 in launching the action for the 40-hour week without consulting the English section of the movement was an indication of this, as was the total inability of the movement to give any organized expression to the rank-and-file unrest in the Triple Alliance at the time of the miners' agitation in February-March, 1919. On this occasion the *Worker*, organ of the Scottish section of the SS & WCM, was forced to admit that only rank-and-file committees would make the Triple Alliance act, yet these were non-existent in the TWF while as for the unofficial movement in the NUR ' . . .so spasmodic and at the same time amenable to any emotional outburst on the part of Mr. J. H. Thomas has it been that it can be written down as the unreliable quantity'.[59] The work of the SS & WCM, or those fragments of it that remained after the war, thus took two lines of development from 1919. Increasingly it tried to establish itself as the focal point for unofficial movements in the unions generally, paying particular attention in this context to the miners and railworkers, and at the same time played an increasingly significant part in the events surrounding the formation of the CPGB. By the early part of 1921 the SS & WCM, now formally united with the newly-formed CPGB, had brought within its scope the important unofficial movements which were developing in virtually all the major coalfields, the vigilance committees on the railways and the rank-and-file committees in the docks, notably Liverpool and Glasgow. In addition, the remnants of the workers' committees in the engineering industry remained

[59] *The Worker*, March 3, 1919.

attached to the movement. In short, the SS & WCM brought into the CPGB all the 'organized' syndicalist movements that existed in the post-war period and brought them in largely on the understanding that the CPGB offered a more effective way of organizing the economic struggle in the workshop or mine. The fact that the Convention of the SS & WCM which met in March 1921 to ratify the alliance with the CPGB formally accepted a constitution which subordinated it to the political control of the party did not alter the fact that the industrial base of the party in its formative years was purely syndicalist in outlook, that many of the leaders of the party were drawn from this industrial base and that no attempt was made in the period of the formation of the party to understand the limitations of syndicalism and to draw the lessons of its weaknesses in a period when working-class struggles in all their forms needed to be fought with a political perspective. On the contrary, the party went out of its way to appeal to industrial militants in purely syndicalist terms. The best example of this was in South Wales where considerable potential existed for building a mass CP given the rapid extension of the unofficial movement there. Appealing to the many thousands of militants who followed the lead of the unofficial movement, the party's South Wales organizer, Alf Cook, wrote:

> The Communist branches in the coalfield areas can be the centres of the unofficial agitation in the Miners' Federation. Communist branches in areas like Cardiff, Newport, Barry, Swansea, etc., can be a connecting link between the miners' unofficial movement and the unofficial movement among dockworkers, seafarers, railway and transport workers, and at the same time being attached to a centralized and disciplined national Communist Party, connect South Wales rebel activities with those of the rest of the country . . .[60]

The tendency to present the function of the party in this way, the very formal character of the understanding of the leadership of the work of the Second Congress of the CI, and the total failure of the party during 1920-1921 to make a thorough analysis of the tendencies in British capitalism and the inevitably political, revolutionary struggles to which these must give rise, meant that the party functioned in a purely syndicalist manner during the great struggles of 1921 occasioned by the miners' lock-out. It must be kept firmly in mind

---

[60] *The Communist*, September 20, 1920. Alf Cook, a veteran SLPer in Cardiff, must not be confused with A. J. Cook.

that the lock-out was, from the start, an objectively political struggle. The collapse of the demand for coal, with the end of the post-war boom, meant that the coal-owners demanded savage cuts in wages and attacks on working conditions to maintain their economic viability, particularly in South Wales, which was hit most severely by the collapse of the export trade. At the same time the Government, in the midst of its deflationary programme, had determined to rid itself of its control of the industry and its attendant obligation to finance the mounting losses of the coal-owners. State and owners were thus united in a move to force down, through decontrol, many hundreds of thousands of miners literally to the starvation level and many thousands more into permanent unemployment. The owners launched the attack on the industrial front; the Government backed them with the full resources of the State in meeting the resistance of the miners. The attack on the miners, moreover, could not be divorced from the mounting pressure in all major sections of industry to destroy the gains made by the working class during the post-war boom; the railwaymen were faced with the decontrol of their industry in the latter part of 1921 and although they were a 'sheltered' trade could anticipate wage cuts and speeding up forced through by railway companies, strengthened by the Government-sponsored amalgamation of 1920, anxious to cut freight costs to industry as a whole. The 1921 depression held the same implications for the dockers, while in engineering and the cotton industry pressures were building up for major rationalization of production. During the latter stages of the miners' lock-out a great lock-out in the cotton industry to reduce wages developed; early in 1922 the defeat of the miners encouraged the engineering employers to launch their attack; the turn of the dockers came in 1923, when the gains of the Shaw award of 1920 were challenged. All these developments were implicit in the miners' struggle, for the miners were the strongest, best-organized of the working class with their leadership kept very much in line with rank-and-file militancy by the activities of the unofficial movements. The breaking of this power made possible the attacks on the other sections of the working class which followed the lock-out.

The CPGB was generally aware of the implications for the working class as a whole if the miners were defeated in 1921, but it approached the struggle with all the syndicalist preconceptions noted above and with all the syndicalist illusions of the unofficial movements attached to the party that the struggle could be fought out in purely economic terms. The aim of the party across the lock-out was to hold the MFGB and its allies in the Triple Alliance to the demands of the miners — for the pooling of the profits of the industry to allow the richer districts to finance those worst hit by the depression. But its role in this process was, as Macfarlane rightly implies, totally negative. Macfarlane quotes the constantly repeated slogan of *The Communist* during the lock-out, 'Watch Your Leaders', and indicates that the party's actual activity was confined to the issuing of admonitions from the sidelines. Certainly in terms of its material resources in the unions, other than the miners', it was not at the outset of the struggle to play a very influential role. On the eve of the lock-out *The Communist* was forced to admit:

> Only in one industry, the mines, is there any real organized 'Left' wing opinion, and even that is of recent growth. Can the same be said of any other industry? With the possible exception of the railways — and that exception only partial — the answer is 'No' . . .The National Administrative Council of the Shop Stewards represents powerful ideas, but it is not a powerful organization. . . .Everything has yet to be done . . .[61]

Yet having admitted this the CPGB did not go on to analyse the very favourable conditions that were being created in the unions by the developments in 1921. The fact that the leadership of the MFGB, and this included some of the left-wing like Ablett, were opposed to a fight explicitly because of its political character, placed the greatest responsibility on the party and its unofficial groups in the MFGB to seize the initiative and work for the consolidation of rank-and-file strength around a definitely political perspective. Such a campaign would, in the conditions of 1921, have driven home in a very clear way the need for powerful unofficial movements in other unions, most notably in the unions allied with the miners in the Triple Alliance. A close examination of the actual developments around Black Friday indicates that in South Wales and other important areas of the country conditions were ripe, had the CPGB been able to take the initiative for the organization of unofficial strike movements in support of the miners, particularly in the NUR. In South Wales, for example, the bitterest condemnation of the action of the executive of the NUR was manifested in a very large number of branches and calls for strike action were wide-spread, yet there was not the slightest evidence that the CPGB or the local unofficial movement attempted to exploit this

---

[61] *The Communist*, March 23, 1921.

situation. The right-wing on the South Wales Miners' executive were well aware of the dangers of the situation immediately after Black Friday; Vernon Hartshorn, the prominent South Wales leader, went out of his way to excuse Hodges' actions on the eve of Black Friday and warned:

> If the miners only remain passive . . .maintaining their resolution not to return to work until they had terms which they could accept, they would be acting perfectly within their rights and the silent pressure they would exert would be far greater than any action of violence.[62]

The most significant feature of the situation around Black Friday was the fact that unless the initiative could be seized at once movements of spontaneous anger amongst the rank and file in the Triple Alliance would fail to develop into effective unofficial action and the mood of militant anger rapidly degenerate into demoralization. It was, however, a week before *The Communist* had any positive advice for the rank and file, other than that they should continue to watch their leaders. It urged that money be sent to the *Daily Herald* miners' fund and that 'decent' officials in the Triple Alliance should resign. Its other advice took the form of a purely propagandist exhortation which explicitly discounted the hope of organizing unofficial action:

> Overhaul the whole (union) machinery from top to bottom [it urged] link up the unofficial movements from industry to industry. Make war . . .on every waverer. . . .

But having made this general point it went on:

> The mining lock-out continues and it seems that the rank and file of other unions will have to express their sympathy in financial help now that their leaders have thwarted for the time being the general strike.[63]

Admittedly, at a Congress of the party on April 24 (i.e. ten days after Black Friday) delegates who were active in the industrial wing of the party agreed to initiate an 'intensified campaign' among rail and transport workers with the aim of bringing them out in support of the miners,[64] but by this stage, inevitably, the momentum of rank-and-file militancy which could have provided the success for such a campaign had largely died away. In South Wales, for example, a conference of the unofficial movement right at the end of April took up this decision of the Congress and decided to co-ordinate action with the railworkers, yet the intense militancy of the South Wales

---

[62] *Merthyr Pioneer*, April 4, 1921.

[63] *The Communist*, April 23, 1921.

[64] *Solidarity*, May 5 1921.

NUR, so apparent at the time of Black Friday, had evaporated. Only two branches out of some twenty which had originally pressed for action agreed to consider the proposals of the miners,[65] and in the event, nothing more was heard of the campaign.

This sketch of the response of the CPGB to the events of 1921 is not meant to detract in any way from the party's militancy and courage in support of the miners during the lock-out. In fact its members bore the brunt of the arrests that were made during the struggle. What it is intended to make clear is the powerful tendency operating in the party, both among the leaders and the membership generally, towards fighting the struggle on purely syndicalist terms. Although Macfarlane indicates implicitly that this was the line adopted during 1921 he totally fails to bring out the very serious effect this had in restricting the very great potential influence the party could have had if it had not succumbed to spontaneity, a-politicism, and the type of 'ginger group' activities which characterized the unofficial movements which made up its industrial wing.

It is of importance to note, in this context and as a conclusion to this characterization of the formative years of the CPGB, that the tendencies evident in the party in 1921 were not solely the ideological product, in some sort of isolated way, of the sects which united in 1920-1921. The powerful impulses towards spontaneity and the various syndicalist forms of action were, as has been pointed out in earlier sections of this article, deeply ingrained in the traditions of important sections of the working class. These traditions had been most firmly established in the years of Labour upsurge before the First World War; in the ferment of the post-war period they revealed how strongly they determined the outlook of 'the Left', both leaders and rank and file, in the Labour movement. The CPGB was as much a reflection of these tendencies as it was a conscious participant in them. If the formation of the party had, by 1921, brought the revolutionary tendencies into organizational relationship with each other around the formal agreement on the policies of the CI, it had, in practice, done little by this period to break down the local autonomy which was so characteristic of the revolutionary movement in Britain up to the formation of the CPGB. A really comprehensive history of the party would inevitably have to show that, despite the movements towards Communist unity in 1920-1921, the CPGB as it emerged in 1921 was

[65] *Merthyr Pioneer*, May 5, 1921.

not a great deal more than a federation of local revolutionary tendencies with a propensity towards forms of action which continued in practice in their day-to-day work whatever the formal decisions of the party nationally on the application of the theses of the CI. This local autonomy had been apparent in the British Labour movement from the formative period of the SDF and ILP; it was inevitable that so strongly entrenched a tradition should carry over into the CPGB and it was to be one of the most fundamental tasks of the party in the early 1920s to fight this tendency through the struggle for a centralized, disciplined party based upon a highly politically conscious membership. In 1921 the success of the unification negotiations meant that the preconditions for the achievement of this task had been established, but only the preconditions; the real fight for the revolutionary party in Britain was still to come. In 1921, therefore, the history of the CPGB is as much the history of the local Communist groups — the movement in South Wales, on the Clyde, on Tyneside or in the various districts of London — as it is a history of the national developments in the party. These local tendencies came very much to the fore in the struggles of 1921 and in reality imposed their own pattern on the activities of the CPGB in this period. With their own conception of the character of Communist work still at a very formal stage, the party leadership was not really in a position to attempt to counteract these localized movements whose ideas on revolutionary practice they themselves shared and reflected.

The present stage of research into the Labour movement in this period does not allow any clear picture to be built up of the way the CPGB in its early years was largely a reflection of local revolutionary tendencies. Had Macfarlane placed his account of the formation of the CPGB in this context and initiated this research the value of his work would have been very greatly enhanced. Evidence that exists on the revolutionary movement in South Wales, however, does show very clearly how the established syndicalist tendencies there did impose themselves very firmly on the work of the CPGB in its formative years and would suggest that a similar state of affairs existed elsewhere.

The post-war boom in the coal trade, particularly in the export field in which South Wales was prominent, placed the South Wales miners in an extremely strong economic position and gave a great boost to the revival of the unofficial movement after its dispersal during the war. This revival of unofficial activity took place within the general context of the impact of the Russian Revolution for which there was widespread enthusiasm among the rank-and-file miners, particularly the younger generation, and at the same time that the unofficial groups began to multiply in the mining valleys under the influence of 'missionary' tours by representatives of the SS & WCM and the local branches of the Labour College movement, important elements of the unofficial movement became involved in the activities between 1919 and 1921 surrounding the formation of the CPGB. The most significant feature of these developments was that the revolutionary movement in South Wales, whether it sided with the BSP and the Communist Unity Groups that formed the CPGB in July 1920 or with the 'left wing' Communist organization of Sylvia Pankhurst[66] was that it centred around a revival, in a far more developed form, of the syndicalism which had been endemic in South Wales since the Cambrian Combine strike of 1910. The great economic strength of the rank and file of the SWMF meant that they were in a most favourable position for wringing concessions on wages and conditions from the local owners and were in a position, furthermore, to force the predominantly right-wing executive of the SWMF to keep closely in line with their demands.

These were conditions in which the tendency for the unofficial movement to function purely as a 'ginger group' upon the union leadership could flourish to the fullest extent. So long as the leaders could be kept in line the long-established aims of the *Miners' Next Step,* which could be summarized as the development of an industrial union with the aim of seizing control of the mines, could be realized. The work of the unofficial movement, and in practice the Communist movement which it dominated, thus came to centre around the task of building up the strength of the union in the mining valleys so that, by progressive stages, the miners would begin steadily to encroach on the power of the owners until, eventually, they would have neutralized the owners' rights of control over production and the work of taking control could be completed. In this context the need for a strongly centralized unofficial movement, closely linked to the overall political strategy of the CPGB, seemed very remote. What mattered was the realization of the full strength of the district organizations of the SWMF in each mining valley for which purpose the agitational enthusiasm of a few local militants in the various unofficial groups

[66] Involved in the latter were A. J. Cook and George Dolling, two leading members of the pre-1914 unofficial movement, who found in Pankhurst's organization the complete expression of their a-political revolutionary syndicalism.

could be considered sufficient; the fact that they were at the same time members of the CPGB made little difference and in practical terms merely served to register their adherence to the idea of revolution. The achievements of the unofficial movement were thus represented in the establishment of 100 per cent trade union membership and the bringing into the SWMF of the various 'craft' grades of miners, enginemen, etc., so that a fully effective industrial union might be established. By 1920 this process had gone a long way, particularly in the Rhondda, which embraced a quarter of the mining population in South Wales. So effective was the trade union organization here under the stimulus of the Rhondda unofficial groups, led by militants like Cook, Horner, Dolling, etc., that the power of the coal-owners was very effectively constrained; for example, on two occasions during 1920 the whole of the Rhondda struck against the victimization of a few union members and forced their reinstatement, and at one point in mid-1920 the unofficial movement was able to bring the whole of the SWMF to the verge of a strike in defence of two miners denied the payment of the minimum wage. It was the experience of this sort of strength which gave so great an impetus to the syndicalist belief that the process of seizing power was well advanced. As the South Wales correspondent of *Solidarity* observed:

> Each and every time the management of a colliery seek to serve notice on any employee they are faced with the prospect of an immediate stoppage of work. ...'Intolerable' is the word used by one coal-owner ...but for the worker it is the first step that has ever been made on the road to real Freedom.[67]

At the meetings of the SS & WCM that took place during 1920, delegates from the South Wales unofficial movement made even clearer their confidence in their strength. Describing the situation in the mining valleys, Charlie Gibbons (one of the original authors of *The Miners' Next Step*) stated:

> They (the unofficial movement) manufactured pretexts and created situations whereby the workers were forced into a spirit of antagonism to the employers. As a result of their efforts there were now 150,000 in the South Wales coalfield prepared to 'do' the employers as soon as the opportunity came. ...[68]

In this context it did not matter that the nationalization campaign of the MFGB had failed in 1919. There was no need to examine the

---

67 *Solidarity*, July 1920.

68 SS & WCM conference, January 10-11, 1920.

political reasons for this failure or to consider the role played in it by the State when the local economic power of the miners was, apparently, increasing so rapidly. It was this situation which prompted a rank-and-file miner to write that:

> Whether the official scheme for nationalization and joint control is granted or not, the South Wales miners are going on quietly with the work of *taking* control. Some day, when the Government at last enacts some scheme of joint control, it will wake up to find that it is only legalizing what already exists in practice.[69]

The circumstances that produced this attitude in South Wales were, of course, purely temporary. The slump which set in from the end of 1920 completely removed the economic conditions which had given the impetus to syndicalism but this rapid change in material conditions did not in any way force a re-assessment of the syndicalist character of the Communist movement in South Wales. The whole work of the unofficial movement in this area in the period leading up to the 1921 lock-out was conducted on exactly the same lines as in 1920. In the propaganda of the movement there was not the least consideration of the inevitably political character of the coming struggle; all that was necessary for success, it was argued, was an extension of the unofficial movement to ensure that the union leaders did not retreat from the policy of the profits pool and the national wages board. Similar considerations dominated the development of the unofficial movement nationally in this period when the SS & WCM was formally uniting with the CPGB. The South Wales unofficial leaders had been arguing during 1920 at meetings of the SS & WCM that what was needed for the realization of their policy for the seizure of the mines was the extension of their type of organization to all the major coalfields. This would ensure that the MFGB followed the policies laid down by the rank and file. In the months before the lock-out the SS & WCM was successful in initiating on quite an extensive scale unofficial movements of this type in all the major coalfields and the formation of the 'British Miners' Reform Movement' in February 1921 seemed to indicate at last that rank-and-file opinions could be impressed on the union leadership and the coalowners and Government defeated in the coming struggle in purely economic terms. In this development the leadership of the CPGB gave its complete support to the conception that the preparations for the

---

[69] *Workers' Dreadnought*, April 17, 1920.

lock-out should be conducted on purely syndicalist lines. At the Convention of the SS & WCM, at the end of March 1921, right on the eve of the lock-out, when the alliance with the CPGB was ratified, there was no consideration given to the coming struggle. Obviously it was held that the work of the party would devolve on the local unofficial groups who would act in a purely spontaneous, 'ginger group' fashion in response to the struggle as it developed. It was because the local, autonomous syndicalism of the unofficial movements imposed itself on the party in this way that the CPGB played so negative a role in the lock-out, as outlined above, and it was this development which prompted the critique of Radek, at the Third Congress of the CI, part of which is quoted by Macfarlane. Radek's comments revealed very clearly how the traditions of the unofficial movements asserted themselves during the struggle: 'In many places,' he noted, 'the Party appears on the scene under the cloak of the "Workers' Committees" and any success that is achieved by the propaganda does not bring the masses near to the CP. . . .' In his further comments, based on interrogations of delegates from the CPGB, he revealed how completely the party had failed to prepare politically for the struggle and had fallen back on the spontaneity of its members:

> To my question, what do you tell the masses, what is your attitude to nationalization? What is your attitude to the present concrete claims of the workers? one of the comrades replied: 'When I ascend the rostrum at a meeting I know as little about what I am going to say as the man in the moon; but being a Communist, I find my way along while I speak.'[70]

It was with this evidence before him that Radek forcibly stated:

> . . . We consider it our duty to say the following, even to the smallest CPs: you will never have any large mass parties if you limit yourselves to the mere propaganda of the Communist theory.

In fact, it was only by assimilating the lessons of 1921, in the context of the critique of the CI and with the guidance of the latter, that the CPGB was to proceed towards the establishment of conditions for effective mass Communist work by 1924-1925. The experience of 1921 was a necessary condition for the escape from the previous syndicalist, sectarian traditions of the British revolutionary movement. It provided the basis for understanding theoretically the limitations of syndicalism in a period of revolutionary industrial struggles

---

[70] *Communist Review*, December 1921.

and for the party to orientate its practice towards mass work in the unions and Labour Party in conscious preparation for seizing the revolutionary initiative in future conflicts. At the same time, for large sections of the organized working class 1921 stimulated intense hostility towards the labour bureaucracy which had featured so prominently in the betrayal of the miners. With the passing of the worst effects of the 1921 defeat the conditions existed in the unions and the Labour Party for a sympathetic response to the CPGB, and a readiness to follow the practical lead of the party which was to be of crucial importance in the events around 'Red Friday', 1925, and which provided the pre-conditions for its development into a mass organization.

Part 4: The degeneration of the Comintern and the General Strike

The realization of this potential in the post-1921 situation depended absolutely on the assimilation by the CP of the lessons of the 1921 experience and its relation to the work of the early congresses of the Communist International (CI). The whole emphasis of the second, third and fourth congresses was on the need to develop, from the groups and parties that adhered to Communism from 1919, parties of the Bolshevik type, based, that is, on the generalized experience of the Russian party and in particular on the experience of 1917. The temporary passing of the post-war revolutionary crisis in Europe had revealed the general inability of the groupings adhering to the CI to provide concrete revolutionary leadership and had underlined the need for basic education of the emergent communist tendencies in the theory of Bolshevism. The work of the third and fourth congresses was particularly important in this context. The emphasis placed by these congresses on the central role of the party, the elaboration of the tactic of the united front, the struggle for the development and application of Marxist theory to the immediate and overall perspectives of the party, all these flowed from the historical experience of the Bolshevik party, combined with the theoretical estimate made of the character of the situation in post-war Europe. In the period of permanent economic crisis ushered in with the 1920s the conditions existed for sharp fluctuations in the consciousness of the working class, for rapid radicalization in reaction to the periodic deepening of the crisis and the predictable attempts of the bourgeoisie to stabilize their system at the expense of the working class. In these conditions the way forward for the constituent parties of the CI could only be through their orientation towards mass work combined with the development of a centralized, disciplined organization and a theoretically trained membership. It was, moreover, only through the constant deepening of theoretical understanding in relation to the work of the party that the relations forged between it and the working class could be strengthened and the conditions for consolidating the practical revolutionary leadership of the class understood and realized.

For the CPGB as it existed in 1921-1922 the emphasis of the CI on the central role of the party meant a complete break not merely from the practice of the party in 1920-1921 but from the traditions of spontaneity and empiricism which had characterized the Marxist and syndicalist groups over the previous generation and which were in many respects the militant expression of trade union politics. The struggle for a party of the Bolshevik type in Britain required the conscious rejection of these traditions; the transformation, in the first place, of the whole character of the party from the loose groupings devoted to spontaneity typical of the syndicalist period to a disciplined party capable of effective communist work in the mass organizations of the labour movement. In the second place, and no less important, a conscious break was required from the formalized, mechanical Marxism of the pre-1920 period (as analysed in Part Two above) and its replacement by an approach to Marxism which emphasized the need for the systematic application of theory to the work and development of the party. The history of the CPGB in the period of 1921-1925 was bound up essentially with the struggle in the party to apply and develop these new methods of work, and in this process the twin questions of party organization and the fight for theory were inextricably connected. This period saw the party move a long way towards overcoming the weaknesses which had attended its inception. With the formation of the National Minority Movement (NMM) in 1924, and the beginning of the Left-Wing Movement in the Labour Party with the launching of the highly successful *Sunday Worker* in 1925, the party began to establish the basic preconditions for its emergence as a decisive political force within the labour movement.

These favourable developments were, essentially, the practical expression of the theoretical lessons derived from the experience of 1921 and the work of the early congresses of the CI. They cannot be seen, however, as the outcome of some straightforward, automatic process of reversal of the party's original weaknesses. The movement towards the creation of mass influence in the period before the General Strike was the outcome of a series of struggles within the party, a process which has to be seen in dialectical terms. By 1925 the party had the potential for rapid growth as a result of its orientation towards mass work, but at the same time it still contained within it, both in the leadership and the branches, a strong disposition towards the empiricist, syndicalist methods characteristic of its formative period. It was still only in a very formal way that the tendencies present at its formation had been overcome by 1924-1925; on questions such as party organization, the relation of theory to practice, the party's grasp of Bolshevik method was necessarily imperfect. By 1925, then, only the pre-conditions for a potentially effective revolutionary party existed, and this was why the experience of 1925-1926, particularly the General Strike, was so crucial. It represented the first decisive test of the political strength of the party as established by the mid-1920s.

The most vital aspect of the development of the CPGB in the early 1920s therefore centred on its ability to apply Marxist theory creatively to the overall work of the party. Without such a development, without the growth of a theoretically trained membership, the work of the party must necessarily be empirical and spontaneous, lagging behind the revolutionary developments in the working class as a whole. In this context, the most striking feature of the CPGB's development was the formal way in which the main aspects of Bolshevik method were adopted. While the permanent crisis in the British economy and the sharp confrontations of workers, employers and the state made clear the vital necessity for a revolutionary solution to the problems confronting the working class, the strongly entrenched traditions of spontaneity, propagandism and empiricism established within the revolutionary movement from the 1900s clashed with, and to some extent negated, the adoption of Bolshevik methods of work. It would, of course, be the purest idealism to consider that the CPGB could develop in any other way than through a conflict between established practice and the struggle to apply communist principles of organization, and it is clear that in shaking off its past practices the party could only develop in a consistently revolutionary direction by reflection upon its past work in the labour movement and conscious efforts to change it in line with Bolshevik principles. Yet although efforts were made in this direction in the early 1920s, the considerable theoretical backwardness of the party meant that in its endeavours to transcend its past it was very heavily dependent on the assistance, theoretical and practical, of the CI; and what was to be of the utmost significance throughout the 1920s was the party's tendency to rely absolutely for theoretical guidance on the CI. While this guidance was to be vital in directing the CPGB into positive revolutionary work in the early 1920s, notably in the establishment of the NMM, the CPGB's dependent relationship to the CI meant that it became quite impossible for the leadership to understand theoretically and resist the complete change of theory and practice in the CI which flowed from the growth of Stalinism and the international consequences of the 'theory' of Socialism in One Country.

The nature of the relationship of the CPGB with the CI is an essential guide to understanding the degeneration of the CPGB from the later 1920s which followed, in the first instance, from its inability to develop the revolutionary potential in the General Strike. It is, therefore, a major failing on Macfarlane's part that he does not really consider, except in a very formal sense, the inter-relationship between the CPGB and the CI. True, he records the campaign of the CPGB against Trotsky in 1925 in accordance with CI policy, together with the role of the CI in the adoption by the CPGB of the disastrous 'new line' at the end of the 1920s, but nowhere does he place these actions in the general context of the Stalinization of the CI or assess the effects of Stalinism on the work of the CPGB. However, it is demonstrably impossible to understand the overall development of the CPGB in the 1920s unless this is closely related to the role of the CI in this period, and this means considering not only what might be called the more 'dramatic' episodes, which Macfarlane uses to good effect, but also the positive revolutionary work conducted by the CI in the early period of its existence.

It is the work of the CI in this early phase, its encouragement to the CPGB through theoretical training and practical assistance, which Macfarlane virtually ignores. But this assistance was of the utmost importance in laying the basis in Britain for the growth of an effective revolutionary party. In fact, the early years of the CPGB were characterized by the persistent efforts of the CI to educate the party's leadership in Bolshevik principles and to fight against the tendency to the purely formal application of these methods. The Executive Committee of the CI (ECCI) was acutely aware, not only in relation to the British party, of the dangers implicit in a rigid, mechanical application of the principles of communist organization as laid down by the second congress that would negate the cardinal principle of democratic centralism. The third congress explicitly warned that:

> ... A formal or mechanical centralization would be nothing but the centralization of power in the hands of a bureaucracy in respect of its domination over other members of the party or the masses of revolutionary workers outside the party...

and it stressed that the formation of centralized, disciplined parties was inseparable from the creation of a theoretically trained membership fully understanding and participating in the formulation of party policy.[71]

The validity of this warning was amply demonstrated as far as the CPGB was concerned. The way in which the theses of the CI on the organization of the party were applied indicated the highly formal, untheoretical approach of the party leadership that was to characterize the relations generally of the CPGB with the CI. Recalling the response of the party to the re-organization in the early 1920s, J. T. Murphy illustrated this point very clearly:

> We were of course far from having put into operation all that was required by the CI resolution to reconstitute the new Communist Party. We had made our political declaration of adherence to its principles, but it is one thing to accept a principle and another to apply it to life. The CP was supposed to be a Marxist party, but there were few in it who had more than a nodding acquaintance with the writings of Marx ...[72]

The significance of Murphy's observation and the warning of the third congress was revealed in the way the re-organization of the CPGB was carried out in 1922-1923, following the presentation of the report of the Reorganization Commission (largely the work of Palme Dutt) to the Fifth Party Congress in October 1922. The material provided by Macfarlane on the Commission and the way its report was applied is of the utmost value in assessing the extent to which the CPGB was still dominated by the old conceptions; devotion to pure propaganda, to loose, undisciplined party organization and spontaneity.[73] Clearly such an organization was totally unsuited to any serious revolutionary work; as the report noted, centralization and a strong leadership were needed.

At the same time, the way the report was drafted and applied displayed a lack of real political understanding and a tendency to

---

[71] *Theses on Tactics.* [72] J. T. Murphy, *New Horizons*, p. 181.
[73] Macfarlane, op. cit., pp. 77-89.

introduce centralization as a purely organizational task divorced from the overall political perspectives of the party. Macfarlane is absolutely correct in pointing out there was no attempt by Dutt to explain how the report related to the political work of the party; as a result, a highly complex, top-heavy structure was imposed on the party in just the way which the theses of the CI had deplored. There was really no attempt at political preparation of the membership and the fact that the centralization scheme was introduced largely through the instrumentality of Dutt and Pollitt was not altogether accidental. The collaboration of these two, the main exponents of the formal and pragmatic approach to party re-organization, marked the beginning of what was to prove a lifetime partnership in the leadership of the CPGB in which they were to play a crucial part in the process of the party's Stalinization. The partnership was an ideal one, based on a division of labour between Dutt, the facile intellectual ready to provide a sophisticated veneer for the policies of Stalinism, and Pollitt, the intensely pragmatic party functionary and speaker. In the immediate circumstances of 1922, of course, their actions were not as yet related to the process of Stalinization, which still lay in the future, but their whole approach to re-organization revealed a conception of party work in general which was at a later date to allow them to play this role very effectively.

The growing volume of criticism in the party press on the way re-organization had been carried out indicated graphically how divorced the process had been from the political perspectives of the party and from the theoretical preparation of the membership. Murphy effectively summed up the essentials of this criticism when he stated that:

> If I were asked what are the principal defects of the party today, I would answer unhesitatingly, formalism, organizational fetishism, and lack of political training . . .[74]

There can be little doubt, from the contributions in the *Workers' Weekly* and the *Communist Review,* that there was serious concern at the abysmal level of theoretical development in the party at the very time when a breakthrough to mass work was being achieved through the formation of the NMM. Yet on the part of Pollitt there was virtually no recognition or apparent understanding of the political problems posed by party re-organization. For him, it was a purely

[74] *Communist Review,* January 1924.

practical task, and he dismissed with evident contempt the vital points raised by Murphy and others:

> The greatest hindrance to the growth of our party is not the lack of political training, it is a number of practical difficulties that our members are meeting with . . .Ask any local organizer in South Wales or Scotland what their biggest problem is, they won't say it was the absence of 'the will to revolution', they will say it was the lack of a common meeting place. Ask them what other things they were up against and we would find it wasn't 'the fetish of mechanical formalism' but lack of finance due to the poverty of the members.[75]

Given this inbuilt bias on the part of a section of the party leadership at national and local level to treat the question of party development in a purely organizational way, it is possible to pose the important question of how far the CPGB entered the period of its most substantial growth in the 1920s, 1924-1926, with a membership conscious of the revolutionary perspectives open to the party and ready to relate immediate issues of party work to an overall theoretical understanding of the chances for revolutionary development associated with the deepening of the economic crisis and the shift to the left among the rank and file of the trade unions and the Labour Party. The point here is not simply that the CPGB inherited from the work of the Reorganization Commission a bureaucratic, unwieldy party structure; in fact, once the worst abuses of re-organization were corrected, by 1924 the party was certainly far more able to carry out effective disciplined work in the labour movement. The crucial issue was whether there was any real attempt after re-organization, to take up the theoretical training of the membership in a serious way. It was quite possible for the party to undertake practical tasks associated with the building of the NMM in the unions and the Left Wing Movement in the Labour Party, but how far was there a developing ability on the part of the membership to understand the theoretical and political considerations from which party practice flowed and to relate this to their day-to-day work?

To some extent this must be an open question as the limited evidence available does not permit any direct examination of the effectiveness of the political training of the party membership. An answer must, however, be attempted insofar as it was the theoretical weaknesses of the CPGB which rendered it so unresistant to the

---

[75] *Ibid.*, February 1924.

process of Stalinization in the CI in the mid-1920s and which prevented it giving any revolutionary lead during the General Strike. There can be little doubt as to the generally low theoretical level of the party leadership in the 1920s. The tendency to apply the policy decisions of the CI in a mechanical way unrelated to the conscious development of Marxist theory was very marked. The Executive Committee of the CI was continually criticizing this failing, and its comments on the weaknesses of the theoretical organ of the CPGB, the *Communist Review*, summed up the approach of the party to theoretical questions in general. The ECCI found, for example, that:

> . . . the aversion to theory revealed itself everywhere in the columns of the *Communist Review* . . Whenever any theoretical questions were touched upon, their presentation and analysis were of a purely descriptive nature. No attempts were made to co-ordinate these questions systematically in conceptions and formulae. As a consequence the officials and advanced workers could gather nothing of the theory of Leninism as the uniform method of Marxism during the present epoch.[76]

In a letter (written shortly before his recent death) J. T. Murphy confirmed the general point implied by the critique of the ECCI, that the party leadership were very much steeped in empirical trade union attitudes and saw Marxism still in the formal way in which it had been approached in the pre-1920 period.

> . . . We were ardent trade unionists, most of us experienced in leading unofficial movements. That was our strength . . .(but) the theoretical equipment of the leadership as a whole was not of a high standard. I remember there [were] only Tommy Jackson and myself who were at all familiar with the philosophical aspects of Marxism.

The clearest expression of the persistence of these long-established empirical traditions was provided in the position adopted by the CPGB over the struggle of Trotsky and the Left Opposition in the mid-1920s against the growth of the Stalinist bureaucracy and its ramifications throughout the international Communist movement. Thus while the struggles in its Russian Party in the 1923-1926 period provoked a sympathetic response among important sections of the major European parties, notably the French, Polish and German, in Britain they aroused virtually no interest. As Macfarlane observes, the sole contribution of the CPGB was the completely uncritical

---

[76] Letter from the Agitprop department of the ECCI, February 24, 1925. *Communist Papers*, Cmd. 2682.

acceptance of the position of Stalin against the Left Opposition; in fact, it was this docile acceptance of the process of bureaucratization which prompted Stalin to hail the CPGB as a 'model party' by 1926. The point was that the CPGB never seriously attempted to understand what was at stake in the struggles in the CPSU. As far as the British leadership was concerned, this was a purely internal affair of the Russian party, having no relevance to the work in Britain. Indeed it was only after specific pressure had been applied by the ECCI[77] that the CPGB took up the issue of the fight against Trotsky and duly echoed the theses of Stalin and the right bloc in the CPSU. The anti-theoretical attitude of the CPGB towards the crisis in the CPSU, and hence towards the overall development of the work of the CI, was clearly demonstrated in such contributions as the party did make to the debate on 'Trotskyism'. These showed a failure to grasp the issues involved and from this failure stemmed the inability of the party to grasp the disastrous international consequences of the 'theory' of Socialism in One Country with its emphasis on the recovery and equilibrium of post-war imperialism. There are definite indications that the CPGB was forced by the ECCI into taking an orthodox line on Trotskyism without seriously debating the issue or attempting to find out the reality of the situation in Russia. This is aptly demonstrated by the initial response of the party to the debate on the New Course in Russia. In 1924 Tom Bell was providing a full and accurate synopsis of the arguments advanced by the opposition against bureaucratization in the CPSU and was recording that:

> ... it was especially Trotsky who brought this discussion to the front which is proof enough to all who have the slightest acquaintance with the Russian Party that this crisis did not represent any danger for the unity of the Party.[78]

This article was mainly designed to answer those elements in the Labour left who were asserting that the Soviet system was on the point of collapse; the significance of it was that it evoked no evidence of contradiction on the part of the CPGB leadership as a whole. It was not until 1925 that the CPGB swung completely to the other side on the question of Trotsky upon the intervention, as noted above, of the ECCI. What was so notable about this change of line, compared with Bell's position in 1924, was that the attack on Trotsky was now conducted on an anti-theoretical and consciously anti-intellectual

[77] *Communist Papers*, p. 33.

[78] *Communist Review*, February 1924.

basis. The most blatant example of this came from MacManus. Reviewing Max Eastman's *Since Lenin Died* (a work which exposed the bureaucratic degeneration occurring in the CPSU written by a member of the American Communist Party who supported Trotsky) he argued that the attacks on and purges of the opposition combined with the recruitment of politically untrained workers to the CPSU (the 'Lenin Levy') were purifying the CPSU and restoring its proletarian character and unity hitherto disrupted by intellectuals.[79] The whole effect of this article was to appeal to the more backward elements in the CPGB still at a trade union level of consciousness to contrast the proletarian common sense of Stalin to the instability and divisive methods of the middle-class intellectuals. This same approach, as Brian Pearce notes,[80] was again clearly displayed in the handling of 'Trotskyism' in the party press and conferences throughout 1925. The significance of these developments must be seen in the context of the overall work of the CPGB in the mid-1920s. The way the CPGB, with virtually no sign of resistance, was pressurized by the ECCI into the campaign against Trotsky was evidence of the extreme theoretical dependence of the party on the CI. In the early 1920s this dependence had helped the CPGB overcome some of its initial weaknesses and orientate itself towards mass work. In the mid-1920s it was responsible in a big way for the subordination of the CPGB to the anti-revolutionary line of Stalin, and for reinforcing the empirical, anti-theoretical tendencies in the party at the very time when its influence was growing rapidly in the labour movement. The failure of the CPGB to prepare any revolutionary leadership for the General Strike was intimately bound up with the campaign against Trotsky and the associated confirmation of the theoretical backwardness of the party. The practical expression of these developments was to be revealed in the party's trade union work in 1925-1926. It was the retreat from the fight for revolutionary politics in the unions into an essentially syndicalist type of trade-union militancy which was at the centre of the failure of the CPGB in its first and, as it proved, only decisive test as a revolutionary party in 1926.

The retreat of the party into syndicalism in the General Strike was all the more disastrous when seen in the context of the substantial advance made from 1921 in developing revolutionary methods of work in the unions. By 1925 the process of forming Minority Move-

---

[79] *Ibid.*, June 1925.

[80] See 'Early Years of the CPGB'.

ments in major trade unions was well advanced and the CPGB was consciously working through the Minority Movements and its own factory and pit groups to politicize the growing industrial militancy of the rank and file. Yet by 1926, although the influence of the CPGB had continued to grow, preparations to provide a revolutionary initiative had been virtually abandoned and the party entered the General Strike as a critical but essentially loyal ally of the TUC. In so doing, it reversed the whole of its revolutionary work from 1921 and the lessons of revolutionary organization learnt during that period.

The ability of the CPGB to prepare seriously for revolutionary work in the unions derived from the inter-relationship of the lessons drawn from its experience in 1921 and the intervention of the CI to correct syndicalist manifestations in the party. Soon after the 1921 conflict the party was aware that the defeat of the miners had been bound up with its own theoretical and organizational inability to give expression to the revolutionary potential in the situation. J. T. Murphy noted self-critically that all sections of the labour movement, including the syndicalist unofficial movements and the CPGB '. . . missed or ignored the revolutionary political significance of the power accumulating in the growth of their organizations . . .The crises of the last three years have delivered smashing blows at all our old conceptions of the struggle . . .Who can now say: This is an industrial issue and that is a political issue?'[81]

Although a correct appreciation of the change in the character of trade union struggles, this remained a purely formal response to the questions facing the CPGB in its trade union work until 1923-1924. While the mistakes of 1921 might be recognized, the party remained in the early 1920s utterly confused as to how to organize effectively in the unions. The depression and mass unemployment had knocked the bottom out of the syndicalist idea of squeezing out the employers by the escalation of pure industrial militancy; at the same time, sectarian and 'dual unionist' ideas persisted among those elements in the party who had come from the SLP, while among party activists in the localities the 1921 defeat and the depression promoted demoralization and disorientation which was matched by that of the trade union rank and file. The practical reflection of this situation was shown by the criticisms made by the party's Control Commission to the Sixth

[81] *Labour Monthly*, January 1922. This point was repeated editorially by Dutt in the April 1922 issue.

Congress (1924). The party's Industrial Department, it stated, had been bandied around from one EC member to another and had not even got down to the basic task 'of ascertaining the strength and co-ordinating the work of the Party nuclei in the Trade Unions and the Trades Councils'.[82] The unofficial movements in the unions had fared no better. Merged with the British Bureau of the RILU in 1922, they had been orientated towards pure propaganda for RILU affiliation by the trade unions and had given no effective lead on basic problems affecting the rank and file. As Lozovsky, head of the RILU, later noted, the British Bureau was totally unsuited to British conditions, not least because it allowed the trade union right wing to accuse the CPGB of splitting the unions by encouraging disaffiliation from the TUC.[83]

The chaos in the CPGB's industrial work was only partly a reflection of demoralization in the trade unions. The miners, badly hit by their defeat, were recovering in militancy by 1923 and became increasingly antagonistic to the collaborationist attitude to the owners on the part of the Executive Committee of the Miners' Federation. Their radicalization preceded that of other major trade unions, but by 1923-1924 there were signs of a general recovery from demoralization and a growth of combativeness on the part of the rank and file. This trend created favourable conditions for the expansion of the party's influence, yet theoretically and organizationally it was not really capable of seizing the opportunity. The intervention of the CI was decisive in this context, and the way it intervened was indicative of the weaknesses of the party leadership at this stage. The first steps towards the formation of an effective opposition block in the unions under party control were taken in 1922. Borodin, the CI agent in Britain, by-passed both the national and district leaderships of the CPGB to obtain information from local party members in South Wales on the way the pre-1921 unofficial movement had operated and how far a revival of its methods would allow an opposition movement to be recreated in the MFGB. From this point he went on to organize party members and sympathizers at the MFGB's annual conference in 1922 into the nucleus of such a movement, now for the first time given the title 'minority government'. The movement's aim was to rally all dissatisfied sections of the rank and file around an agitation for the

---

82 Macfarlane, op. cit., pp. 121-122.

83 E. H. Carr, *Socialism in One Country*, Vol. 3, part 1, pp. 121-122.

overthrow of the 1921 agreement, the winning of a living wage and the destruction of the pernicious leadership of Hodges.[84] Initially the movement was confined to South Wales, but by the latter half of 1923 minority movements were developing in other coalfields and by January 1924 an effective national movement was formally established.

The encouragement of this type of unofficial movement did not amount to a tacit encouragement of syndicalist methods. Via Borodin, the CI was endeavouring to orientate the CPGB towards the immediate problems of the trade union rank and file, to advance policies which would maximize opposition to the existing collaborationist union leaders and thereby bring the rank and file towards the party as a necessary preparation for politicizing their industrial militancy and thereby recruiting to and building the party. In line with this the immediate programme of the NMM started from the existing level of consciousness of the rank and file, but by advancing demands based on the desire of the rank and file for major improvements in conditions, the NMM sought to develop a revolutionary consciousness on the understanding that these demands were basically incompatible with the private ownership of industry, and that the unions could fight for them only through the growth within them of a revolutionary opposition to the union bureaucracy.

On the basis of the growing success of the Miners' Minority Movement the CI sought to convince the CPGB of the urgent need for the adoption of this method of organization generally in the party's trade union work. At a meeting of the party leadership with the ECCI and the RILU in Moscow in mid-1923 the CPGB was censured for its failure to make any real attempt to form revolutionary minorities in the unions and was urged to set about the immediate task of organizing them into a cohesive national movement.[85] It was a sign of the continuing confusion in the party leadership and the strength of the attachment to the earlier syndicalist and sectarian methods that, even though the British Bureau was reorganized and Gallacher put in charge of it with the specific task of organizing a national Minority Movement, it was not until the latter part of 1924 that its first national conference was held.[86]

---

84 Information based on interview with member of the CPGB in the Rhondda in the 1920s; also see *The Times*, December 23, 1926.

85 Carr, op. cit., p. 121.

86 These developments are detailed in M. Woodhouse, 'Syndicalism, Communism and the Trade Unions', in *Marxist*, Vol.4, No. 3.

Significantly, one of the factors inhibiting the party leadership in the rapid implementation of the Minority Movement policy was the deep-rooted belief that it represented a purely reformist tactic unrelated to the revolutionary aims of the party. It was later observed that:

> . . . at the beginning of the National Minority Movement considerable time and energy had to be expended to fight down the belief that there was no room for a movement dealing with immediate and 'narrow' economic issues . . .and that such an organization would stand in front of and hide the party from the workers.[87]

The existence of this attitude was an indication of the basic difficulty of developing in the party at this stage a real appreciation of the necessary relationship between the 'pure theory' of Communism and practical mass work. Yet while the party was never able to overcome fully this tendency to compartmentalism in its thinking on questions of theory and practice, there was all the same a sense in which the development of the work around the NMM from 1924 did take the CPGB a long way towards realizing the necessary conditions for creating a mass party by the mid-1920s.

1924 saw the start of a marked radicalization among the working class which was to build to a peak in 1925-1926. The election of the Labour government was only one sign of this; it was accompanied by a clear tendency on the part of organized labour to fight for a restoration of the gains lost after the defeats earlier in the 1920s which took sections of the working class to the verge of a direct confrontation with the Labour government and produced, on the part of the miners, a build-up in militancy, stimulated by the NMM, which resulted in the winning of a ten per cent wage increase in the new agreement signed in mid-1924. Taken together with the disillusionment bred by the Labour government and the return of a strengthened Tory government in the autumn of 1924, these developments served to promote a leftward swing in the labour movement expressed, initially, through the strengthening of centrist tendencies in the trade unions and Labour Party (the election of the 'left' union leaders, Purcell, Hicks, *et al.*, to the TUC General Council; the growth of the Maxton grouping in the Independent Labour Party) but related, basically, to the growing readiness to challenge the employers and their state through mass industrial action. Accompanied as it was by a down-turn in the economy and a particularly acute situation in the mining industry, the

---

87 *Communist Review*, Vol.4, 1932.

growth of rank-and-file combativeness presaged a profound intensification in the class struggle and the opening of a period of industrial conflict bound, objectively, to challenge the private control of industry and lead to a direct confrontation between organized labour and the state. It was the fact that a clear tendency in this direction was established during 1924, implied particularly in the mood of the miners after the conclusion of their new agreement, which allowed the CPGB to reach a clearer understanding of the significance of the trade union policy which flowed from the establishment of the NMM and the way forward to the development of a revolutionary leadership in the unions.

The advances made by the party since the early 1920s shaped the way it approached the deepening industrial crisis in 1925. From the failure of the miners to win their full objective in the 1924 agreement, the living wage, the CPGB drew the conclusion that it was impossible for the miners, or any other individual trade union, to win advances in the prevailing economic conditions through isolated action. The way forward must be through the formation of an offensive alliance of trade unions which could take joint action around a common programme. Behind this alliance should be ranged the TUC and the overall direction of the mass movement placed in the hands of the General Council, mandated by and responsible to the rank and file.[88] The proposal was made more concrete by the formulation of a definite programme by the first annual conference of the NMM, August 1924, which centred on the £4 minimum wage and the 44-hour week,[89] and by the development of a widespread movement for wage advances from the start of 1925 by a number of the bigger unions, the NUR, AEU, Shipbuilders and T&GWU among them. The most striking feature of the campaign by the CPGB to bring these developments together into a unified, offensive trade union movement was the fact that from the start the party fought against any tendency for its activities to become entangled with the centrist currents so strongly evident in the labour movement after the collapse of the Labour government and fought, too, against any syndicalist trend in the work of the NMM which would merely serve to strengthen the opportunism of the official left wing in the unions. For the CPGB, the policy

[88] The first proposals for such an alliance were made in mid-1924, *Workers' Weekly*, June 6, 1924.

[89] The conference had been preceded by the formation of MM groups in the rail, dock and engineering industries as well as mining.

of the industrial alliance was understood wholly in the context of the building of the party in preparation for the revolutionary turn which the coming industrial struggles must take. In its work in the unions the CPGB and the NMM did not operate with the idea of gingering the union leadership into militant actions from below but rather with the fundamental perspective of establishing rank-and-file control over the leadership through their day-to-day work among the rank and file and winning them to a revolutionary position. The practical work of the CPGB in the unions was therefore directly related to the deepening class conflict in Britain and the chances this created for the expansion of the party. As the Resolution on the Minority Movement adopted by the CPGB's 6th Congress put it:

> In the actual fight to achieve their immediate demands the workers will be brought up against the whole organized power of capitalism — the State Therefore, as the struggle develops, the importance and absolute necessity of the Communist Party to the working class becomes more and more clearly revealed. The opposition movements can only go forward under the leadership of a powerful Communist Party. Out of the struggle of the opposition movements of today will be forged the Communist Party of tomorrow.

The resolution then went on to warn, very emphatically, against the dangers of syndicalism in the work of the NMM:

> . . . the Communist Party, while working inside the minority movement will on no account sacrifice its separate existence or limit its freedom of agitation and propaganda. By this means it will win the workers to the Party in ever-increasing numbers, and prepare the working class for the real problems that confront them, that of the conquest of power.[90]

It flowed logically, and correctly, from the 6th Congress and the contemporaneous launching of the NMM, that the CPGB should be cautious towards and critical of the leftward movements in the official leaderships of the trade unions, as demonstrated at the 1924 Congress of the TUC. While the Congress was marked by the active association of the 'lefts' with proposals for international trade union unity and the strengthening of the powers of the General Council to co-ordinate

---

[90] That this resolution was indicative of the fact that the CPGB had, at least formally, learnt the lesson of its syndicalist trade union work in 1920-1921 was underlined by the observation of J.R. Campbell that ' . . .the chief danger is that it (the NMM) will develop into a purely industrial movement concerned only with union problems unrelated to the general struggle of the workers. That is . . .a marked trait of the old left official leadership. It is no less marked amongst the active rank and file in many of the unions.' *Communist Review*, October 1924.

trade union action in Britain, the CPGB saw this tendency as a reflection of the pressure building up from the rank and file for effective mass industrial action and an adaption to this mood by the official left-wing. In itself, the activity of this left wing was of little value unless it led on to the formation of an industrial alliance under rank-and-file control. If the 'lefts' were to associate themselves with the NMM programme their support would be welcomed and every effort must be made, argued the CPGB, to win them to this position. At the same time this should in no way be made a substitute for the winning of the leading position among the rank and file by the party.

> It would be a suicidal policy, however for the Communist Party and the Minority Movement to place too much reliance on what we have called the official left-wing [wrote J.R.Campbell]. On problems of TU organization this element is fairly clear, on other problems it has not broken away from the 'right' position. It is the duty of our Party and the Minority Movement to criticize its weaknesses relentlessly and endeavour to change the muddled and incomplete left wing viewpoint of the more progressive leaders into a real revolutionary viewpoint. But the revolutionary workers must never forget that their main activity must be devoted to capturing the masses.[91]

The CPGB therefore approached the crucial year 1925, the year which saw the acceleration of industrial militancy and the anticipation of the General Strike in the events around 'Red Friday', in a potentially strong theoretical and organizational position. At the same time the party was placed in an increasingly contradictory position in 1925. In a period when the CPGB was beginning to make a decisive breakthrough in the establishment of its influence in the unions and the Labour Party it was subject to pressures emanating from the Stalin bloc in the CPSU for the adoption of an uncritical approach towards the centrist tendencies in the union leaderships. At the very time when the crisis of British capitalism was deepening, Stalin was seeking, through the intermediary of Tomsky and the Russian trade unions, a *détente* with British imperialism via the Anglo-Russian Trade Union Committee. While the Committee had obvious relevance to the RILU's strategy of seeking membership of the Amsterdam Trade Union International, the main emphasis came to be placed on the Committee's utility to the diplomatic interests of the emergent bureaucracy in the CPSU, and the CPGB was consequently placed in a

---

91 *Ibid.*

position where it would be obliged increasingly to support, and in a practical sense identify with, the centrist currents considered so favourable by Stalin to the interests of the USSR. It would be a-historical to suggest that the course on which the CPGB was launched from 1924 was negated in any immediate sense by this development, but across the period between 1924 and the General Strike the international implications of the policy of Socialism in One Country served in the British context to confuse and neutralize the important steps which the CPGB was taking in the mid-1920s towards a full understanding of Bolshevik methods of party work.

It is a crucial failing on the part of Macfarlane that he almost wholly ignores the significance of this development for the work of the CPGB before and during the General Strike. While he throws valuable light on the struggles between Trotsky and Stalin in the context of Trotsky's fight in the CPSU and CI for theoretical clarity on the approaching revolutionary crisis in Britain, and indicates how, in its theoretical agnosticism, the CPGB aligned with Stalin in adopting a non-revolutionary interpretation of the British situation, he appears ignorant of the fact that the adoption of this line by the CPGB flowed directly from the policy of Socialism in One Country and amounted to a complete rejection of the fight for revolutionary politics in the trade unions which the CPGB had been carrying on at least until 'Red Friday'. Macfarlane explicitly attacks the arguments put forward by Brian Pearce[92] to the effect that the CPGB came to subordinate its independent, revolutionary line to the official left wing in the TUC and denies that the CPGB in any way played down its critique of the TUC up to the General Strike or departed from its own independent preparations for the strike. In so doing, Macfarlane adopts a basically a-historical approach. He employs the technique of selective quotation to demonstrate criticism of the TUC by the CPGB up to the General Strike but fails to show how the party prepared in any concrete practical way (as opposed to exhortation to the TUC) for the role of independent leadership during the strike. He also seems unaware of the fact that the quotations he produces are self-contradictory, some indicating uncritical support for the TUC left wing, others expressing criticism, but the whole in fact displaying the ambiguity and confusion in the party's attitude to the TUC which Macfarlane appears to share, and certainly fails to understand.

---

92 B. Pearce, 'The Early Years of the CPGB'; Macfarlane, p. 154.

There is, in fact, the clearest evidence that, as it came to articulate more definitely the line towards the TUC emanating from the CI, the CPGB did gradually abandon its revolutionary position and assume instead the role of a critical, but essentially loyal, component of a bloc with the official left wing in the TUC; that instead of working on a tactical, united front basis with this left wing, in which context the party sought to advance its influence among the rank and file, the CPGB became involved in an opportunist relationship with the left wing which allowed the leadership of the General Strike to remain in their hands and lost the opportunity to seize this leadership which potentially existed.

The only way in which Macfarlane's distortions of the historical reality can be corrected is by looking at the work of the CPGB in the unions as it evolved in the period preceding the General Strike. The first point which must impress itself on any investigator is the marked contrast between the party's role before and after the events which led up to 'Red Friday'. Before August 1925 the CPGB was attempting consciously to develop a clear revolutionary lead in the unions in preparation for what it felt must be a direct confrontation between the unions and the state in July. Thereafter, gradually at first but with increasing emphasis, it moved steadily closer to the official left wing and turned its work in the unions away from its revolutionary perspective of 1925 and towards the reinforcement of the official apparatus of the unions in anticipation of what it assumed must now be a purely economic, industrial conflict in May 1926. This reversal of the party's earlier work was doubly disastrous in view of the great increase in support gained by the CPGB in the preceding period; the mass demonstrations for the release of the party leaders imprisoned at the end of 1925 were the surface manifestations of the deeper-going relationship being formed between the party and the organized working class in the period following 'Red Friday' and were indicative of the way the practical leadership of the party was being strengthened through the growth in influence of its press, its nuclei in the factories and mines, and through the work of the NMM and the Left Wing Movement. There can be little doubt, when these developments are seen as a whole, that the CPGB was in the process of establishing itself in a position before the General Strike where it had the potential for providing a possible alternative to the inevitable betrayals of the TUC; the line it actually adopted, however, allowed it to realize very little of this potential.

The contrast between the position ultimately adopted by the CPGB in 1926 and that with which it approached the onset of the pre-revolutionary crisis in 1925 could not be clearer. The party's attitude towards the official left-wing at the start of 1925 was indicated by the way in which it initially reacted to the setting up of the Anglo-Russian Trade Union Committee. For the CPGB the formation of the Committee was welcomed only insofar as it provided a means for furthering the process of revolutionizing the British working class. An alliance between trade union leaders alone would be useless and the party made clear that it would in no way subordinate its activities to the diplomatic requirements of this committee; as the *Workers' Weekly* observed editorially:

> Unity that only means a polite agreement between leaders is useless unless it is backed up by mass pressure. Unity that confines itself to negotiations between Amsterdam and the Russian Unions only touches the the fringe of the question . . .Vast masses of workers everywhere are moving slowly forward. Those leaders who stand in the way are going to be swept aside. The class struggle cannot be limited to an exchange of diplomatic letters.

Effective unity, the paper went on to argue, could only be built up by the work of the CPGB and the NMM.[93] The implication of this attitude was of considerable significance for the immediate work of the CPGB in the context of the growing industrial militancy of the organized working class in Britain, for the CPGB saw the moves of the official left wing towards Russia and their left-wing phraseology in relation to the industrial situation in Britain, as the pale reflection of the confused, contradictory but quite definite movement among the trade union rank and file towards a revolutionary position. While the official left wing must therefore be urged on from below to translate their militant promises into practice, the CPGB must in no way compromise itself with the hesitations and confusions of this left wing but rather intensify its activity to clarify the rank and file on the developing revolutionary situation. The meaning of this approach for the practical work of the party was very clearly demonstrated in its trade union agitation in the months culminating in 'Red Friday'. From the start of 1925 there was a very favourable situation for the formation of a new trade union alliance to replace the defunct Triple Alliance. The miners were well aware, after their frustrations over the 1924 agreement, that hopes of future gains rested on the formation of

[93] *Workers' Weekly*, January 2, 1925.

such an alliance, and from the latter part of 1924 the NMM, with the backing of A. J. Cook, was working for an alliance which would unite major trade unions around a common programme for offensive action. Yet in supporting, indeed largely initiating, this trend it was vital that the CPGB should avoid entanglement with the opportunism inherent in the position of the trade union left wing and that it should relate the agitation for the industrial alliance directly to the question of the revolutionary education of the rank and file. This it went a long way towards doing in the first part of 1925, for while it encouraged the militancy of the sympathetic union leaders, it made the main emphasis of its trade union work the formation of an alliance under direct rank-and-file control in conditions where the CPGB and the NMM had the practical revolutionary leadership of that rank and file.

In line with this, the CPGB called constantly, up to 'Red Friday', for the formation of an alliance of the miners, the AEU, the NUR and the Transport Workers,[94] but at the same time it made its main contribution to the formation of the alliance its campaign at local level for the creation of joint committees of rank-and-file miners, dockers, railworkers and engineers. These committees were designed not simply to pressurize the official union leaders into national action to conclude the alliance; their primary function was to revitalize the trades councils and convert them into Councils of Action for the direction of trade union action in the districts in the coming mass struggles. After an intense propaganda campaign on the need for such committees persistent efforts to set them up in all major industrial areas were made by the CPGB from April 1925. The response to the party's initiative was generally favourable. Within a month joint committees had been formed in all parts of the country and the conversion or preparation to convert trades councils into Councils of Action was almost as widespread,[95] these developments being considerably assisted by the recent rejection of the wage demands of many groups of workers, the engineers, shipbuilders, post-office, rail and

---

[94] Moves to form the alliance were made by the miners, the AEU, the T&GWU and the Rail Unions between April and June 1925, but the negotiations were overtaken by the events which led up to 'Red Friday' when the main question became that of securing the backing of the TUC as a whole for the miners . Formal moves to establish the alliance continued thereafter but broke down in practice through the deliberate attempts of J. H. Thomas to wreck unity and the hesitations of the left in the AEU leadership who did not organize a ballot on the proposed constitution until the eve of the General Strike.

[95] *Workers' Weekly*, May 1925, *passim*.

transport workers amongst them. At the same time, the CPGB was laying the basis for a further considerable expansion of its influence among the working class through its drive to form party groups in factories and mines.[96]

Anyone attempting to argue that the CPGB did not change its line towards the trade union leadership between 1925 and the General Strike could point to an apparent similarity in the agitational work of the party both before 'Red Friday' and the General Strike itself. The attempt would be an exercise in eclecticism little related to the historical reality. In contrast to its activity before the General Strike, the CPGB was, in this period in 1925, clearly relating its work in the trade unions directly to the creation of a revolutionary consciousness in preparation for the acute crisis which would arise with the outbreak of the conflict in the mining industry. It showed that it had learnt from the syndicalist weaknesses of the early 1920s and that it was now concerned *not* to become a mere 'ginger group' devoted simply to pressurizing the more sympathetic left-wing union leaders; on the contrary, it sought to create a revolutionary leadership in the approaching conflict and win the initiative from the official left-wing. At the height of the party's preparatory campaign, immediately prior to the events of 'Red Friday', the leadership emphasized this point quite unambiguously:

> The success of the Minority Movement [wrote C. M. Roebuck (T. Rothstein)]is in reality a sign that the workers are coming to look upon the unions less and less as a means of improving their individual well-being within the framework of the capitalist system, and more and more as a weapon of struggle against the capitalist class. For this reason the Minority Movement cannot be compared with previous 'unofficial', 'vigilance' and 'reform' movements in the era of capitalist vigour . . . There can be no doubt that . . . many reformist leaders would rather swim with the current than against it. Without pushing away anyone who will fight, the task of the Communists in the Minority Movement is to see that this does not obscure in the eyes of the workers the fact that their fight is a class fight against a class enemy, and not a fight for small reforms . . .[97]

There was, furthermore, no tendency for the CPGB to see the approaching conflict as a purely economic struggle, as it did in May 1926, or to separate the problems of the miners from those of the working class as a whole. In contrast with the position before the

---

[96] On the eve of 'Red Friday' 120 had been formed. *Workers' Weekly*, July 31, 1925.

[97] *Communist Review*, June 1925.

General Strike the CPGB was highly critical of the TUC before 'Red Friday' not simply because of its slowness to rally support for the miners but quite basically because the TUC's approach to the crisis was incapable of measuring up to its revolutionary implications. Thus Tom Bell commented editorially shortly before 'Red Friday':

> All talk, such as the statement of Citrine, the acting secretary of the General Council of the TUC, that this is an 'economic dispute' is a definite sabotage of the working-class defence against capitalist attack. The miners' crisis is part of the general economic crisis in British industrialism. For that reason it has passed beyond any purely economic stage. It is a definitely political crisis and can only be solved by revolutionary political means.[98]

The events of 'Red Friday' did nothing immediately to undermine this estimate of the crisis. Although the government, under the threat of a possible general strike, backed down, provided a nine-month subsidy for the coal industry and set up the Samuel Commission to investigate the industry's problems, it was quite clear that this was a delaying tactic only. For British capitalism the mining crisis could be solved only at the expense of the miners and the Commission was merely a device for adding respectability to the brutality of the owners' demands while making suggestions on the behalf of private industry as a whole for the necessary rationalization of the industry. The conflict had therefore been postponed for nine months, not avoided, and when it eventually came it would have the same implications as that in July 1925. A general strike, the CPGB warned, would be inevitable in May 1926, and the party and its supporters must prepare accordingly.

> But let us be clear what a general strike means [warned J. T. Murphy]. It can only mean the throwing down of the gauntlet to the capitalist state, and all the powers at its disposal. Either that challenge is a gesture ...or it must develop its challenge into an actual fight for power ...[99]

It was completely in the context of these analyses of the mining crisis and its revolutionary implications that the CPGB approached the crisis as it initially developed in July 1925. Although a conference of the potential members of the Industrial Alliance was held on July 17 to consider a possible constitution, and although a special conference of the TUC on July 24 agreed to support the miners through an

---

[98] *Ibid.*, August 1925. (The issue went to press on the eve of 'Red Friday'.)
[99] *Ibid.*, September 1925.

embargo on the movement of coal, the CPGB was highly sceptical as to whether these moves in themselves would lead on to any positive action. They could do so, in the party's estimation, only through the mobilization of the rank and file under the party's leadership to force forward a mass strike from below and to develop the ensuing conflict into a revolutionary challenge to the state. Given the small size of the CPGB in mid-1925 and the fact that the growth of its organized influence among the trade union rank and file was still in its early stages, there was objectively no certainty that such a conflict could be precipitated by the party alone at this stage, but the CPGB entered the struggle with the aim at the very least of laying the basis for a mass membership through the political education which such a struggle must produce in the working class. As it stated when calling for the expansion of the embargo into a general strike, 'through the efforts of its members it (the CP) will be able to convince the workers that not the least of its tasks is that of building a mass Communist Party in Great Britain.'[100] The way in which it set about the realization of this aim was indicated in the strategy which it evolved on the eve of the implementation of the embargo by the TUC. The whole work of the party was to be directed towards the mobilization of the rank-and-file committees and Councils of Action previously established to call out the trade union rank and file and thus convert the action over the embargo into an unofficial general strike. The coal embargo, stated the *Workers' Weekly*, was a challenge to the government. 'Once you challenge the government you must go all out to win', and this led logically to a general strike. To achieve this the rank and file must prepare, under the party's lead, for immediate action.

> Immediately a section of workers comes out on strike, mass demonstrations must be organized by the Councils of Action in conjunction with the strike committees of particular unions. If the miners come out there must be mass demonstrations to the docks and railway centres, where the workers should be told to form section and job committees and prepare for action. If the docks and railways are stopped then there must be a mass demonstration to the power stations and factory committees set up which will take unofficial action if official action is not called for.[101]

That this was not a mere propagandist posture on the eve of the expected embargo action but a considered statement of the party's intentions based on previous preparation of the party membership

---

[100] *Workers' Weekly*, July 24, 1925 [101] *Ibid.*, July 31, 1925.

was indicated by the fact that in one area at least, South Wales, there had been full discussion at an aggregate meeting some time before 'Red Friday' of the implications of the coming crisis and preparations made for action exactly on the lines laid down by the *Workers' Weekly*. Here, to enthusiastic applause, Frank Bright (a leading Rhondda member) declared that 'far more important than the fight for wages is the struggle for power' and went on to urge that 'in the event of them [the TUC] failing to give a proper lead we must be prepared to organize unofficial action by way of mass demonstrations of miners from the valleys to the steelworks, the big railway centres and the docks . . .To do so entailed work, sacrifice and danger. We shall be met by the armed forces of the State. Nevertheless, the work had to be done.'[102] It seems highly unlikely that similar preparations were not made by other aggregates elsewhere, although they were not reported, and what was so very significant about these preparations by the CPGB on the eve of 'Red Friday' was that, in contrast to May 1926, they showed the party's readiness for independent leadership with no subordination of party policy to the opportunist elements in the union leaderships.

There are many indications that the CPGB and the NMM had created a situation by their agitation in the unions whereby it would have been impossible for the TUC to back down in July 1925 without letting the control of the struggle fall into the hands of the party. The significance of the events of 'Red Friday' did not, however, lie simply in the immediate effects of the party's work on the union bureaucracies. The experience undergone by the party in its campaigns up to July 1925 had done much to help it emerge from the position which it had occupied on the sectarian fringe of the labour movement in the early 1920s. The theoretical lessons of the earlier period would seem to have been assimilated and greatly enriched in this first experience of practical mass work. Yet there was no sense in which the way forward for the CPGB from 'Red Friday' was simple or clear-cut. The development of mass work on the scale apparent by mid-1925 created considerable problems in terms of the maintenance of a clear theoretical conception of the party's revolutionary strategy in relation to its day-to-day agitational work. The danger existed in particular that an immediate tactic might be elevated into a general perspective, that the agitational work of the NMM on questions of immediate trade union

---

102 *Ibid.*, July 24, 1925.

significance might come to be seen by the party membership as their main work and its relationship to the building of the party and the fight for a revolutionary perspective lost sight of, or at best understood in a purely formal way. While there were indications that the party was aware of these dangers as it began to engage in mass work from 1924, there was always the possibility that the pressures operating on the party from the conditions in which it was working during 1925 might well nullify this necessarily formal understanding unless there was a constant deepening of its theoretical grasp of the revolutionary opportunities opening up in the period around 'Red Friday' and a constant struggle to develop the practice of the party in relation to this understanding.

As it was, the CPGB was operating under increasingly contradictory conditions from the latter half of 1925. While it had fought for a revolutionary perspective in the period up to 'Red Friday', it was at the same time subject increasingly during 1925 to the pressures emanating from the CI for the development of a working relationship with the left opportunist elements on the General Council of the TUC. While, on the one hand, it was attempting to actualize the revolutionary potential of the union rank and file, it was, on the other, obliged to adopt towards the TUC an attitude which would not embarrass the working of the Anglo-Russian Committee. The long-term outcome of these contradictions was that, when the General Strike took place in May 1926, the understanding which the CPGB had been developing of its role in the revolutionary situation into which the unions must be pushed was neutralized and the party placed in a position where, objectively, it had to act increasingly as the supporter at rank-and-file level of the official left wing on the General Council. The initiative in the deepening revolutionary crisis from mid-1925 was therefore allowed to pass from the CPGB, which had really made the running up to 'Red Friday', and forced on the TUC from below, to the opportunistic element in the union leaderships who, in their turn, assisted the right-wing in their sabotaging role during the strike. It was this process which allowed J. T. Murphy, who had written of the coming revolutionary crisis in September 1925 (see above), to place, on behalf of the Central Committee of the CPGB, the whole initiative in the hands of the TUC on the eve of the General Strike. In complete antithesis to the line of the party in July 1925 he then wrote:

> Our party does not hold the leading positions in the Trade Unions. It is not conducting the negotiations with the employers and the government. *It*

> *can only advise and place its forces at the service of the workers – led by others* . . . Those who do not look for a path along which to retreat are good trade union leaders who have sufficient character to stand firm on the demands of the miners, but they are totally incapable of moving forward to face all the implications of a united working-class challenge to the State.
>
> To entertain any exaggerated views as to the revolutionary possibilities of this crisis and visions of new leadership 'arising spontaneously in the struggle', etc., is fantastic . . . [103]

These comments adorned the front page of the *Workers' Weekly* three days before the start of the General Strike; they were fully representative of party policy and put the party in a manifestly absurd position both in view of the objective conditions which must operate during the strike and the correct stand taken by the party on this question only a few months earlier. Yet while Macfarlane quotes this article, he totally ignores its implications, both for the actual character of the strike and the revolutionary role of the party, which he clearly fails to comprehend. The crucial point is that Murphy's statement was an admission of sheer theoretical confusion. Only a few months earlier Murphy and other leading party members had been at pains to emphasize the necessarily revolutionary character of a general strike and in the period intervening between 'Red Friday' and May 1926 the Baldwin government had made it quite evident that it was preparing for the coming conflict with its revolutionary implications very much in mind. Yet, despite all this, the CPGB could still adopt on the eve of the strike a position which basically denied the whole function of the party.

It would be a-historical to suggest that the party's approach to the General Strike came about through some dramatic reversal of policy. What did happen in the period from July 1925 was that the tendency associated with the Anglo-Russian Committee made itself more clearly apparent, that this occurred in circumstances where centrist and opportunist tendencies in the labour movement were reinforced by the TUC's support for the miners on 'Red Friday' and where there was a widespread belief among rank-and-file militants that the TUC must act firmly again in May 1926 when the postponed crisis would come to a head. In these conditions there was the strong possibility that the membership of the CPGB, particularly those

---

[103] *Ibid.*, April 30, 1926. My emphasis. The latter part of the statement was clearly an implicit attack on Trotsky who was at this point warning the CPGB of the dangers of under-estimating the revolutionary character of the situation.

working in the NMM, would be affected by the general mood of euphoria and opportunism after 'Red Friday' and that they would come to share in, or at least compromise with, the general belief in the efficacy of the official left wing. At the very time when the party needed to fight such illusions and false optimism most vigorously it was increasingly inhibited from doing so by the line emanating from the CI. Even before 'Red Friday' there were signs of confusion about the role of the official left-wing in certain areas of the party's work. In the period before the build-up to the events of July 1925 the *Sunday Worker*, the paper of the Left Wing Movement, ran a series of articles on the left-wing leaders in the unions uncritically extolling their virtues and fostering considerable illusions about their role in the TUC. Typical of these was the comment on Swales, chairman of the General Council, and his forthcoming address to the Scarborough Congress of the TUC:

> . . . it will be something stated in plain blunt language and will give the whole movement a bold and clever lead. It will personify the simple and rugged strength of a far-seeing and courageous leader.[104]

Attitudes of this sort towards the official left wing were not pronounced in the party as a whole before 'Red Friday', but thereafter there appeared a confused and vacillating attitude to their role on the part of the party leadership which marked the emergence of what was to be an increasingly uncritical approach to them in the period immediately before the General Strike. Characteristic of this was the CPGB's reaction to the events of 'Red Friday'. Very correctly the leadership observed that there was no occasion for euphoria; a temporary truce only had been won, preparations for a fight must continue and 'One thing that every worker and every workers' leader, must now recognize, and must openly and fearlessly face, is that the struggle for wages involves the struggle for power'. But it then went on to compromise this formally correct estimate with the confused, and confusing, assertion that 'The leadership [of the events of 'Red Friday'] passed into the hands of good proletarians like Swales, Hicks, Cook and Purcell. And this proletarian leadership and the proletarian solidarity it was capable of organizing and demonstrating was the real big thing that came out of the struggle.'[105] Such an estimate was valid only if it was related to the task of converting the centrist tendency predominant in the unions into a consistent

---

[104] *Sunday Worker*, May 24, 1926. [105] *Workers' Weekly*, August 7, 1925.

revolutionary position through the expansion of the party's work to force centrist tendencies either to work consistently with the party or to expose them for not matching up to their revolutionary protestations. The CPGB went in the other direction, however. What it came to do increasingly after 'Red Friday' was to work on the assumption that the TUC, under pressure from the official left wing and its Communist allies, would perform the same role in May 1926 as it had done in 1925, that there would be, in the last analysis, a division of labour between the leadership of the struggle by the official left-wing and the supporting role of the CPGB among the rank-and-file.

The emergence of this tendency on the part of the CPGB was illustrated by its reponse to the TUC's Scarborough Congress in September 1925. The Congress was marked by the passing of left-wing resolutions on imperialism, trade union unity, workshop committees and the increasing of the power of the General Council to lead joint trade union struggles; it was marked, also, by the attendance of a well-organized NMM-CPGB fraction which played a leading part in the discussions and was influential in the decisions of the Congress. But while the Congress seemed to mark a further stage in the movement of the left wing towards the Communist position, it posed the CPGB with a considerable dilemma. It was forced to note that on many of the crucial issues the official left wing had been almost wholly silent and the running had been made by the party delegates.[106] Pollitt observed of the Congress that the left wing had been curiously silent in the face of the right wing who had been strengthened on the General Council by the return of Thomas and Clynes. 'There is now the greatest opportunity in our history,' he wrote, 'for those leaders claiming to be left-wingers to come out boldly and take a prominent place in the revolutionary movement — they must do this, or they, too, will be forced to take up a position no different from that of the right wing . . .'[107] There were, in fact, increasingly clear indications from the 1925 Congress on that the left wing were retreating, yet the party failed to draw the relevant conclusions, despite Pollitt's comments. The post-Scarborough line of the party was not to develop the type of independent initiative in the unions evident in July 1925 but to press for the TUC to implement the left-wing resolutions of the Scarborough Congress and for the General Council to take steps to

---

106 See, e.g., the comments of J. R. Campbell, *Communist Review*, October 1925.
107 *Labour Monthly*, October 1925.

assume full controlling powers over the unions in anticipation of May 1926. The whole approach of the CPGB from the autumn of 1925 was thus based on the assumption that the real leadership of the coming strike would be in the hands of the General Council; the party's task would be solely that of pressurizing it from below. As Pollitt observed, in summing up this approach:

> In view of the overwhelming decision for complete solidarity registered at Scarborough, the new General Council will simply *have* to prosecute more vigorously the fight on behalf of the workers. True, the right-wing of the Council is strengthened by the return of one or two people who do not give support to the idea that we are engaged in a class struggle, but I think that the mass pressure from behind will force even them to toe the line.[108]

From this point, then, the whole tendency of the CPGB in its work in the unions was to subordinate its activities to the TUC leadership, and such criticisms as it made of TUC policy (and they were often vigorous in tone) took the form basically of exhortations to the TUC to prepare for action more effectively and were accompanied less and less by independent preparations by the party among the rank and file for the approaching struggle.

The first clear indication of the practical implications of this trend for party work came from J. T. Murphy's observations on the resolution on workshop committees passed by the Scarborough Congress. The whole context in which the resolution had been passed had indicated that, for the General Council, it was a piece of pious resolution-mongering not committing the TUC in any concrete way to the encouragement of committees of rank-and-file workers at workshop level. The only way it could have been implemented would have been by serious agitation by the CPGB in the unions and Trades Councils locally to set up what would have been important centres of working class organization in preparation for the General Strike. As it was, the party, via Murphy, placed the whole initiative for their formation on the General Council and pleaded with the latter to live up to their Scarborough commitments.

> The initiative [wrote Murphy] should come from the General Council of the TUC and its sub-committee of trades councils . . . Both need, of course, the complete co-operation of the trade union executives and this ought not to be difficult to obtain if they are at all intent on defending their own interests.[109]

---

[108] *Sunday Worker*, September 20, 1926. [109] *Labour Monthly*, November 1925.

In the months preceding the General Strike the trend became even clearer. It was impossible for the party to ignore the fact that the TUC was doing nothing to prepare for the anticipated strike and certainly nothing to implement the recommendations of the Scarborough Congress. As Citrine later made clear, the General Council as a whole expected that the Samuel Commission would result in a permanent settlement of the mining crisis and in particular on the Industrial Committee, set up by the General Council to consider further support for the miners after 'Red Friday', this idea was very prevalent. While the Committee had a right-wing majority it contained at the same time prominent left-wingers, notable Swales and Hicks and others of a leftish character, yet despite this the Committee met only twice between Scarborough and early 1926 and decided at its second meeting that there was no need to take up the proposals of the Scarborough Congress for increasing the General Council's powers. It was a fair indication of the treacherous character of the official left-wing that the four members present at this meeting included Swales and Hicks.[110] The left wing on which the CPGB was coming to place such reliance was thus completely involved in that process whereby the attempt was made by the General Council (both before and during the General Strike) to force the miners to accept the proposals of the Samuel Commission Report, proposals which meant wage cuts for the miners and the rationalization of the industry on an increasingly monopolistic basis under private control.

The CPGB might be excused for ignorance of the decisions behind closed doors in the TUC but any misconceptions on this account were soon dispelled by the TUC itself when it notified the affiliated unions by letter of its decision not to seek the extra powers suggested at Scarborough to conduct a general strike. The response of the party to what it called 'this amazing circular' was significant of the extent to which it had departed from any independent preparation for the coming General Strike, for while the party protested at the circular and called on union branches and trades councils to oppose the TUC's decision, it drew no lessons from the TUC's action and in no way revised its attitude to the role of the TUC in the rapidly developing crisis. In fact, all that it had to suggest in a practical sense was that the issue should be taken up at the next congress of the TUC not due until

110 A. Bullock, *The Life and Times of Ernest Bevin*, pp.289-290.

the autumn, a suggestion totally irrelevant to the immediate crisis and avoiding any criticism of the role of the left wing in the TUC's decision.[111]

It could easily be suggested by Macfarlane and Stalinist critics that this point ignores the fact that the CPGB did expend much energy in the months preceding the General Strike in agitating for the type of trade union preparation necessary for the conflict. True enough, the party did conduct a vigorous propaganda campaign on this issue; the vital point, however, is to understand the content of this propaganda, not merely its form, for despite the fact that the party stressed that the Scarborough decisions existed on paper only and that the NMM had the responsibility for seeing that they were put into effect, and despite the special NMM conference in March devoted to the question of 'preparedness', there is very little concrete evidence that the party did anything to break out of the limitations placed on preparation imposed on the rank and file by the trade union apparatus or that it saw its role as anything more than 'gingering up' the official leaderships. In short, its activities were devoted to the exhortation of the TUC to act, not to preparing for an independent initiative in the light of the wholly likely betrayal by the TUC in the coming conflict. Stalinist writers are in the habit of making great play with the fact that it was the CPGB alone, at the March conference of the NMM, which urged the unions to prepare for the approaching General Strike. A look at the decisions of the conference dispels this myth, as far as any practical developments from the conference were concerned, for while it was characterized by the display of much militant rhetoric it made no concrete plans whatsoever for definite action by the rank and file to organize its strength for the strike and certainly it was altogether unconcerned, as the CPGB had been in July 1925, with seizing the favourable opportunities at rank-and-file level for furthering the revolutionary role of the party. The nearest the conference came to this was in the resolution on 'The Capitalist Offensive', moved by Horner, in which delegates were urged 'to go back to their branches and not only report but gather round them the active membership and force their unions to inaugurate a militant policy in spite of the leaders . . .'[112] But the suggestion was left in mid-air; no concrete proposals for action to rally the rank and file flowed from it and had they done so there would have been signs of a drive by the party and the NMM to

---

111 *Workers' Weekly*, March 19, 1926. 112 *The Worker*, March 27, 1926.

implement them. As it was, the party leadership seemed utterly complacent about the coming struggle, confident that the TUC must continue to support the miners and anxious mainly to avoid 'sectarian' action by the NMM and party activists in the unions which would separate the party from the official union apparatus. The point was underlined by George Hardy, acting general secretary of the NMM, who when interviewed after the March conference of the NMM, had nothing at all to say about any campaign to rally the rank and file behind the lead of the party and was content merely to talk complacently about a summer campaign of outdoor meetings as though the General Strike was an issue of no great importance.[113] In fact, for Hardy, as for the party leadership as a whole, the coming strike was now seen as a purely industrial issue in relation to which the role of the party was not that of fighting for a revolutionary lead but rather of ensuring the maximum of trade union solidarity at local level wholly within the context of the official union apparatus and under the established union leadership. Hardy was thus acting quite logically when he ordered the NMM to subordinate itself entirely to the TUC and its local affiliates on the eve of the General Strike:

> . . . we sent out from Minority Movement headquarters instructions to our members to work for the establishment of Councils of Action in every area. We warned, however, that the Councils of Action were under no circumstances to take over the work of the trade unions . . . *The Councils of Action were to see that all the decisions of the General Council and the union executives were carried out* . . .[114]

Given these trends in the party leadership it was highly probable that the lessons of the preparation for struggle gained by the party membership in the period before 'Red Friday' were undermined and destroyed and that in place of the emphasis then placed on seizing the revolutionary initiative the party activists in the unions were allowed to fall back into the type of 'rank and filism' which had characterized the CPGB's unofficial trade union movements in the early 1920s. The point was, of course, that the whole trend of party policy towards the TUC between July 1925 and May 1926 meant that that work of the NMM had to be orientated increasingly towards the pressurizing of the existing union leadership and not to the development of an alternative revolutionary leadership prepared for the betrayals to which

---

113 *Workers' Weekly*, April 9, 1926.

114 G. Hardy, *Those Stormy Years*, p. 185. My emphasis.

orthodox trade unionism, however militant, must lead in a political confrontation of the type witnessed in the General Strike. In other words, the party membership was not being trained for the task of revolutionary leadership across the nine months; it was, by contrast, being encouraged to lapse into the 'ginger group' operation of the old type with the result that in the objectively revolutionary circumstances of the strike it was unable to see any way of transcending the methods of orthodox, militant trade unionism.

In circumstances where working-class consciousness developed very rapidly and where the task of the party was to provide concrete leadership to give this radicalization a revolutionary means of expression, the party inevitably lagged behind the developments among the working class; it was theoretically unprepared for them, unprepared for the treacherous role of the official left wing and unprepared for the movement of the General Strike towards a necessarily revolutionary challenge to the state. The result of this for the party's role in the strike was that it was unable to mobilize to the full the combativeness of the rank and file, unable effectively to develop the great potential for leadership which had been building up through its work in the unions since 1924. Looking back on the situation, George Hardy later admitted to the great theoretical confusion with which the party entered the strike:

> Although we knew of what treachery the Right Wing leaders were capable, we did not clearly understand the part played by the so-called 'left' in the union leadership. In the main they turned out to be windbags and capitulated to the Right Wing. We were taught a major lesson; that while developing a move to the left officially, the main point in preparing for action must always be to develop a class-conscious leadership among the rank and file.[115]

The tragedy of the CPGB in 1926 was that it was precisely with this theoretical concept of the role of the party that the NMM had been launched in 1924 and had operated in the first part of 1925. Now it was caught in the contradiction of the policy emanating from the CI and its own inability to fight the implications of this. The outcome, as was later implied by the party itself, was a complete antithesis between the party's call for 'preparedness' on the eve of the General Strike and its subordination in practice to the leadership of the TUC:

> In this, however, it [the CP] displayed a certain inconsistency, for while in

[115] Hardy, op. cit., p. 188.

itself it [the call for preparedness] was an organized protest against the defeatist policy of the General Council and was one of the principal instruments for exposing this policy, it nevertheless issued the slogan of concentrating the leadership of all the unions in the General Council . . .[116]

The contradictory position of the CPGB did much to prevent it maximizing its influence during the General Strike. The previous growth of the NMM and the propaganda for 'preparedness' had indeed done much to make it impossible for the TUC to back down from supporting the miners, but when the conflict had begun the fact that the CPGB had approached it in a purely trade union sense did much to neutralize its potential effectiveness. The clearest indication of this was the fact that from the start the party leadership was virtually paralyzed, for while the party might not have seen the strike as a potentially revolutionary struggle, the government was acutely aware of its implications with the result that the party bore the brunt of government repressive actions and its leadership was consequently able to function in only the most limited way. The Central Committee's Report to the Eighth Congress later admitted that:

> Communications were a problem at the outset, as it became clear that we had not sufficiently mobilized even the very scanty resources at our disposal and the question was complicated by the fact that, on top of the General Strike, the Party Centre after the first day or two was semi-illegal . . .

The point was that the leadership was paralyzed not, as Stalinists suggest, because prominent party leaders had been imprisoned in October 1925 (six were released on the eve of the strike and the party had set up an alternative leadership) but because the CPGB had failed to understand the revolutionary implications of the strike or prepared accordingly. Moreover, party policy during the strike indicated the way the party lagged behind developments, tail-ending the working class and subordinating itself essentially to spontaneity, both phenomena being products of its own theoretical backwardness. As the Report to the Eighth Congress indicated:

> The Party entered the General Strike with political and organizational slogans that were inevitably defensive in character . . .once the masses were on the streets the business of the Central Committee was to extend these slogans, at the same time making them more aggressive in character.

---

[116] *The Communist International Between the 5th and 6th World Congresses*. CPGB, July 1928.

What this meant in practice was the advancing of the demand for the resignation of the Baldwin government, its replacement by a Labour government and the nationalization of the mines; but besides the anachronistic character of these slogans at a time when the strike was developing into the initial stages of a situation of dual power and the urgent need was to extend and link up the Councils of Action, the fact was that they were political demands and completely contradicted the party's previous assertion as to the purely economic character of the struggle. The slogans were, in fact, purely spontaneous reactions to events; they were unrelated to any previous political preparation of the party membership and had no effect on the course of the strike.

The considerable potential which the CPGB possessed for playing the leading role in the strike was therefore largely unrealized. There is no questioning the party's great local influence — its members were active in leading positions on the great majority of Councils of Action — but the crucial issue was how this potential was to be realized when, until the very end of the strike, the party was subordinating its activity to that of the General Council. The party could, then, do no more than play a militant but essentially limited part during the strike and the influence which it was able to exert over the rank and file was of a basically syndicalist rather than revolutionary kind. As a result, the CPGB was quite unready to mobilize the rank and file against the action of the TUC in calling off the strike at the very moment when later reports showed that it was just reaching the peak of its effectiveness. In fact, the party completely shared the astonishment and bewilderment of the rank and file, the *Workers' Weekly* commenting in a tone of aggrieved surprise:

> We warned our readers of the weakness and worse of the Right Wing on the General Council — but here we confess that reality has far exceeded out worst forebodings . . . The CP had in fact consistently warned the workers that such was likely to happen, but even the CP can be forgiven for not believing it to be possible that once the struggle had begun these leaders should have proved themselves such pitiful poltroons as to surrender at the very moment of victory.[117]

In fact, the CPGB had no reason for sharing in the rank and file's bewilderment. The betrayal of the General Strike was essentially bound up with the movement of the party into an opportunistic relationship with the TUC left-wing and the fact that it had lent itself

---

[117] *Workers' Weekly*, May 21, 1926.

to the task of creating illusions about the character of the strike and the role of the TUC among the rank and file which had objectively assisted the General Council in its treacherous role. This may seem a harsh judgement; certainly it is in conflict with Macfarlane, who considers that the party's line was the only one 'practicable' under the circumstances. The point is, however, that a revolutionary situation places on the revolutionary party the responsibility for absolute theoretical clarity and complete firmness in carrying into practice the practical work which flows from this understanding. The CPGB failed in its first, and, as it proved, only decisive test as a revolutionary party precisely because of its inability to deepen theoretically its necessarily formal understanding of Bolshevik methods of work in the period when it began to emerge as a decisive force among the working class. It was only through a ruthless critique of centrist politics and the opportunistic relationship to these of the line of the CI that the CPGB could have prepared for the General Strike and educated its membership for the revolutionary possibilities inherent in the situation. Without this the CPGB necessarily became involved in the confused centrist tendencies which were so pronounced in the Labour movement in the mid-1920s and which rested on a certain opportunism in the working class which it should have been the work of the party to counteract, not appease.

It can be suggested, then, that the significance of the study of the origins and early history of the CPGB derives from the necessity for Marxists to make more concrete their understanding of the crucial role of revolutionary theory in relation to political practice in a period of acute class conflict. It is for the elucidation of this question that Marxists look to Macfarlane's work, but while they will find information of considerable value there hitherto unavailable for the study of the CPGB they will find no explanation of why the CPGB failed as a revolutionary party. Indeed, by implicitly lending support to the Stalinist line of the mid-1920s, Macfarlane helps perpetuate the myths propagated by the CPGB about its role in the General Strike ever since 1926. This is why his book (certainly the section up to 1926) is quite acceptable to his Stalinist reviewer, Monty Johnstone.[118] The aim of this set of articles, based partly on the material in Macfarlane's book, partly on new research, has been to indicate the main tendencies

[118] *New Left Review*, 41, January-February 1967.

which went to make the CPGB, which shaped its empirical, syndicalist character in the 1920s, and made for its weakness as a revolutionary organization. Above all, the aim has not been simply to indicate the historiographical aberrations of Macfarlane but to suggest to Marxists who read his book the parallels which can usefully be made between the work of the CPGB in the 1920s and the present problems associated with the construction of the revolutionary party in Britain.

Some Past Rank and File Movements

by Brian Pearce

> The trade unions of our time can either serve as secondary instruments of imperialist capitalism for the subordination and disciplining of workers and for obstructing the revolution, or, on the contrary, the trade unions can become the instruments of the revolutionary movement of the proletariat. (L. D. Trotsky, *Trade Unions in the Epoch of Imperialist Decay,* 1940).
>
> All sections of the Fourth International should always strive not only to renew the top leadership of the trade unions, boldly and resolutely in critical moments advancing new militant leaders in place of routine functionaries and careerists; but also to create in all possible instances independent militant organizations corresponding more closely to the problems of mass struggle in bourgeois society; not stopping, if necessary, even in the face of a direct break with the conservative apparatus of the trade unions. If it be criminal to turn one's back to mass organizations for the sake of fostering sectarian fictions, it is no less so to passively tolerate subordination of the revolutionary mass movement to the control of openly reactionary or disguised conservative ('progressive') bureaucratic cliques. Trade unions are not ends in themselves; they are but means along the road to proletarian revolution (L.D. Trotsky, *The Death Agony of Capitalism and the Tasks of the Working Class,* 1938).

The source of rank-and-file movements is the conflict between the struggle of the working class for better conditions and a new social order, and the increasing reconciliation between the leaders of the trade unions and the capitalist class, their growing integration into the upper reaches of bourgeois society. In Great Britain we find the first appearance of such movements in the years shortly before the first world war, and it is significant that this phenomenon was preceded and accompanied by a good deal of comment on the declassing of trade union officials.

In 1892 the 'civil service' of British trade unionism numbered between 600 and 700. After the Reform Act of 1867 and the Ballot Act of 1872 had created an important working-class electorate largely immune to older forms of pressure, the ruling class began to pay special attention to trade union leaders. Engels observed in 1874 that 'the chairmen and secretaries of trade unions ...had overnight become important people. They were visited by MPs, by lords and other well-born rabble, and sympathetic inquiry was suddenly made into the wishes and needs of the working class'.[119] On the advice of the Liberal politician Mundella, the Trades Union Congress held at Nottingham in 1872 was officially welcomed by the city corporation, the delegates were banqueted and invited to the homes of leading citizens, and so forth — the first time such things had happened. Trade union leaders were pressed to accept seats on Royal Commissions, and in 1886 the general secretary of one of the most important unions stepped into a job in the Labour Bureau formed by Mundella as President of the Board of Trade, an organization from which the Ministry of Labour later developed. During the 1880s outstanding trade union leaders were more than once entertained by the Prince of Wales (later Edward VII) at Sandringham. In 1890 Broadhurst, secretary to the Trades Union Congress, was exposed as having accepted a gift of shares from Brunner, the chemicals industrialist, in return for political support at an election.

The years of comparative industrial peace, between the 1850s and 1880s, had seen 'a shifting of leadership in the trade union world', as the Webbs put it, 'from the casual enthusiast and irresponsible agitator to a class of permanent salaried officials expressly chosen from out of the rank and file of trade unionists for their superior business capacity'.[120] To the epoch of 'defence, not defiance', corresponded the emergence of a generation of trade union leaders of a different type from those who had laid the foundations in the bitter days of the Combination Acts and Tolpuddle. It was between these 'sober, business-like' men and sections of the capitalist class 'that the political alliance was forged which, in different forms and phases, has been with us ever since — "the bourgeoisie cannot rule alone". The system which J. H. Thomas admired for "making me what I am" was fairly launched'.[121]

These trade union leaders saw their task as essentially one of

[119] F. Engels, 'The English Elections' (February 22, 1874), *Marx and Engels on Britain* (1953), p. 467

[120] Sidney and Beatrice Webb, *History of Trade Unionism* (1920 edition), p. 204

[121] Dona Torr, *Tom Mann* (1941 edition), p. 12

peaceful negotiation with the employers, and this gave rise to a whole network of social relations separating them off from their original class. Assured of a permanent position with a secure income, the trade union officials — 'a closely combined and practically irresistible bureaucracy', as the Webbs called them in their book *Industrial Democracy*[122] which Lenin translated while in exile in Siberia — soon found their different life-experience reflected in a different outlook on the class struggle. In the Webbs' *History of Trade Unionism* the account of the career of a typical official given to the authors in 1893 by a member of one of the great craft unions is quoted:

> Whilst the points at issue no longer affect his own earnings or conditions of employment, any disputes between his members and their employers increase his work and add to his worry. The former vivid sense of the privations and subjection of the artisan's life gradually fades from his mind; and he begins more and more to regard all complaints as perverse and unreasonable. With this intellectual change may come a more invidious transformation. Nowadays the salaried officer of a great union is courted and flattered by the middle class [i.e., in the language of those days, the capitalists]. He is asked to dine with them, and will admire their well-appointed houses, their fine carpets, the ease and luxury of their lives ... He goes to live in a little villa in a lower-middle-class suburb. The move leads to dropping his workmen friends; and his wife changes her acquaintances. With the habits of his new neighbours he insensibly adopts more and more their ideas ...His manner to his members ...undergoes a change ...A great strike threatens to involve the Society in desperate war. Unconsciously biased by distaste for the hard and unthankful work which a strike entails, he finds himself in small sympathy with the men's demands and eventually arranges a compromise on terms distasteful to a large section of his members.[123]

Brought constantly into friendly intercourse with well-to-do business men, civil servants and capitalist politicians, trade union leaders, the Webbs observed, were tempted to bring their spending power up to the same level as that of their associates by making 'unduly liberal charges' for their travelling expenses, and even 'to accept from employers or from the government those hidden bribes that are decorously veiled as allowances for expenses or temporary salaries for special posts'.[124]

---

[122] 1920 edition, p. 28 [123] *History of Trade Unionism* (1920 edition), pp. 466-70.
[124] *Ibid.* pp. 589-90. The authors, of course, saw this as a problem arising from the *inadequacy* of trade union officials' salaries, with the remedy to be found in increasing them!

This situation, thus already recognizable in the 1890s, is still with us today. The authors of a sociological study of a Yorkshire mining area, published in 1956, write of the trade union bureaucracy: 'These officials exist on salaries and with expense accounts which must be comparable with those of people with whom they have to deal from day to day, they grow used, of necessity, to the same kind of life and entertainment as other executives in bureaucratic organizations.'[125] Men who as miners had virtually no prospect of 'social mobility' find themselves very differently placed as trade union officials:

> Not only is there the possibility of promotion in the union itself, with at each level the various conferences and meetings in very pleasant places and good hotels, the chance, for those of such inclination, of coming into the public eye through public meetings, the Press, and even the radio and television. In addition, men with trade union administrative experience are more and more thought suitable for posts in management, particularly in the nationalized coal-mines. Here are real prospects of individual success.

As between the National Coal Board and the officials of the National Union of Mineworkers, 'the personnel of the two sides becomes over a period similar to a greater degree than there is similarity between the interests of the officials of the union and its basic rank and file'.[126]

Parallel with the rise of the corps of permanent officials was the weakening, during the years of 'the servile generation',[127] in trade union democracy. Such institutions as the referendum and the initiative 'withered away'. The shifting of the basis of the branch in many unions from the place of work to the place of residence helped to atomize the membership and increase their dependence on the officials. The Trades Union Congress of 1895 saw a conscious and open

---

[125] According to B. C. Roberts, *Trade Union Government and Administration* (1956), the total number of full-time officials of the eighteen large unions was in 1952 about 1,600. Roberts states that the commonest level of general secretaries' salaries was between £800 and just over £1,200 a year, while the general secretary of the Trades Union Congress got £2,000 a year. Average annual payments to executive council members in attendance fees, hotel expenses, etc., ranged from such figures as £200 in the National Union of General and Municipal Workers to £1,172 in the National Union of Railwaymen (pp. 288, 306, 367, 443).

[126] N. Dennis, F. Henriques, C. Slaughter, *Coal is Our Life* (1956), pp. 114-16.

[127] Raymond Postgate's phrase, in *The Builder's History* (1923). He uses it in the sense that in the period between the 1850s and 1880s the British workers in the main accepted the capitalist order and merely sought to protect or at most improve a little their position within it.

move by the officials to cut away a possible line of rank-and-file control over their doings, by excluding the representatives of the trades councils, the very bodies which, less than thirty years earlier, had summoned the TUC into existence.

> The trades councils were in fact shut out partly in order to exclude 'agitators' whom the trade union leaders regarded as irresponsible busybodies, and partly in pursuance of a definite policy of centralizing industrial control in the hands of the national trade union executives. Obviously a Congress in which two or three million votes might have been cast by the delegates of local bodies would have been a great deal more difficult for the platform to manage than a Congress in which a very small number of national trade unions would cast, under a system of block voting, a majority of total votes. The TUC might have been a very different body if the trades councils had retained their original place in it. That, of course, is precisely why they were not allowed to retain it.[128]

Just as the emergence of a caste of privileged officials, cosily coexisting with capitalism, was reaching completion, a new phase of history opened, that of imperialism, passing into that of the general crisis of capitalism. The conditions characteristic of the second and third quarters of the nineteenth century were swept away for ever, and the workers found themselves under steady and intense attack, at first especially by means of rising prices. Round about 1909, when E. J. B. Allen published his pamphlet *Revolutionary Unionism,* wide sections of the workers became aware that the militant policy their new circumstances urgently demanded was being sabotaged by their officials. Allen listed a number of examples of what he called the 'treachery of officials' in preventing necessary strikes on various pretexts. He wrote:

> This kind of business is notably on the increase, particularly since the workers have been fools enough to pay this kind of official £200 and more per year [1909 money!] to do nothing in Parliament except betray their interests and run around after different capitalist politicians . . .in order to be remembered when there are some government jobs going.

Fred Knee, of the London Society of Compositors, remarked bitterly in 1910 that 'there are some trade union leaders who are so prosperous that they at any rate have in their own persons achieved the harmony of the classes'.[129]

---

[128] G. D. H. Cole, *British Trade Unionism Today* (1945), p. 192.

[129] In the *Social-Democrat,* November 15, 1910; reprinted in *Labour Monthly,* June 1950.

The 'Labour Unrest', 1910-14

Growing dissatisfaction with trade union officialdom was coupled from about 1910 with a mood of disillusionment with parliamentary politics. This was caused by the functioning of the Labour group in the House of Commons as a mere adjunct to the Liberal Party, all other considerations being subordinated to keeping the Liberals in and the Tories out. Syndicalist ideas from America and France found fertile soil among British trade unionists and such bodies as the Socialist Labour Party, the Syndicalist Education League and the Plebs League came into being and began developing rank-and-file sentiment for militant industrial policies in an organized way. Tom Mann, James Connolly, Noah Ablett, Richard Coppock, A. A. Purcell and A. J. Cook were among the leaders of the new trend. It was on the initiative of these men that the wave of great strikes began which shook Britain on the eve of the first world war.

The movement began with the unofficial strike of the Northumberland and Durham miners in the early months of 1910. These miners were bitter against their officials for having accepted a change from a two-shift to a three-shift system. The summer saw a similarly unofficial stoppage on the North-Eastern Railway, provoked by a case of victimization. Then, in the autumn, came the Cambrian Combine strike, begun against the will of the South Wales Miners' Federation executive. Of the 1911 strike in the docks, Sir George Askwith, the government's conciliation officer, observed: 'The Labour leaders were taken by surprise. Some quickly headed the movement and tried to regain their lost authority. Others frankly expressed astonishment, and could not understand the outbreak.'[130] The railway strike of 1911 began under unofficial leadership in Liverpool, 'in spite of the fact that the executives of the railwaymen's unions were opposed to any railwaymen leaving work or making demands, the officials arguing that they were tied down by the decisions of the conciliation boards, which they had accepted.'[131] Finally, the general miners' strike of 1912 began as an unofficial movement — and one of its

[130] G. R. Askwith, *Industrial Problems and Disputes* (1920), p. 177. For a good general survey of this period see G. Dangerfield, *The Strange Death of Liberal England* (1936); see also Tom Mann, *Memoirs* (1923).

[131] Tom Mann, *From Single Tax to Syndicalism* (1913), ch. vi.

results was the ousting from the South Wales miners' executive of the leaders who had opposed the strike, and their replacement by syndicalists.

A number of economic gains resulted from these strikes, but the outcome fell far short of what might have been. As Trotsky stated in *Where is Britain Going?* 'The vague shadow of revolution hovered over Britain in those days. The leaders exerted all their strength in order to paralyse the movement . . . strengthening the bourgeoisie and thus preparing the way for the imperialist slaughter.' Ralph Fox, writing during one of Stalinism's left zig-zags, summed up the experience thus:

> Practically every one of the great strikes from 1911 to 1914 was begun as an unofficial, spontaneous movement of the workers, rapidly spreading throughout the industry concerned. Only then did the reformist trade union bureaucrats lend the strike the official support of the union, while their swift acceptance in every case of the 'mediation' of the Liberal Government doomed the strike at once to semi-failure.[132]

Among the most important achievements of the 'Labour unrest', as the capitalist Press called it, were two moves towards the unification of the workers' forces: the amalgamation of three railway organizations in the National Union of Railwaymen, and the formation of the Transport Workers' Federation, the germ of the Transport and General Workers' Union of today. Amalgamation was one of the chief demands of the militants, who wanted all craft and sectional interests to be subordinated to the needs of the working class as a whole, and had one union for each industry as their ideal. A metal, engineering and shipbuilding amalgamation committee was set up in 1912, to carry on 'propaganda in the workshops and trade union branches with a view to bringing pressure to bear from below on the national executives',[133] in favour of fusing the unions catering for workers in the industries named. Similar movements sprang up in other industries. This amalgamationist trend 'was for the most part a "rank-and-file" movement of a Left-wing character, keenly critical of the attitude and conduct of the permanent trade union officials'.[134] Nowadays the concentration of the bulk of trade union membership into a few great, powerful amalgamations is taken for granted, and it is

---

[132] Ralph Fox, *The Class Struggle in Britain, 1880-1914* (1932), p. 71.

[133] W. A. Orton, *Labour in Transition* (1921), pp. 93-4.

[134] G. D. H. Cole, *Workshop Organization* (1923), p. 17.

worth recalling that the struggle to bring this about was at first an affair of 'Left-wingers' and 'unofficial movements'.

Coupled with the fight for amalgamation was the fight for workshop organization. In the early stages of trade unionism the branch had largely coincided with the place of work, but with the expansion of the unions a territorial basis for branch membership had been established in many unions. The militants believed that organization on the basis of the workshop made for greater effectiveness of the unions as fighting machines — and less 'atomization' of the rank and file in relation to that compact bureaucracy at the top which they had learnt to distrust. Before the first world war, the shop stewards in a number of centres had already begun to come forward as leaders of their members in conflict with the employers, and shop stewards for different unions had begun to come together informally, constituting an 'amalgamated' leadership at local level. The tremendous class battles of 1910-14 inevitably fostered this development, by revealing the inadequacy of the type of trade union structure which had set hard in the decades of relative social peace.

Linked with amalgamation of the unions and the building up of workshop organization was the aim of limiting the power of officials to go against the will of the rank and file, and subjecting these officials to more effective control from below. A comparatively moderate expression of this idea was given by a writer in Tom Mann's journal the *Industrial Syndicalist:*

> Our leaders must be elected by a ballot of the membership by direct vote, elected for a definite period with definite instructions, *and they must prove their competency by being successful* ...We can afford no more lasting failures, even in high places. The only test of competency in this connection is success.[135]

Much more advanced views than this were widespread in the Labour movement at this time. A definitely anti-official, anti-leadership outlook was reflected in one of the rules of the Socialist Labour Party, which wielded great influence among Clydeside militants, that its members must not occupy any official position in a trade union. The most finished formulation of the extreme view is found in the famous pamphlet *The Miners' Next Step,* brought out in 1912 by the Unofficial Reform Committee active among the South Wales miners. Trade union officials, it was claimed, were wedded to the

---

[135] W. F. Hay, in the *Industrial Syndicalist*, November 1910.

policy of industrial conciliation regardless of their members' interests. They were opposed to any increase in rank-and-file control over themselves, because their possession of arbitrary power gave them social prestige and ensured the 'respect' of the employers, with all that that implied. When the Cambrian Combine men had demanded a ballot on the agreement accepted in their name in 1910 the leaders had talked of a 'growing spirit of anarchy'. The remedy was not to be found in a mere change of leaders, for former agitators who became leaders went the same way as those they supplanted. (The element of truth in this was to be seen in the later career of A. J. Cook, one of the co-authors of this pamphlet!) 'Leadership implies power held by the Leader . . .All leaders become corrupt, in spite of their own good intentions. No man was ever good enough, brave enough or strong enough to have such power at his disposal as real leadership implies.' Consistently with this view, the authors demanded a reorganization of their union so that 'all the initiative for new proposals, policies and tactics remains with the lodge' and the executive (from which officials should be excluded) was to be reduced to merely administrative functions.[136]

The First World War and the Shop Stewards

With the outbreak of the imperialist war, which their braking of the 1910-14 struggles had helped to make inevitable, the trade union officials entered into an agreement with the government which virtually abolished trade unionism 'for the duration'. In exchange for this they were taken on to all sorts of committees and given such social recognition as they had never enjoyed before. The war years were a period, wrote the Webbs, of 'revolutionary [they mean, of course, counter-revolutionary] transformation of the social and political standing of the official representatives of the trade union world', when the trade union machine was recognized as 'part of the social machinery of the State'.[137] While prices rose steeply, wages were kept down and employers were allowed to chisel away at hard-won rights and safeguards on the plea that the 'war effort' necessitated sacrifices.

[136] Cf. James P. Cannon, Introduction (1931) to L. D. Trotsky, *Communism and Syndicalism:* 'The slogan of "no leaders" — that slogan of demagogues who themselves aspire to leadership without qualifications.'

[137] Sidney and Beatrice Webb, *History of Trade Unionism* (1920 edition), p. 635.

What the Judases of trade unionism, enjoying their statesmanlike status, looked like at close quarters we see in Beatrice Webb's notes on the Trades Union Congress of 1915:

> The Congress is no better, in fact less hopeful, than in old days, if we assume it to be representative of advanced working-class opinion. The leading men have grown fatter in body and more dully complacent in mind than they were twenty years ago; the delegates have lost their keenness, the rebels of today don't get elected to Congress and the 'old hands' know, from long experience, that it is more of an 'outing' than a gathering for the transaction of working-class affairs. What the delegates enjoy is a joke, it matters not what sort of joke so long as it excites laughter. Indignation, righteous or unrighteous, is felt to be out of place. There is no anti-government feeling, no determination to get evils righted . . .I listened to two officials over their big cigars in the hotel lounge this afternoon. 'The wages are cruel,' said one to the other, 'perfectly scandalous.' It was the largeness of the [workers'] earnings, it appeared, they were complaining of! . . .In so far as there is any feeling it is reserved for jealousy between leaders or for the disputes between the unions.[138]

The workers' impatience with the situation created by their traitor leaders broke through into direct action first on the Clyde in February 1915. 'Amalgamationists' among the engineers, together with members of the various Marxist groupings in Glasgow, took the lead in getting an unofficial ban on overtime imposed until the employers agreed to a wage increase that would meet the rise in the cost of living. When the union leaders opposed them, the workers concerned set up a Central Withdrawal of Labour Committee on which all the unions in the engineering trade were represented by their shop stewards, and called a strike. This lasted eighteen days before the combined pressure of the government and the union leaders forced the men back. The committee resolved to remain in being as the Clyde Workers' Committee and its members actively promoted the formation in each workshop in the area of a shop stewards' committee covering all sections. The success of this movement caused tremendous alarm in capitalist circles, and pretexts were found to arrest the chief 'agitators' and deport them from Clydeside and also to suppress the shop stewards' paper, *The Worker*.[139]

---

[138] Beatrice Webb, *Diaries 1912-1924* (1952), pp. 44-5.

[139] The best accounts of this and other industrial struggles of 1914-18 are given in W. Hannington, *Industrial History in Wartime* (1940), and J. T. Murphy, *Preparing for Power* (1934). See also W. Gallacher, *Revolt on the Clyde* (1949) and T. Bell, *Pioneering Days* (1941).

Hardly had the noise of battle died down on the Clyde, however, when it broke out in Sheffield. The calling up to the army of an engineering worker belonging to an exempt category was taken as a test case by the engineers of that city. Shop stewards improvised a local organization which brought 10,000 men out on strike in November 1916, and sent delegates to other engineering centres to have the strike extended. The War Office hastily released their victim in order to get the men back to work in the munitions factories. Out of this struggle emerged a network of permanent workshop committees in Sheffield, and a trend towards the unification of these into factory committees and into a workers' committee covering the entire district. The struggle for amalgamation became primarily concerned with building up unity from below at the point of production: 'Make the amalgamation of unions incidental, the amalgamation of the workers fundamental.'[140]

All through the years 1916-18 there was a succession of strikes in one centre after another, particularly in engineering but also in other industries, notably in the South Wales coalfield, in every case led by unofficial groups. But there was little co-ordination between these actions. Thus, the engineers' strike which began at Rochdale in May 1917 and spread rapidly, did not affect such important centres as Clydeside and Tyneside. The unofficial leaders faced enormous difficulties, every possible obstacle being put in their way by the government, the employers and the union officials. As they began to overcome them and to hold successful national conferences of shop stewards — and as news of the February revolution in Russia and its consequences began to come in, along with news of mutinies in the French army and other signs of the times — the official leaders of the Labour movement started to vary their tactics. Union officials intervened with the authorities to get arrested shop stewards released and concessions granted to various sections of the workers. The charade of the Leeds Convention took place, at which men like MacDonald and Snowden talked of setting up councils of workmen's and soldiers' delegates in every locality to work for peace and the emancipation of Labour. The unions of the miners, the railwaymen and the transport workers formed a Triple Alliance and made vigorous-sounding pronouncements about 'conscription of wealth', so that many workers looked to the leaders of this new official grouping of unions as the

---

[140] J. T. Murphy, quoted in W. A. Orton, *Labour in Transition* (1921), p. 96.

advance-guard in the war on capitalism, making unofficial, rank-and-file organization unnecessary.[141]

When a national leadership of the various shop stewards' committees and amalgamation movements at last came into being, in August 1917, it was hamstrung by the syndicalist prejudice against any kind of effective leadership which their experience of corrupt officialdom had fostered in so many rank-and-file trade unionists. What was set up was a merely administrative council without any executive powers: all decisions had to be referred back to the rank and file before action could be initiated, and the council functioned as little more than a reporting centre for the local committees.

By allowing the official leaders of the working-class movement to make some 'Left' gestures, and by granting some real concessions, British imperialism was able, aided also by confused ideas in the workers' ranks, to survive the war intact. But what would happen after the war, when the 'patriotic' considerations which had held back many workers during the hostilities with Germany ceased to apply, and the demobilized soldiers demanded that 'land fit for heroes to live in' which they had been promised? 'With the coming of the Armistice in November 1918 organized Labour was left in what was probably the strongest position it had ever occupied . . .Moreover, for a halcyon breathing-space of eighteen months Labour was in a much stronger position than it had dared to hope.'[142]

The 'full-employment' period which lasted until the slump began in the latter part of 1920 presented a wonderful opportunity to the militants, and the capitalists were hard put to it to fend them off. Though the opportunity was taken, with the 'rephasing' of the munitions industry, to get rid of as many shop stewards as possible and thereby break up the movement in its war-time strongholds, it continued to advance on a number of sectors of the industrial front and its ideas were widely discussed. The shop stewards' movement, wrote a contemporary observer, 'is at once the demand for greater autonomy for the rank-and-file workers as against the control of the central

[141] One workers' leader who saw the fallacy of relying on the Triple Alliance — a mere pact between top officials — was James Connolly, who wrote in the *Workers' Republic*, February 12, 1916: 'The frequent rebellion against stupid and spiritless leadership and the call of the rank and file for true industrial unity seems to have spurred the leaders on, not to respond to new spirit but to evolve a method whereby under the forms of unity [it] could be trammelled and fettered . . .a scheme to *prevent* united action rather than facilitate it.'

[142] M. H. Dobb, *Trade Union Experience and Policy, 1914-18* (1940), p. 24.

official, and for more effective organization against the power of the employer' — demands which 'are not easily separated for the second may depend largely on the first'.[143] In those days 'it looked as though some fundamentally new form of trade union structure was going to replace the established forms'.[144] J. T. Murphy's pamphlet *The Workers' Committee* (1918) sold 150,000 copies. Its central idea was the election of workshop committees cutting across the boundaries between unions, but given official recognition by the unions; committees which should link up into district workers' committees, which 'should not usurp the functions of the local trade union committees but attend to the larger questions embracing all the trade unions in the industry'. These committees would be 'similar in form to a trades council, with this essential difference — the trades council is only indirectly related to the workshops, whereas the workers' committee is directly related'. The formation of these committees, it was argued, would render the union machinery more and more responsive to the needs of the members 'at the point of production', and would facilitate the desired trend towards amalgamation.[145]

After the head-on clashes which occurred in Glasgow and Belfast early in 1919 the main method followed by the capitalists, together with the government and the trade union bureaucrats, was the method of concessions, both real and apparent, to tide over the awkward period pending the slump. Railwaymen were given the 48-hour week, engineers and shipbuilders the same. A commission to investigate the possibilities of nationalizing the coal industry appeased the miners. Substantial wage increases raised the general level of real wages above that of 1914. An 'Industrial Conference' of representatives of trade unions and employers' federations agreed upon an imposing programme of social legislation. The Amalgamated Society of Engineers made an agreement with the employers which accorded a definite status to that union's shop stewards in the works.[146] The

[143] C. M. Lloyd, *Trade Unionism* (1921), p. 244

[144] J. I. Roper, *Trade Unionism and the New Social Order* (1949).

[145] Typical of the many committees formed unofficially in this period was the River Thames Shop Stewards' Movement, which embraced all trades and grades engaged in shipyard work. It had a membership card, and formed local committees in each shipyard. The organizer was a boilermaker, the secretary an electrician, the editor of the movement's paper a woodworker (H. Pollitt, *Serving My Time*, 1940, pp. 92-3).

[146] 'The recognized shop stewards were representatives only of a particular union, and were precluded from acting with representatives of other unions, except with the consent of the union's district committee. The shop stewards' movement, where it

amalgamation of the ASE with other unions into the Amalgamated Engineering Union seemed to give promise of reorganization for battle on one important sector, while the Triple Alliance could be trusted to look after most of the others. Much of the workers' confidence in the official machinery and leadership was restored.

Among the militants themselves the confusion of ideas continued. The National Guilds movement enjoyed a brief but deadly vogue and led important groups of building workers into costly, fruitless and discouraging attempts to take over their industry by setting up in business in rivalry with private builders. Similar notions were widespread in other industries, diverting workers' minds from the need for political struggle against the capitalist state. As regards the attitude to be adopted towards the trade unions, on the one hand there was the tendency, especially marked in the unions of the Triple Alliance, to confine oneself to 'vigilance' work, making propaganda for militant policies and warning against the danger of sell-out, while on the other, the prejudice against 'leaders' caused many outstanding shop stewards voluntarily to hold back from contesting union elections and fighting to win footholds within the official machine.[147] The principal Marxist groups did not come together into a united Communist Party until January 1921, and then remained very much under the influence of their sectarian traditions and did not try systematically to become rooted in industry until the reorganization of 1922-23 got under way. By then the slump had set in, unemployment existed on a mass scale, and a succession of industrial defeats (especially 'Black Friday' in 1921 when the Triple Alliance showed its true worth, and the engineering lock-out of 1922) had smashed what remained of the war-time shop stewards' movement and compelled the militants to start painfully building up again almost from scratch.

---

survived, became officialized; it lost its revolutionary character, and its inclusiveness as a class movement' (G. D. H. Cole, *British Trade Unionism Today*, 1945, p. 169).

[147] 'The Workers' Committee elements were in opposition to trade unionism! They saw the trade unions as centres of Labour corruption, and were obsessed by the enormous growth of the unofficial movement during the war and the power it had been able to wield. Lenin here insisted on the necessity of combating the corrupt leaders of the trade unions but also stressed the importance of work in the trade unions and recognition of the trade unions as the mass organizations of the working class' (T. Bell, *The British Communist Party*, 1937, pp. 58-9).

The Minority Movement

The regrouping of the militant forces took place under the guidance of the Communist Party, working mainly through what was called the British Bureau of the Red International of Labour Unions, headed by Tom Mann.[148] The RILU fully understood at this time that there could be no question of forming new unions in Britain, nor was there much to be gained by campaigning for affiliation of existing unions to the RILU. The South Wales Miners' Federation, where the 'Reform Committee' elements were strong, declared for affiliation in 1921, but retracted when threatened with expulsion from the Trades Union Congress. Under the guidance of the RILU communists began working, industry by industry, to rally the workers on the basis of specific programmes related both to the problems of the given industry and to the actual structure of the trade union machine. In sharp contrast to the attitude taken up in a later phase (1929-31), the fact that many workers had left the unions, either through fear of victimization in a period of slump or out of disgust with the betrayals by the bureaucrats, or for other reasons, was not seen as the end of the trade union epoch, justifying militants in turning their backs on the unions. On the contrary 'Back to the unions!' was one of the slogans of the British Bureau of the RILU, coupled with 'Stop the retreat!' which was a call to end the policy of surrender to the employers' offensive. *All Power*, the Bureau's paper, had a circulation by the end of 1922 of 12,000. Rank-and-file organizations, known as 'minority movements' — from a complaint by some bureaucrat regarding 'the minority of troublemakers' — were brought into being anew among the miners, the engineers, the transport workers and other sections, and these were eventually, in 1924, gathered together into the National Minority Movement.

I have discussed elsewhere[149] this movement's record in 1924-27 and here wish only to draw attention to certain of its features. In the early phase great stress was laid on the need to make trades councils directly representative of the workshops instead of merely consisting of delegates from trade union branches which were often remote and

[148] A. J. Cook and Richard Coppock were among the members of this Bureau.
[149] In 'The Early Years of the CPGB', and 'British Communist History'.

unrepresentative, to secure the restoration of the trades councils' representation in the Trades Union Congress, and in every way to strengthen the element of rank-and-file control in trade union structure, so as to ensure that the unions functioned for the purpose they had originally been formed to serve.

> The task of the Minority Movement was to make the unity of the trade union movement a real one, to build up the shop and local organization which should be able to control from below this great mass machine, to fight at every step the apostles of 'civil peace', and uniting the workers, organized and unorganized, on the widest possible front in their everyday economic struggles, build up such a rank-and-file movement as should make impossible a repetition of 'Black Friday'.[150]

Unfortunately, although the Minority Movement became an influential centre of propaganda and a ginger group which injected new life into many trade union branches and trades councils, and thereby forced the trade union leaders to put themselves at the head of strikes and to make various 'Left' gestures, as in 1917-20, it did little in practice to establish the workshop and factory committees of which so much was said. In the main it proved able only to spread the idea and urge it upon the official leadership. The root of the trouble here was probably that the transformation of the Communist Party on to a factory-group basis 'was only begun in earnest towards the end of 1924' and by May 1, 1925, there were only sixty-eight communist factory groups, embracing a mere 10 per cent of the party membership.[151] By the time that the political driving force in the Minority Movement had organized itself sufficiently to begin setting up new kinds of mass organizations in the factories, the Anglo-Russian Unity Committee had come into existence, and the Stalinist leadership of the world communist movement had decreed that nothing be done that might disturb the goodwill of the 'Left' bureaucrats. At the party congress in May 1925 a Sheffield delegate observed:

> A. J. Cook's speech at the recent miners' conference was completely out of tone with the speeches he had previously been making [i.e., before he had been elected to the secretaryship of the Miners' Federation, with Minority Movement support]. After we have praised and said nice things about these Left-wing leaders, what will the masses say about the Communist

[150] Ralph Fox, *The Class Struggle in Britain, 1914-1923* (1933), p. 82.

[151] Report of the Seventh Congress (1925) of the Communist Party of Great Britain, pp. 148, 201.

> Party when these leaders fail them? We must give the necessary qualifications to our support of these Left-wingers.

A Glasgow delegate warned of the need to be suspicious of certain trade union leaders who were acquiring an easy reputation for 'Leftness' through prominence in the movement for international trade union unity. Pollitt replied that there was 'just a little danger of overstressing this point ... The Russian trade union leaders are interested, leaders who have proved their worth to the working-class movement and in whom we have complete confidence'.[152]

The end of this road was the betrayal of the General Strike, with the Communist Party and the Minority Movement unable to do anything against it but protest and call upon the traitor leaders to mend their ways. It revealed 'the weakness of a Left which could only make propaganda, and which was not so firmly organized in the factories and localities that it could take the lead in action'.[153] A hint of realization that the movement had been shunted on to the wrong path in 1925-26 appeared in Wal Hannington's pamphlet *What's Wrong in the Engineering Industry?* published by the National Minority Movement in 1927, where he wrote, after urging the need for a change of leaders in the unions:

> To those who say 'We have seen leaders turn before and what guarantee is there that they will not continue to do so?' we reply, the Minority Movement must be strong enough inside the unions not only to make leaders, but also to break them, if and when they reject the policy upon which they were elected.

But Stalinist policy remained unchanged right down to the end of 1927, and the decision not to resist the TUC General Council's ultimatum to trades councils to disaffiliate from the Minority Movement virtually killed it.

> So died the Minority Movement, much as the General Strike had died. Ernest Bevin and his colleagues had called off the General Strike to avoid open warfare with the government; Harry Pollitt called off the Minority Movement to avoid open warfare with the TUC and many executives of trade unions.[154]

---

[152] *Ibid.* pp. 29, 73-4.

[153] John Mahon, *Trade Unionism* (1938), p. 53.

[154] J. T. Murphy, *Labour's Big Three* (1948), p. 137. The national executive committee of the movement reported to the fifth annual conference, in 1928, that 'it has become increasingly clear that we made a grave mistake last year in recommending the trades councils to withdraw their affiliation from the Minority Movement'.

The 'Third Period'

Thanks to the policy imposed upon it by Moscow from the spring of 1925 onwards, the Minority Movement had done just enough to incur the resentment of the bureaucracy without acquiring the power to fight back effectively. The bureaucracy was able very thoroughly to combine its proscription and bans with the employers' victimization of militants in that black period of the British working-class movement which followed the General Strike, and so to stamp out the Minority Movement for most practical purposes. For all its weaknesses and opportunist errors, the Minority Movement of 1924-27 had been a genuine expression of a trend in the working class, with real roots in the masses and a relationship to the traditional organizations of British Labour. Between the end of 1927 (Fifteenth Congress of the Soviet Communist Party) and the middle of 1929 (Tenth Plenum of the Executive Committee of the Communist International) a change of policy was put through in the international communist movement which caused British Stalinists in their industrial work to take off into realms of fantasy and adventure, not to mention crime and treason to the working class.[155] This episode is largely responsible for the attitude of reserve and suspicion towards anything calling itself a 'rank-and-file movement' which is sometimes met among old trade unionists who are by no means bureaucrats.

The original Minority Movement based itself on affiliation by trade union branches, district committees, etc.; individual membership was treated as transitional until the individual concerned had won his branch to affiliate. It was careful to emphasize that it was not an anti-union movement but on the contrary expected its supporters to work for 100 per cent trade unionism wherever they had influence, and could point to many an achievement in this respect. One of the last expositions of the movement's purpose before the entry into what Stalinist jargon called 'the third period' is found in a pamphlet by Fred Thompson called *Maintenance for Dockers*, published by the Transport Workers' Minority Movement in 1928.

---

[155] For some account of the ultra-Left phase of Stalinism in Britain at the end of the 1920s and the beginning of the 1930s, see 'The Communist Party and the Labour Left, 1925-29', and Henry Pelling, *The British Communist Party* (1958).

> The Minority Movement is an organization of militant trade unionists who, realizing the extent to which the present leadership have committed themselves and the unions unreservedly to class collaboration, have banded themselves together to restore the original purpose and fighting spirit on which the trade unions were founded, to secure a new leadership with a policy based upon a realization of the class struggle, and a complete reorganization of the trade unions on lines that will admit of this policy being given effect to.

From mid-1929 onward for a period of over two years, this approach was replaced by a totally different one. Not merely was the Minority Movement in its new guise uninterested in winning 100 per cent trade unionism, it declared the trade unions to be cracking up and on their way out, and a good thing too. Not merely did it turn away from the task of winning trade union branches for militant policies, it deliberately sought to *exclude* branch officers from strike committees and rank-and-file *ad hoc* committees of all kinds. Special 'red' trade unions were created and then launched by their communist leaders into 'prestige' strikes, the need for which was not understood by the members (though these affairs looked impressive in the periodical reports to Moscow), so that militancy was discredited among those sections of the workers closest to the Minority Movement.

It was of this period in Stalinist industrial policy that Trotsky wrote (in *Communism and Syndicalism*, 1929) that:

> ... the struggle for the party's influence in the trade unions finds its objective verification in whether or not the unions thrive, whether or not the number of their members increases, as well as in their relations with the broadest masses. If the party buys its influence in the trade unions only at the price of a narrowing-down and factionalizing of the latter — converting them into auxiliaries of the party for momentary aims and preventing them from becoming genuine mass organizations — then the relations between the party and the class are wrong.

The Communist Party was showing 'an adolescent tendency to make itself master of the working class in the briefest time, by means of stage-play, inventions, superficial agitation, etc.'; nothing good would come of 'political hysteria which does not take conditions into account, which confuses today with yesterday or with tomorrow'.

Characteristic of the 1929-31 period was a growing disparity between slogans and achievements. During the Bradford woollen strike of 1930, for instance, the Minority Movement shouted to bewildered workers about 'the struggle for power' — but proved incapable of setting up a single independent mill committee. While the Red International of Labour Unions demanded that the movement become 'a real mass organization based on dues-paying collective and individual membership', setting itself up as an alternative trade union centre to the TUC, the tactics of frenzy were in fact resulting in the isolation and even expulsion of those groups which had retained some mass influence from the General Strike period (e.g., the expulsion of the Mardy lodge from the South Wales Miners' Federation). Arthur Horner himself eventually spoke out within the party against what was happening: 'Artificial strike committees, really Minority Movement groups, were set up as alternatives to the lodges, without mass contact, resulting only in our isolation ...The revolutionary movement was effectively bankrupt from every angle.'[156] For this statement he was, of course, reprimanded and removed from the leadership of the Miners' Minority Movement. The shouting to the workers to come and be led, with a general strike as 'the next step', grew louder and shriller, especially as the international Stalinist leadership kept impatiently contrasting the poor showing of the Minority Movement with what was happening in Germany (where the Nazis were now a substantial and growing force) — there, forsooth, 'all mass movements are conducted under the leadership of the party'.

Those who criticized the suicidal tactics of the 'third period' were dismissed as 'Trotskyist yellow-bellies', just as those who had criticized the opportunist errors of the previous phase had been 'Trotskyist wild men'. After the damage had been done, and without, of course, any acknowledgement to those who had been right at the time, Wilhelm Pieck admitted on behalf of the Executive Committee of the Communist International, in his speech of July 26, 1935, at the Seventh Congress of the CI, the justice of these criticisms:

> The most glaring example of sectarianism in the trade union movement was provided in Great Britain, where in the face of the sharp attacks of the Right members of the General Council and the vacillations of the Left trade union leaders the communists adopted [in fact had pressed upon them by the Executive Committee of the CI! — B.P.] such clumsy and sectarian tactics that the Minority Movement actually fell to pieces. Adopting the course of independently leading the economic struggles, the communists, as a result of former Right mistakes and the inadequate organizational consolidation of the Minority Movement, transferred their main work from the trade union groups to individual members and from the

[156] Quoted in *Communist Review*, April 1931.

trade unions to the unorganized workers, and set up their scanty forces against the whole trade union movement. These mistakes were aggravated by the fact that the communists regarded the Minority Movement as the nucleus of new trade unions and discontinued recruiting workers to the trade unions, issuing appeals to join the ranks of the Minority Movement. It must be borne in mind that these mistakes were committed by our comrades in a country where the reformist trade unions possess the oldest traditions. Under such circumstances the communists were found to become entirely isolated from the trade union movement, and the Minority Movement collapsed. It is only with great difficulty that our British comrades, having realized their mistakes and correspondingly altered their trade union policy, are managing to regain their influence in the trade union movement.

The January Resolution and After

It was the outcome of the government crisis of 1931 that gave a salutary jolt to the Communist Party and to its mentors in Moscow, inducing some new thinking on industrial policy. The collapse of the Labour government provided a model opportunity for communist advance, but the actual development of events merely served to highlight the isolation and impotence of the communists.

Meanwhile, the fact had to be faced that, independently of the surviving Minority Movement groups, now left high and dry, workers in a number of industries were forming unofficial organizations and carrying on the struggle in their own way — regardless both of the top officials of their unions and of the theories of the Communist Party. In South Wales the big strike against the 'Schiller Award' was led by the militant Llwynypia lodge of the union. A Builders' Forward Movement arose, based on thirty-two London trade union branches. An unofficial movement in the British Iron and Steel and Kindred Trades Federation held a conference at which sixty-one branches were represented, drew up a programme for democratizing the union, reducing officials' salaries etc., and issued its own duplicated news-sheet. A Members' Rights Movement appeared in the Amalgamated Engineering Union, a Reorganization Committee among the boilermakers, and a Rules Revision Committee among the furniture workers. All these developments began in the latter part of 1931, before any change was made in Communist Party policy; they were in no sense created by the Communist Party, as was later alleged by the Right wing and implied in communist propaganda. On the contrary, not only were they largely ignored by the communists but in some cases they were resisted and opposed as rivals to the Minority Movement![157]

On the initiative of the Red International of Labour Unions, the British Communist Party now undertook an important modification of its industrial policy. This was expressed in what came to be known as 'the January Resolution', adopted by the Central Committee in January 1932. This decision called for a turn towards the real movements going on among the workers, with abandonment of notions and forms of organization that constituted a barrier between the communists and these movements. The communists must cease to appear as a self-appointed leadership coming from outside, usually rather late in the day, and trying to impose programmes they had invented independently of the workers concerned. They must cease, too, to seem to wish to weaken and even to destroy the trade unions. In British conditions strike struggles, to be successful, must involve trade union branches, and the party should strive to win influence in the branches and among branch officers — who should no longer be put on the same level as the head-office bureaucrats. The trade union branches must be transformed 'from organs of class collaboration into organs of class struggle'. One of the tasks of Communist Party members must be to win unorganized workers to join the unions, as part of a general line of strengthening organization for struggle.

This change of outlook on major problems naturally produced much discussion in the party. It was during this discussion that the Balham group of the Communist Party was expelled, to become the original nucleus of the Left Opposition in Britain. In a series of thoughtful contributions to the *Daily Worker* (April 14, May 27, June 10), mild in tone though perhaps somewhat abstract and rigid in presentation, these comrades explained that while they welcomed the January Resolution as a step in the right direction of a critical examination of the party's policy and methods, they were worried about the way the resolution put the unions and workplaces on the same footing as fields of work. 'We recognize the great value of work in the trade unions and realize that we should make use of every opportunity afforded to us inside the trade union branches. We see the possibilities for work in the unions as well as the limitations.' The structure and

[157] See articles in *Daily Worker*, May 26, 1932, and *Communist International*, August 15, 1932.

constitution of the trade unions made them unsuitable as organs of class struggle; these must be built directly in the workshops and factories. 'We do not deny . . .that the branches can be of great value in building the job organizations, but the emphasis in the resolution is upon the unions.'

King Street had been worried about the Balham group for some time, being aware that a number of its members were studying Trotsky's criticisms and counter-proposals regarding Comintern policy, and was happy to seize the opportunity of expelling the group on an issue where it could be made to look like a centre of Left-sectarian resistance to necessary changes in party work. The Balham comrades were in fact far from being alone in warning against the danger that the correction of Left errors might, unless very carefully understood and explained, open the way to Right ones. No less an authority than R. P. Dutt himself noted, in contributions to the *Daily Worker* of September 14 and 19, 1932, that:

> . . . under cover of the absolute and agreed necessity of strengthening a hundredfold our work in the reformist trade unions there has begun to appear increasingly a very different tendency — a tendency to preach confidence in the reformist trade unions and in the reformist trade union machine as organs of working-class struggle.

He stressed that 'we stand for a powerful united revolutionary trade union opposition, firmly based on the trade union membership, on the lower trade union organs, and on factory organization, which will break the power of the reformist trade union bureaucracy and lead the way to the future powerful united revolutionary trade unionism'. Not surprisingly, J. Shields pointed out in the *Daily Worker* of September 30 that 'Comrade Dutt objectively comes out on the side of the Balham group'.[158]

For a considerable period after the January Resolution the Communist Party's industrial work made little progress, and may even, on balance, have declined. A process of 'falling between two stools' was going on. On the one hand, the Minority Movement, which had

---

[158] To correct any anti-trade union tendency in their ranks, the British Left Oppositionists published in their paper the *Communist,* September 1932, part of a reply written by Trotsky in the previous year to a letter from British friends. The latter had expressed the view that the trade unions were falling to pieces. Trotsky sharply disagreed and went on to demand: 'How can the revolutionization of the working class take place outside of the trade unions, without changing their physiognomy and failing to call forth a selection of new leaders?' Trotsky: *Collected Writings and Speeches on Britain,* Volume 3, p. 52.

become a caricature of its former self, was dropped by many militants to whom it had become an embarrassment. ('Following upon this resolution, group after group of the MM that still existed went out of existence, the comrades claiming that they understood it now to be the line of the party that the MM should be liquidated', wrote W. Allan in *Communist Review,* October, 1932.) On the other, the persistence of sectarian habits — and of the workers' distrust of the communists arising from these — meant that the successful implementation of new methods of work did not come easily

> All the party activities in the big weavers' strike in 1932 were *outside* the union. The 'Solidarity Movement' formed out of the strike had no real roots in the lower organizations of the union, and was mainly composed of individual communists. It was inevitable that such a movement could not live long.

So wrote Idris Cox three years afterwards.[159] So late as October 1932 it was still necessary for the leadership of the Metal Trades Minority Movement to pass a resolution calling on all its members to 'link up with and actively work amongst' the Members' Rights Movement, which had the support of 120 trade union branches and four area councils of the AEU and published its own monthly paper the *Monkey Wrench,* with a circulation of 5,000.[160] John Mahon reported in the same period that a number of the unofficial movements in the trade unions had been allowed to decline or to go out of existence and that 'one tendency regarded these movements as dangerous competitors with the Minority Movement, and in pursuance of this theory the Builders' Forward Movement was liquidated'.[161] At the Twelfth Congress of the Communist Party, held in November 1932, it emerged that virtually no progress had been made in striking roots in the factories. 'Most of the new members who joined are unemployed; most of the members who left are unemployed.'

There was an outstanding exception, however, amid the disappointments in the field of rank-and-file work. This was the work carried out among the London busmen, which became a 'model' for successful unofficial organization. The London Busmen's Rank-and-File Movement arose in August 1932 out of dissatisfaction with

---

[159] *Communist International,* February 5, 1935.

[160] *Weekly Worker,* October 22, 1932; *Communist International,* October 1, 1932.

[161] *Daily Worker,* October 20, 1932; *Weekly Worker,* November 19, 1932.

the trade union officials' attitude to the employers' proposals, and by November it was issuing a printed monthly paper the *Busman's Punch*. Pollitt wrote in the *Labour Monthly* of January 1933:

> The experience of the London Busmen's Rank-and-File Movement should be carefully studied by the militant workers in every industry. The determination of the mass of London's busmen (shown in a four-to-one majority ballot vote to resist the company's terms) was expressed through the setting up of a rank-and-file committee consisting of branch representatives who reported back to the branches and secured confirmation of the committee's decisions. Funds to carry out a propaganda campaign were raised through the branches; leaflets, pamphlets, and the *Busman's Punch* were sold through the branches; speakers from the rank-and-file committees addressed the branches. . . . And all this work was carried out by a committee drawing its authority from the garages and branches, who looked to it to lead the fight against the company *independently of the trade union officials, but with the full force of the trade union branches and garages behind it.*

In the case of the busmen, the branch coincided with the place of work, the garage, so that the problem whether to work mainly through the branches or mainly on the job itself, whether to try to transform the branch or to set up a special 'factory committee', hardly existed. The busmen were, moreover, all members of one union. Another favourable circumstance was the existence as part of the official set-up of the Central Bus Committee, composed of representatives of the branches; through their success in the branches the militants automatically obtained a majority on this committee, which then became a powerful instrument for extending their influence and providing leadership to the London busmen as a whole. V. L. Allen notes, in his *Trade Union Leadership:* Based on a Study of Arthur Deakin (1957):

> The National Minority Movement was based on an individual membership of trade unionists; it was a body outside of the trade union movement and, as such, it could be proscribed by unions, and trade unionists who belonged to it could be disciplined. This was not so easily done in the case of the Rank-and-File Movement, for it was based on the support of trade union branches and shop stewards' organizations and had no individual membership. The communists concentrated on getting powerful lay trade union committees to affiliate to the Movement. In the Central London Area Bus Committee they found one such committee which fairly quickly came under the control of the London Busmen's Rank-and-File Movement. From then onwards its policy ran counter to that of the union

executive and there was no way in which the executive could change it except by suspending the machinery, declaring the movement subversive, and taking disciplinary action against its leading members (pp. 64-5).

George Renshaw, analysing the success of the busmen's movement in the *RILU Magazine* (February 1, 1933), described how it had all grown from the work of militants in one branch who had got this branch to pass a resolution and then to circulate it to all the garages and call a mass meeting, through which they made new contacts and launched the *Busman's Punch* — at first as a duplicated sheet.[162]

Inspired by the example of the London busmen's movement, the 'Vigilance' movement on the railways made considerable progress in the early months of 1933 and was expected to prove as viable, but it was soon dragged down by difficulties which did not exist for the London busmen — inter-union rivalries and the problems connected with setting up an organization cutting across union membership, and the absence of an official leading centre which could be 'captured' as the Central Bus Committee had been. Nevertheless, the agitation carried on by the 'Vigilance' movement, especially through its widely-circulated paper the *Railway Vigilant,* forced the railway National Wages Board, for the first time since 1921, to reject a demand made by the railway companies, and the movement led numerous successful local strikes.

As the militancy of the workers revived, with signs of recovery from the depths of the depression, during 1933, and as the communists began seriously to apply themselves to work on the new lines, the trade union bureaucracy started to crack down on rank-and-file activities with greater determination than for several years. They recognized that a serious threat to their position was developing. Twelve London members of the Amalgamated Society of Woodworkers who organized, through a committee representing thirty branches, a rank-and-file conference in June 1933 for the purpose of working out a fighting programme for building workers, were expelled from the union. Ernest Bevin began to introduce amendments to the rule-book to trip up lower officials of his union who associated with unofficial movements. In union after union the clash grew sharper, culminating in the Black Circulars issued by the Trades Union Congress General Council in March 1935, attempting to make

[162] For a detailed account of the history of the London Busmen's Rank-and-File Movement, see H. A. Clegg, *Labour Relations in London Transport* (1950).

affiliated unions and trades councils deprive their communist members of delegation rights.[163] It was widely remarked that the 'reds' whom the union leaders were persecuting were among the best workers for 100 per cent trade unionism. Bert Papworth, who as secretary of Chelverton Road branch initiated the London busmen's movement, had just been decorated with his union's silver medal for recruiting 170 new members. Communists were to the fore in a series of strikes in unorganized factories in the Birmingham area and elsewhere (notably Firestone's, Brentford, and Pressed Steel, Oxford) which resulted in trade unionism getting footholds in previously black spots. The aircraft section of the engineering industry was practically unorganized in 1934 but within three years every important factory was over 90 per cent organized, an achievement mainly due to the Aircraft Shop Stewards' Movement, which issued its own paper the *New Propellor*, and in twelve months conducted fourteen important unofficial strikes, most of which were successful.

When the Thirteenth Congress of the British Communist Party took place, in February 1935, both the general situation in industry and the position of the communists in the trade unions were markedly different from what had obtained at the previous congress. Trade union membership had begun to increase for the first time for many years. The militancy of the workers caused *The Times* to write of 'the spirit of 1926' showing itself again. Of the 294 delegates to congress, 205 were employed: 234 were trade unionists, and of these nearly two-thirds held positions at some level in their unions. Not long afterwards, speaking on August 20, 1935, at the Seventh World Congress of the Communist International, J. R. Campbell could with reason depict Britain as being on the eve of great mass struggles, with the workers increasingly impatient of the restrictions imposed on them by the bureaucracy, and substantial prospects for a broad militant movement in industry.

[163] It was in the 1935 Birthday Honours that Pugh, of the Steelworkers, and Citrine, general secretary of the TUC, received knighthoods. They were not the first trade-union knights; but what was new was that they were knighted specifically for their trade union work, that Citrine had many years of such work ahead of him, and that the honours were bestowed by an anti-Labour government. Indicative of the strong position which the communists had built up between 1933 and 1935 was the narrowness of the General Council's majority when the Black Circulars came up for approval at the Trades Union Congress in September 1935: voting was 1,869,000 to 1,274,000. Peter Kerrigan could correctly claim, at the Seventh World Congress of the Communist International, that 'the change in our trade union work . . .has entirely altered the attitude of the majority of trade unionists to the party'.

Consequences of the 'People's Front' line

It is hard to reconcile the position that had actually come about by the eve of the war, in 1938-39, with the prospects confidently discussed in 1935. The rank-and-file movements which had been surging up again and again in industry in spite of official repression and intimidation, and causing panic among the bureaucrats, had either disappeared or become unrecognizably tame and respectable. The expected major class conflicts had not occurred. G. D. H. Cole writes in his *Short History of the British Working-Class Movement* (1948):

> In the early months of 1937 there were all the symptoms of developing Labour unrest . . . The workers were beginning to feel that, unless they took action immediately to secure improved wages and shorter working hours, their opportunity would very likely be gone; for already economists were beginning to speak of the imminence of a new recession, as soon as the intensive building of new factories for purposes of rearmament had passed its peak. Actually, there was a recession after the relatively high industrial activity of 1937, and even increased rearmament activity in 1938-39 did not quite restore conditions to the level reached in 1937. Thanks, however, to these activities, the recession was much less severe than it would otherwise have been, and the recovery of trade unionism continued at a slow pace up to the outbreak of war in 1939. Right through these years the trade union movement retained its essentially pacific policy. Strikes and lockouts were few and for the most part small, and the trade union leaders gave them little encouragement.[164]

When all due allowance has been made for objective factors, it seems clear that decisive significance attaches to a change in 1935-36 in the political 'line' of the Communist Party, which had by then got itself and its fellow-travellers widely accepted as the leaders of the militant movements in industry. As things turned out, the Stalinists headed these movements only to behead them at a crucial stage, because in accordance with Stalin's disastrous diplomacy they assumed the task of seeking alliances with 'progressive capitalists' and holding back the working-class struggle within strict and strangling limits.

---

[164] Cole, *op. cit.* p. 444. Cf. Arthur Horner, *Trade Unions and Unity* (April 1937): 'The trade union movement is in the throes of a great revival. Tens of thousands of workers

Characteristic was the line of development in South Wales. October 1935 saw a tremendous struggle against company unionism, led by the Ocean Combine Committee, which culminated in the 'stay-down' strike at Nine Mile Point for removal of the blacklegs imported during a recent dispute. Several other collieries came out in sympathy, and so also did the railwaymen at Merthyr. An attempt by the SWMF officials to close the struggle down was rebuffed and it was brought to a successful conclusion. On the basis of this and previous militant movements in the coalfield, Arthur Horner was elected president of the SWMF in 1936. A splendid opportunity for combining the efforts of communists in official positions with the fight of the rank and file seemed to have been created. Yet, after 1936, rank-and-file activity died down in South Wales. As John Mahon put it, in the *Labour Monthly* of July 1937, 'the Left' was now 'in control' there: 'The union machine is used to express the workers' demands.'

A bitter struggle in the Nottinghamshire coalfield, the other major stronghold of company unionism, ended with a compromise between the Miners' Federation and the company union. According to the communist pamphlet *Notts United* (June 1937) 'this agreement is, it is true, a compromise, but if we examine it soberly and refuse to allow ourselves to be led away by talk of "sell-outs" and "betrayals", it is obvious that it represents a tremendous step forward'. Mick Kane and other leaders of the Nottinghamshire miners had been arrested at Harworth and given harsh sentences under the new Public Order Act, allegedly passed to restrain the Blackshirts. These arrests roused intense indignation throughout the working-class movement, which was canalized by the Stalinists into a petition campaign. (Kane, sentenced to two years' hard labour, was eventually released in August 1938.)

The rank-and-file movement on the London buses, which appeared to be so firmly based, was out-manoeuvred and smashed by Bevin in the 'coronation strike' of 1937. He deliberately allowed the rank-and-file-controlled Central Bus Committee to take over direction of the strike in order that they might discredit themselves. Similar rank-and-file success to that achieved among the London busmen had not been won among the tram and trolley men, nor

---

are joining the unions every week. Branch meetings were never better attended. There is hardly a section of organized workers which has not received some slight increase in wages, and most sections are beginning to ask for more . . . The workers feel that they have a golden opportunity in the next two years and they intend to use it.'

among the provincial busmen,[165] and all these groups were effectively held back by Bevin, making the defeat of the strike inevitable. The leaders of the rank-and-file movement could then be ousted from office and their organization broken up. All this was accepted with surprising resignation by the Communist Party, and the *Busman's Punch* closed down after the October-November issue. Non-communist leading figures of the rank-and-file movement, bewildered and frustrated, followed the call of W. J. Brown to form a breakaway union.

Study of the literature of the other rank-and-file movements of this period, notably those among the aircraft workers and building workers, shows increasingly narrow concentration on recruitment to the unions and propaganda for amalgamation of the unions. Exposures of the officials and campaigning for democratization of the unions both faded away. Nothing more was heard after 1935 of the need to work towards a linking-up of all the rank-and-file movements on a national scale, which had frequently been indicated as the goal to be kept in view when communist leaders discussed these movements in 1933-34.[166] The articles about Britain in *International Press Correspondence* from 1936 onwards contain little about the industrial front, and the same is true of the *Communist International*. The British Communist Party monthly *Discussion* ran articles in its issues of June and July 1936 pouring cold water on the conception of rank-and-file movements: maximum use of the facilities provided by the trade union machinery was the thing, and unofficial movements must never be conceived as permanent in character. At the party congress in May 1937, J. R. Campbell, reporting on the industrial front, said:

> We insist that the trade union leaders stop fighting their own militants and start mobilizing the working class to storm the Bastille of unorganized labour . . .Our demand is for the calling of a conference of trade union executives . . .A growing number of comrades are being elected to trade union executives and to paid official positions.

One looks in vain in the communist publications of this period for any echo of an idea which had been commonplace not long before and

---

[165] Pollitt had pointed out so far back as 1933, in an article in the *Communist International* of November 1 of that year, that the Achilles' heel of the London busmen's movement was that it was confined to busmen and to London, and indicated the need to extend it to other passenger-transport workers in London and to the provinces.

[166] E.g., J. R. Campbell, 'The Future of Rank and File Movements', *Labour Monthly*, March 1933, and Pollitt in *Communist International*, January 15, 1933 and December 5, 1934.

which can be illustrated by two quotations from the *Communist Review:*

> It is clear from experience . . .that many militants still believe that we can force the leaders to head a real fight. In actual practice mass pressure forces the leaders to *manoeuvre* and to head strikes in order to retain negotiating authority and to betray the strike (October 1933).
>
> If we can take the reformist unions out of the hands of the reformist leaders, then there is no need for independent organs of struggle and for building a revolutionary trade union opposition . . .We need a Minority Movement because we stand as much chance of capturing the trade union machine and using it for our own ends as we do the capitalist State (October 1932).

At the 1938 Congress of the British Communist Party no report was given on industrial and trade union work as such. J. R. Campbell, who had usually given this report, devoted his time to explaining the menace of 'Trotskyism'. In the report of the Central Committee prepared for the next congress, which was to have been held in October 1939 but never took place owing to the outbreak of war, we read:

> The preoccupation on questions concerning war or peace may seem at first to have led to a dampening down of the struggle against capitalism at home . . . It is not possible to record any big mass movements on the industrial field . . .In the main there has been no real advance made in raising the standards of workers as a whole . . .In many districts there has been serious neglect of this work.

The story of the years immediately preceding the war is a cautionary tale for industrial workers today, with two morals: the need for rank-and-file movements, and the fatal consequences of allowing the Communist Party to get control of such movements. For just as the trade union bureaucracy came closer and closer to monopoly capitalism, so the Soviet bureaucracy, whose agent the Communist Party is, not only lost all interest in promoting workers' revolution but from the mid-1930s onward became more and more actively opposed to it.

British Communist History

by Brian Pearce

In July 1956 the Executive Committee of the Communist Party decided 'to proceed with the preparations for the publication of a history of the party'. In September the composition of the Editing Commission for this work was announced — with Harry Pollitt as chairman and R. Page Arnot as executive officer. Since then no news has been given out as to the progress or prospects of the party history.* It is hardly surprising that a number of comrades have been doing some digging on their own account without waiting — 'it may be for years, and it may be for ever' — for something to emerge from the Commission. One such freelance effort has already been published — my short study of *The Communist Party and the Labour Left, 1925-29*, which came out in April as *Reasoner* Pamphlet No. 1. Since I wrote it I have read, discussed and thought further on the period and the problems involved, and am glad to have this opportunity of presenting, in *Labour Review*, some self-critical considerations which I hope may prove helpful to comrades studying the history of the party, and may perhaps stimulate original work by others.

The principal shortcomings of the pamphlet seem to me to be twofold. First the *international setting* of the developments in Britain in 1927-29 is not shown sufficiently — the changes of a similar kind that were made in other Communist Parties in this period, as part of a world-wide 'turn', with more or less equally disastrous consequences in the various countries concerned. In this connection, comparison with China is especially striking and instructive. Second, the years 1925-27 are dealt with somewhat sketchily, and in particular, those weaknesses of a 'right-opportunist' nature in Communist policy

* James Klugmann was eventually appointed to write the history. Volume I appeared in 1968 and Volume II in 1969, dealing with the period up to 1927; nothing further has since emerged. Thus it has taken 19 years for the first 7 years of party history to be written! — *Ed.*

which, by leading to setbacks and defeats, provided the basis for the 'left-sectarian' turn that began at the end of 1927. Here, too, there is a significant parallel with what happened in China.

Comintern policy in China, following the betrayal of the national revolution first by Chiang Kai-shek and then by the Wuhan Government, took a violent swing to the left, signalized by the Canton insurrection of December 1927. While the revolutionary tide had been sweeping forward, the slogan of soviets had been banned, the workers held back from anti-capitalist actions and the peasants from seizing the land. Now, with some of the best cadres of the communist movement annihilated, the masses stunned and reaction in the saddle, an adventurist, putschist policy was suddenly adopted, resulting in further heavy losses, to no purpose. The Canton affair coincided with the Fifteenth Congress of the Communist Party of the Soviet Union, and a spokesman of the Stalinist majority there hailed the news as evidence that an era of direct struggle for working-class power was opening in China. A few months later, experience having shown the tragic folly of such a claim, the Sixth Congress of the Comintern characterized Canton as 'an heroic rearguard action'. . . The 'New Line' in its Chinese edition led to the destruction of virtually all Communist positions in the cities and towns of China for a long time to come, dooming the Chinese revolution to take the long way round through a series of peasant wars unassisted by urban struggles. (Another consequence was the provision of ample scope in China for several years for the expansion and strengthening of Japanese imperialism. Not for the first time, or the last, a Stalinist policy 'justified' by the needs of the defence of the Soviet Union produced results full of danger to the Soviet Union.)

Anyone can be wise after the event, but it should be more widely realized that the 'left-turn' of 1927-29 was warned against *at the time* by L. D. Trotsky, both in relation to China and in relation to Europe, including Britain. The conventional image of Trotsky presented by Stalinist propaganda since 1935 shows a man whose political wisdom consisted in always trying to push Communist policy leftward, regardless of circumstances. It is fascinating to observe the ingenuity with which J. R. Campbell conceals from his readers in his widely-read *Soviet Policy and its Critics* (1939) and other anti-'Trotskyist' writings the fact that Trotsky denounced the 'social-fascist' nonsense of 1928-34 from start to finish and never stopped urging that a united front of all workers' parties against fascism should be the aim of the Communists in Germany. At the time, every effort was made by the Stalinist leadership of the British Communist Party to prevent knowledge of Trotsky's critique of Comintern policy reaching the members at large. Comrades in South-West London who in 1932 printed (in *The Communist,* a sort of predecessor to *The Reasoner*) Trotsky's views on the situation in Germany, and urged that, in Britain, the party should at least stop calling on the workers to spoil their ballot papers rather than vote Labour, were slandered and expelled....

In his letter to the Sixth Congress of the Comintern (1928), Trotsky offered the opinion that 'nothing is more fruitless than showing one's fist after the battle' and argued that, contrary to the official 'Third Period' thesis, 'an inter-revolutionary period of indefinite duration' was opening, to which Communist activities must perforce be adjusted in a realistic manner. Now this situation had not come about by itself, but as a result of a series of blows suffered by the working-class movement internationally — above all, the betrayal of the General Strike in Britain and that of the revolution in China. These defeats, in turn, were not unconnected with the flaws in communist policy in the 1925-27 period; and it is to this theme, in its application to Britain, that I would now direct attention.

The slow growth of the Communist Party in Britain in the early twenties made impatient the Zinoviev-Stalin leadership of the Comintern, producing in them a sceptical attitude to the party and a tendency to seek alternative instruments for revolutionary policy in this country. Already in 1924 at the Fifth Congress of the Comintern, Zinoviev hinted at what was to come in the following year:

> In Britain we are now going through the beginnings of a new chapter in the Labour movement. We do not know exactly whence the communist mass party of Britain will come, whether only through the Stewart-MacManus door [Bob Stewart and Arthur MacManus were prominent British Communists. — B.P.]or through some other door. And it is entirely possible that the communist mass party may appear through still another door — and we cannot lose sight of that fact.

Knowing his Zinoviev and recognizing the instinctive preference of the Soviet bureaucracy for influencing world affairs through pacts with other bureaucrats rather than through developing mass movements, already in the same year Trotsky warned in his *Lessons of October:*

> It is true that the British trade unions may become a mighty lever of the proletarian revolution; they may, for instance, even replace workers'

> soviets under certain conditions and for a certain time. They can, however, fill such a role not apart from a Communist Party and certainly not against the party, but only on the condition that communist influence becomes the decisive influence in the trade unions.

Looking back on the period 1925-27 in his essay *On the Draft Programme of the Comintern* written in 1928, Trotsky observed that: 'The point of departure of the Anglo-Russian Committee . . .was the impatient urge to leap over the young and too slowly developing Communist Party.' This Anglo-Russian Committee was a joint committee of the British and Soviet TUC General Councils formed in 1925 to promote world trade union unity in general and closer relations between British and Soviet trade unions in particular, for the common cause of Labour. On it there served, from the British side, a group of trade union leaders, Purcell, Hicks and Swales, who rapidly acquired a reputation as left-wingers almost entirely on the basis of their attitude to the USSR. In this same period the British communists were steadily and painfully building up the Minority Movement in the trade unions, that broad alliance of militants which at the height of its development embraced a quarter of the total members of the trade unions. The Minority Movement was essentially a *mass* movement; it worked for and achieved the election to office of militant trade unionists, notably A. J. Cook, who became the miners' secretary with Minority Movement support, but it never degenerated into a mere election-winning caucus. Together with the National Left-Wing Movement which arose among Labour Party members after the Liverpool decisions, as described in my pamphlet, it represented a tremendous potential force for leftward progress in the British working-class movement. Now, Purcell and the others held aloof from the Minority Movement: where Cook was a friend of the Soviet Union *and* a fighter for militant policies in Britain, Purcell was a 'Left' strictly in the international sphere, and his friendly relations with Russian communists did not modify his coolness towards the home-bred variety. But the importance attributed to the Anglo-Russian Committee by the Russians and the confidence they showed in Purcell and his colleagues inevitably had its effect on the view taken of these men by the British communists and militant workers generally.

It may be doubted whether the leaders of the CPSU really believed that the implications of Purcell's willingness to sit on a committee with Soviet trade unionists were as revolutionary as their propaganda around the Anglo-Russian Committee seemed to suggest. Already by this time they saw the central task of the workers outside the USSR as that of ensuring good relations between their respective countries and the USSR, and they probably thought of their alliance with a group of established, influential British trade union leaders as first and foremost a factor for good Anglo-Soviet relations, of much more practical value than anything the rank-and-file militants could offer. Experience was to disabuse them sharply of this illusion; but in its heyday Zinoviev spoke with unbounded enthusiasm of the Committee as 'one of the surest guarantees against intervention', as well as 'a guarantee that in the course of time we shall render European reformism harmless'. Trotsky's view of the line of development was a different one. In his book *Where is Britain Going?* (1925)[167] he wrote:

> The British bourgeoisie take unerring account of the fact that the chief danger threatens them from the trade unions, and that only under the pressure of these mass organizations will the Labour Party, after radically renewing its leadership, be transformed into a revolutionary force.

The trade unions could be won through the Minority Movement, under Communist leadership, and the Communist Party would 'take that place in relation to the Labour Party which at present is occupied by the Independent Labour Party' — then the principal political organization within the Labour Party.

Under the pressure of the rising tide of militancy led by the Minority Movement, the TUC General Council defied the Baldwin Government and the mine owners on 'Red Friday', July 31, 1925, forcing a postponement of the showdown over miners' wages and hours till May of the following year. Instead, however, of mobilizing all the workers' forces to ensure victory when the showdown came, the Labour leaders at once began taking steps to break up the movement that had obliged them unwillingly to make a stand. The Liverpool Conference ban on Communists in the Labour Party followed directly from Red Friday. A. J. Cook campaigned for preparation against the fateful day, but none of the alleged 'Lefts' of Anglo-Russian Committee fame would join him. In his *History of the British Communist Party* (1937), Tom Bell, one of the party's leaders of the time, wrote:

---

[167] When the English version of this book first appeared, a reviewer in the *Labour Monthly* wrote: 'A challenge may safely be issued to the critics to name a single book by a single English author or politician, bourgeois or Labour leader, which is as close to the essentials of the English situation as Trotsky's book. It cannot be done.' The reviewer was R. Palme Dutt. (See *Collected Writings and Speeches on Britain*, Volume Two, New Park Publications, 1975, for both the book and the review.)

> The Labour leaders made no effort to prepare for action. They lulled the trade unions into a false sense of security by encouraging reliance on the findings of the Coal Commission. At the same time in many places it was tacitly assumed that secret preparations were being made by the General Council. The fact that there was a Left wing on the Council (comprising Purcell, Swales, Hicks, Tillett and Bromley) lent colour to this idea.

One may add that the source of this notion, accepted by the British Communists as well as by others, that there was a Left wing on the General Council, was the association of the individuals named with the Anglo-Russian Committee, and the illusions which were being built up around this Committee. R. Page Arnot, in his study of *The General Strike* (1926) writes:

> Knowledge of the existence of this Left wing was at once a stimulant and a narcotic for the masses. It gave them a rallying ground, lent confidence to their leftward mood; but, then, it put vigilance to sleep, and led to overtrustfulness, so that when the breakdown of May 12 came, workers in the localities were looking at one another in dismay, naming the individual leaders of the Left and complaining that it was these men who were responsible in chief.

It is important to realize that from the end of 1925 onwards the membership and prestige of the British Communist Party was rising rapidly. Given the mood of the workers, the arrest and imprisonment of some of the party's leaders produced exactly the opposite effect to what had been intended by the Government. A greater opportunity than ever before since the days of 1920 was coming to the British Communists. One observer wrote (*Bulletin Communiste*, January 1, 1926) that where the party had had ten sympathisers before the arrests, now there were a hundred. But the attitude to the 'Left' TUC leaders inculcated on the basis of their membership of the Anglo-Russian Committee prevented the party and the Minority Movement from striving for the leadership of the workers and even weakened essential measures of preparation for the coming struggle. At the Comintern Executive's plenary meeting in February 1926 Aitken Ferguson defined the role of the Minority Movement as being 'to bring pressure to bear upon the reactionaries and to stiffen up the hesitating and wobbly elements', and George Hardy admitted that the formation of factory groups of the Minority Movement was still 'something which we have to tackle'.

In an article published in the *Communist International* shortly after the General Strike, 'Problems of the British Labour Movement',

Trotsky quoted passages from his correspondence of January-March 1926, which are of great interest in enabling the historian to see with the eyes of a contemporary 'what went wrong' in these vital months preceding May Day, 1926. He pointed to the danger that 'the forming of the proletarian vanguard might lag behind the development of the revolutionary situation. Faced with the necessity for decisive action, the proletariat might be unable to find the necessary political leadership'. There was a risk of taking the 'Lefts' in the General Council too readily at their own valuation. 'The masses are immeasurably more Left than the Left-wingers themselves.... In the British Labour Movement, international questions have always been the line of least resistance for the "leaders".' They used the prestige gained in the international sphere to impose a reactionary policy in domestic, class-struggle spheres. If the British Communists were not to miss the boat as the Germans had done in 1923, they must 'aid the Left wing to find the proper orientation for action (the *real* Left wing and not Lansbury or Purcell)'. Apart from private correspondence, Trotsky managed to bring into an article in *Inprecorr* for March 11, reviewing events in Britain during the year since the publication of his book, a call for 'systematic unmasking' of the 'Left' leaders. King Street remained, however, under the guidance of the dominant faction in Moscow, blind to this aspect of the situation. George Hardy, who was acting secretary of the Minority Movement during the General Strike period, records in his memoirs (*Those Stormy Years*), that, when the strike was called, 'at first many of us gave the Left wing on the [General] Council the credit for this victory, which seemed to bring into being that solidarity which we had worked so hard to create'. (After describing the betrayal of the strike, Hardy remarks: 'Although we knew of what treachery the Right-wing leaders were capable, we did not clearly understand the part played by the so-called Left in the union leadership'; and draws the conclusion that 'the main point for preparing for action must always be to develop a class-conscious leadership among the rank and file'.)

In the midst of the General Strike itself, Trotsky wrote (May 6) in his preface to the second German edition of his *Where Is Britain Going?* that the success of the struggle depended on the extent to which the workers realized the need to change their leaders and succeeded in doing this.

> An English proverb says that one must not change horses while crossing a stream. This practical wisdom is true, however, only within certain limits.

> It has never yet been possible to cross a revolutionary stream on the horse of reformism, and a class which enters battle under opportunist leaders is compelled to change them under the enemy's fire.[168]

The common betrayal of the strike by 'Rights' and 'Lefts' alike on the General Council came as a surprise to the British Communists, and, in the words of J. T. Murphy (*The Political Meaning of the Great Strike*), 'the shock . . . was too great to make any quick throw-up of a new leadership possible'. The workers turned towards the party in greater numbers than ever in the months immediately following the betrayal, and by October 1926 the membership was double what it had been in April. Thereafter, however, especially with the forced surrender of the miners, a drift out of and away from the party began which was to continue steadily for many years. And the party has never since recovered the standing it enjoyed among the workers in 1925-26, even though paper membership from about 1936 onward has markedly exceeded the figure of that period. As Trotsky had warned it could, 1926 proved as tragic a year of 'might have been' for Britain as 1923 for Germany. A prominent member of the Communist Party in the General Strike period, in a so far unpublished manuscript, sums up the lesson like this:

> It is my considered opinion, in the light of after-happenings, that if the workers of Britain had been equipped with a leadership at all equivalent to their splendid courage, resolution and sense of solidarity, May Day, 1926, would have been the opening day of a proletarian revolution. Unhappily, history shows us by many examples that, if such a chance is missed, it takes long and many years before it can be induced to return.[169]

The Anglo-Russian Committee had been formed to ensure mutual aid and support between the trade unionists of the two countries. But after the workers of the USSR, amid scenes of tremendous enthusiasm, had levied themselves to the extent of £1,250,000 to help the British strikers, this money was flatly rejected by the General Council. Hicks, one of the actual members of the Anglo-Russian Committee, was widely reported as denouncing 'this damned Russian gold'. It was a slap in the face which evoked moods of confusion and

[168] One may compare with this J. H. Thomas's statement in the House of Commons on May 13: 'What I dreaded about this strike more than anything else was this — if by any chance it should have got out of the hands of those who would be able to exercise some control, every sane man knows what would have happened. I thank God it never did.'

[169] This was in fact the work of the late T. A. Jackson, and the manuscript of his second volume of autobiography is still unpublished — *Ed.*

disappointment among the Soviet workers, feeding the cynicism about the world revolution which had already been implanted by the failure in Germany in 1923 and which was the main moral foundation for Stalinism. They had been led to believe that Purcell, Hicks, etc., were the men who were going to bring about the social revolution in Britain — and here these men were, rejecting the solidarity of the Soviet working class. A few days later these same men betrayed the strike. And, from the Soviet point of view, there was worse to come.... A demonstrative break with the General Council might have helped to rally the British workers by stripping the last shred of political respectability from the pseudo-Lefts. That, however, would have meant that Trotsky and the Opposition, who were calling for this very action, were right. So it was not done, and the Soviet trade union leaders added to the confusion among the British workers by continuing to hob-nob with the strike-breakers for a year after their curt rejection of Soviet aid.

The Anglo-Russian Committee was kept alive on the initiative of the Soviet partner alone, the attitude of the British leaders growing colder and colder. The spectacle of the Soviet trade union leaders running after the British had its effect in blunting the edge of the militants' criticism of the latter. In August a meeting of the Committee broke up without any agreement being reached on a Russian proposal for a joint international campaign for aid to the miners. Yet the Committee remained in being; and this undoubtedly influenced the Minority Movement's spokesmen in their adoption of a mildness of tone in their criticism of the General Council, at the Trades Union Congress not long after, for its responsibility for the failure of the General Strike, a mildness which bewildered great numbers who had been hoping for a bold lead on that occasion. A few months later, the General Council issued an ultimatum to trades councils, forbidding them to affiliate to the Minority Movement. Some of the largest trades councils in the country, such as Glasgow, Sheffield and Manchester, were opposed to this ultimatum, and a defiance could have been organized which might have stirred the trade unions to the depths, revived the spirit, now fast draining away, of the Nine Days, and brought a salutary change of leadership. But no, King Street advised the trades councils to submit without a fight. As J. T. Murphy, one of the party leaders of that time, puts it in his *Preparing for Power* (1934): 'The workers could not understand this new alliance of the Communists and the General Council, and their resistance was killed.'

Now came the final phase in the story of the Anglo-Russian Committee, and the real value of this fetish to which so much had been sacrificed was at last put to the test. In April 1927 the Committee met in Berlin. The Opposition in the CPSU demanded that the Russian representatives call for immediate action against British intervention in China. But the question was not even raised; instead, the Russians accepted a new paragraph in the Committee's constitution, demanded by the British side, forbidding any criticism of their conduct by the Russians. Even this they were now ready to swallow, though the Comintern 'theses' on the General Strike had made a point of mentioning that 'the trade unions of the USSR entered the Anglo-Russian Committee without in any way tying their hands in the matter of criticism'. This was the price they were prepared to pay for the support of the General Council against those Tories who were working for a break with the USSR. On May 12 came the Arcos raid, and shortly afterwards the breaking-off of diplomatic relations. The Soviet trade unions called for an emergency meeting of the Anglo-Russian Committee to plan action to force a reversal of this move — and were refused. The house of cards had collapsed. The Anglo-Russian Committee was dead. What was supposed to function as 'the organizing centre for the international forces of the proletariat in the struggle against all attempts of the international bourgeoisie to start up a new war' had gone absent just when it was most needed.

In an article dated May 16, 1927, Trotsky recalled that 'the Opposition foretold in its writings that the maintenance of the Anglo-Russian Committee would steadily strengthen the position of the General Council, and that the latter would inevitably be converted from defendant into prosecutor'. 'Our real friends, the revolutionary workers, can only be deceived and weakened by the policy of illusions and hypocrisy.' If the Soviet trade unions had broken with the General Council in good time, 'such a policy would have forced the Left capitulators of the General Council to fight for the remnants of their reputation . . .in a word, to show the workers that they, the Left, are not half as bad as the Moscow people present them'. At the Central Committee of the CPSU on August 1, Trotsky showed how the Stalinist leadership had preferred to rely in its British policy upon the Anglo-Russian Committee rather than upon the Minority Movement: 'You rejected a small but sturdier prop for a bigger and utterly rotten one'. Comparing what had happened in Britain and what had happened in China, he went on: 'Your present policy is a policy of rotten props on an international scale. . . . Each of these props broke at the moment when it was most sorely needed. Thereupon, first you said "This is utterly incomprehensible!" in order to add on the very next day: "We always foresaw this".' (In his reply Stalin affirmed that 'the importance of the British Communist Party is growing from day to day' — something which had been true twelve months previously but had now for some time sadly ceased to be so.) 'What We Gave and What We Got: The Balance Sheet of the Anglo-Russian Committee' was the title of Trotsky's article of September 23 reviewing the story of the whole sorry episode after the TUC had formally wound up the Committee, and drawing the political lessons from it.[170] The General Council had utilized the moral support of the Soviet trade unions to help it over the politically difficult period following the General Strike; then, when securely back in the saddle again, it had kicked the Russians away with the minimum of protest among the bewildered and disappointed rank and file. This was the inevitable penalty for trying to skip over the necessary stages in building up the British Communist Party and its influence, in favour of would-be clever manoeuvres of a diplomatic character with sections of the trade union bureaucracy. What was at best a temporary and auxiliary device had been made the pivot of international Communist policy in relation to Britain, so fostering dangerous illusions and sowing confusion among the genuine Left elements in Britain, Communists and others. Trotsky called for publication of all the documents of the controversy around the Anglo-Russian Committee, so that comrades might judge for themselves and decide what political conclusions to draw.

In place of this, what happened was the expulsion of the Opposition from the CPSU in December 1927, and along with it a somersault to the left in international Communist policy. Having burnt its fingers in China with Chiang and in Britain with Purcell (also, incidentally, in Poland with Pilsudski) the Stalinist leadership rushed into the ultra-Leftist excesses of which my pamphlet gives some account so far as Britain is concerned. Just when, as a result of the 'Right' mistakes of the period 1926-27, the Communist Party had lost its former ascendancy and social-democratic ideas were re-establishing themselves among the workers, so that a policy of strengthening links with the masses (such as the National Left-Wing Movement) was more than ever necessary, the order went out to the Communists to retreat into

[170] Published in *Collected Writings and Speeches on Britain,* Volume Two, Part 3, pp. 222-240

isolation and separate themselves from the broad movement. The genuine Left, Cook, was to be reviled as unrestrainedly as the pseudo-Left Purcell had been praised. Trotsky, with his characteristic bitter humour, spoke of people who could not distinguish the face of a revolution from its backside, and recalled 'the very well-known hero of a Russian folk tale who sings wedding songs at funerals and funeral hymns at weddings. He gets a sound thrashing in both places.' Unfortunately, it was the Communist Parties of the world and the working class generally that paid the price for the unprincipled zig-zags — 'zigging', as somebody said, 'when they should have zagged, and zagging when they should have zigged' — carried out by the Stalinist bureaucracy. Study of the history of the international communist movement may help us to avoid the repetition of old mistakes, at least, in new situations.

Early Years of the Communist Party of Great Britain

by Brian Pearce

Julian Symons has done a service to the British working-class movement by writing *The General Strike* (Cresset Press). At this time when great clashes between Capital and Labour are in prospect it is particularly valuable to have a fresh and thorough study of the major industrial conflict of our age, for examination of the history of the General Strike can help to clarify understanding of the dangers and possibilities that confront us now.

Besides the printed materials,[171] Mr. Symons has used the Transport House records and a mass of private letters and diaries which were made available to him by participants in the struggle, both strikers and strike-breakers. The two strongest impressions left by the book are, first, that contrary to what the author calls 'a much cherished myth' of the British bourgeoisie the strike was not weakening but actually growing stronger at the moment when it was called off (figures are given that show how 'the railway services were chaotic, and functioned with only a small fraction of their normal efficiency'); and, second, the sharp contrast between the behaviour of the leadership and that of the rank and file. Not only had the General Council totally failed to prepare for the conflict or even to draw up a strategic plan — some of its members, and especially J. H. Thomas, worked deliberately, from the start, to betray their followers. The mass of the strikers meanwhile displayed both enthusiasm (groups not called out pressing the leadership to call them out) and that amazing power of self-organization that is so characteristic of the British working class in an emergency. Mr. Symons shows the anxious concern of the General Council to prevent the rank and file getting out of hand:

> The problem of controlling provincial activities much engaged the General Council. It was feared that in some provincial towns and cities extreme

[171] Omitting, however, the valuable pamphlet *The Reds and the General Strike*, published by the Communist Parity in June 1926.

Left-wing elements might take control and conduct the strike as a purely political affair. Hence, the Strike Organization Committee tried from the first to maintain a control over provincial activities which was, in the circumstances, simply unworkable, and which contrasts markedly with the Government's plan to give the greatest possible degree of autonomy to Civil Commissioners. (p.64)

The chairman of the Strike Organization Committee was that A. A. Purcell who had been given such a build-up as a 'Left' by the Communists in the preceding twelve months, on the strength of his membership of the Anglo-Russian Trade Union Unity Committee.[172] Another of these alleged Lefts, Swales, was one of the committee of three who negotiated with Baldwin on the eve of the strike, and Mr. Symons notes that he, 'who might have been expected to protest' against the Government's proposals, 'was the least vocal of the three'. Summing up on the 'Lefts', the author writes:

The left-wing trade union leaders played what seems in retrospect a strikingly timid part. They were outnumbered, but they occupied important positions. One of them, Purcell, was chairman of the Strike Organization Committee; Purcell, was chairman of the Strike Organization Committee; George Hicks, John Bromley, Ben Tillett and A. B. Swales were leading figures on various committees. After the strike was over some of them spoke brave words to the effect that it had been a class struggle, yet during the nine days there is no suggestion that opinion in the General Council was seriously divided at any time. (pp. 135-136)

It is implicit in the story of the General Strike as set forth in this book that the Communists, though they worked devotedly and were the object of special persecution by the police, played no special role in the strike and certainly did nothing to justify the fears of the General Council that they might try to take over the leadership. Reactions to my article 'British Communist History' have shown that this is an unfamiliar conception to many Communists and also to ex-Communists of recent vintage. When they appreciate that it is nevertheless true, the usual comment is either: 'Well, anyway, it was Thomas and Co. who betrayed the strike, not the Communists', or: 'What was to be expected? After all, the party's leaders were in jail in the vital period'.

---

172 An adulatory obituary of Purcell, without one word regarding his role in 1926, was contributed to the *Labour Monthly* of February 1936 by John Mahon. ('Purcell's thoughts on the betrayal of the General Strike are not to be found in speeches or writings. They must have been bitter.')

To the first of these comments I would reply that one of the jobs that Communists are sent into the world to do is to save the workers from being betrayed by the Thomases; and to the second, that it does an injustice both to Communists generally and to the British Communists of 1925-26 in particular. Lenin was on the run and Trotsky in prison when Kornilov launched his attack on Petrograd, but that did not prevent the Bolsheviks from turning the tables upon him, in spite of everything, Kerensky included. So far as Britain in 1926 was concerned, George Hardy writes in his useful memoirs *Those Stormy Years* that, though the arrests were 'a severe blow', nevertheless 'plans for an alternative leading group had been made. Bob Stewart stepped into the breach as acting general secretary and several members, including myself, were brought on to the Political Bureau'.

That the Communist Party failed to play the role in the General Strike which most people, friends and foes alike, had expected it would play, was a commonplace in the period immediately ensuing. For example, Harold Laski wrote in his book *Communism* (1927): 'It was noteworthy that in the British General Strike of 1926 the communists played practically no part at all', and Hamilton Fyfe, in his diary of the conflict, *Behind the Scenes of the Great Strike* (1926) noted: 'The communists have kept very quiet.... On the Continent, in America even, it is the extremists who come to the top in crises. Here they have sunk out of sight'. The suggestion that there might have been some foundation for the Government's alleged fear of revolution was firmly rebutted by T.H. Wintringham, in the *Communist Review* for June 1926: 'The Communist Party knew, as the TUC leaders knew, that this was not the time for anything but solid resistance to a deliberate attack.' George Hardy acknowledges that 'the Councils of Action, with a few exceptions, functioned only in a limited way'. E.H. Brown, reporting to the Organization Conference of the CPGB in October 1926, said: 'It must be admitted that our factory groups were weak and did not function properly during the General Strike. In some districts the groups stopped functioning altogether' (quoted by Piatnitsky, in *Communist International*, June 15, 1927). 'A British Communist' wrote, approvingly, in the Paris monthly *La Révolution Prolétarienne* for July 1926 that 'the acting general secretary called upon the members of the party to behave as loyal trade unionists and carry out the instructions of the General Council — which they did'. P. Braun, in the *Labour Monthly* of January 1927, declared that it was 'quite obvious that during the days of the General Strike, when millions of workers came out to fight for the cause of Labour against the Government, the Communist Party believed that the General Council would not dare to betray such a magnificent fight. It is a fact that, even after Baldwin made it perfectly clear in the House of Commons that the representatives of the TUC were prepared to discuss the formula drafted by Birkenhead which definitely mentioned wage reductions, the *Workers' Bulletin* (the official organ of the Communist Party during the period of the General Strike) of May 7 expressed the hope that the leaders of the General Council would frankly admit that they had made a mistake, and that they would stand solidly by the miners' slogans'.[173]

Trotsky summed up the chief lesson of the General Strike in the sentence:'The entire present "superstructure" of the British working class, in all its shades and groups without exception, is an apparatus for putting a brake on the revolution.'[174] To this judgment the Executive Committee of the Comintern sharply retorted in its resolution of June 8: 'The attempts to include the Communist Party of Great Britain in the arsenal of "brakes on the revolution" do not bear criticism'. It is not my purpose in this article, however, to go further into the history of the debate which took place in the international communist movement on the conclusions for the subsequent period to be drawn from the defeat of the General Strike in Britain, though I am well aware that I only touched the fringe of the subject in the article 'British Communist History'. What I wish to do here is to reinforce my account in that article of how the CPGB *arrived at* the lamentable political position indicated above, showing that the beginning of the decline and fall of this party as a revolutionary Marxist party is to be dated from 1925; and briefly to consider, in the light of the history of the first five years of the party, how far this downfall was 'inevitable' and to what factors it was due.

---

[173] See also the quotation in the editorial in the *Communist Review* for October 1926 from an unpublished article received from an unnamed comrade, reproaching the party leaders for 'failing to take steps to provide an alternative trade union leadership nationally, in anticipation of the breakdown of the General Council . . .[This was] the whole party feeling during the General Strike: the feeling that the party was not responsible for the central lead — that had already been given by the General Council and we could not alter it.'

[174] *Pravda,* May 26, 1926.

The Struggle against Sectarianism

Though formed in August 1920 (with adhesion of some further groups in January 1921), the British Communist Party remained for its first year or two of existence little more than an amalgamated and enlarged version of the propagandist sects which had preceded it. It took the moral pressure of Lenin himself to bring about the fusion of the various sects into a single party in the first place (*'Left-Wing' Communism* and *Letter to Sylvia Pankhurst*), and from the beginning Lenin, Trotsky and the whole Comintern leadership of 1920-23 had to struggle against the rooted sectarianism of the British Marxists. At the convention where the Communist Party was established strong opposition was expressed to Moscow's advice that the party apply for affiliation to the Labour Party: the Russian comrades did not know what they were talking about, said some, and the vote, taken after a debate in which most of the speakers opposed affiliation, was the narrow one of 100-85 in favour. The first application for affiliation was couched in terms that invited rejection, and when this duly came, the party leadership's relief was unconcealed. *The Communist* of September 16, 1920, wrote: 'So be it. It is their funeral, not ours.' A message from the Comintern compelled the British Communists to reconsider this estimate of what had happened, and a week later the same paper explained that 'it is the duty of the communists to work where the masses are. That may mean going into reactionary organizations, but that is better and easier than creating brand new organizations in the hope that the masses will leave the old ones and come to the new'.

The basic attitude of the CPGB, derived from pre-war Social Democratic Federation traditions, remained unchanged, however, and this was shown in the activities which it launched towards the end of 1920 and in early 1921. The unemployed workers' committees which were set up on Communist initiative did a tremendous job in bringing pressure to bear on local authorities, stopping blacklegging and agitating against overtime, but the achievements of the unemployed movement were far less than could have been won with a less sectarian approach. There was little sustained effort to establish links with the trades councils and achieve recognition by the organized Labour movement. Satisfaction with unemployed 'separatism' was combined with a tendency to neglect steady work and concentrate on stunt demonstrations.[175] Then there was the East Woolwich by-election, when the party stumped the constituency calling on the workers to abstain because Tory and Labour were 'two of a kind' and *The Communist* of March 5, 1921, boasted that the Labour candidate's defeat (by 683 votes in a poll of 27,000) was due to the Communist campaign. This sort of thing prevented the party from winning the political influence among the workers that the valiant work of many of its members during the 'Black Friday' period might otherwise have secured, and provided the Right-wing leaders of the Labour Party with ready-made arguments against affiliation which they kept bringing up for years afterward.[176]

The persistent 'Leftism' of the West European Communist Parties in this period found its supreme expression in the so-called 'March action' (1921) in Germany. Had the Comintern leadership not given a sharp rebuff to attempts to justify this semi-putschist approach to politics and set the course unmistakably towards the united front and the winning of the masses, 'perhaps within a year or two only splinters of Communist Parties would have been left'.[177] What Soviet Russia needed was successful revolutions in the West, Lenin and Trotsky pointed out to all concerned, and these would not be brought nearer by futile self-immolations of the revolutionary minority. The Comintern's calls during and after the Third World Congress (1921) for serious and self-sacrificing efforts for the working-class unity 'came to the party in Britain practically as a shock', admitted J. T. Murphy at the succeeding Congress in 1922.

Under the guidance of the Comintern, the CPGB began in the autumn of 1921 to set its house in order and take serious steps towards becoming the leader of the working class. A campaign was launched to popularize a scheme of reorganization of the TUC ('A Parliament of Labour') whereby, in addition to delegates of the national trade unions, it should contain representatives of the trades councils and

---

[175] See E. Stanley, *Communist Review*, December 1924: a critical review of the experience of the unemployed movement.

[176] In August 1921 the CPGB stood Bob Stewart against a Labour candidate in the by-election at Caerphilly. In his election address he declared: 'We oppose the Labour Party for the simple reason that it is not a Labour Party at all.' Though the South Wales Miners' Federation had just affiliated to the Red International of Labour Unions, Stewart found himself at the bottom of the poll.

[177] L. Trotsky, Introduction to *The First Five Years of the Communist International*, Vol. 1, New Park Publications, 1973.

also direct representation of the workers in the workshops.[178] In the demoralization following 'Black Friday' great numbers of workers had torn up their union cards and a successful employers' offensive was under way. The Communists set themselves to reverse this trend, with the slogans: 'Back to the Unions!' and 'Stop the Retreat!' When the engineering lock-out began, in April, 1922, the party for the first time, instead of *merely* denouncing the trade union bureaucrats, put forward a number of practical, specific proposals. In each locality the Communists strove to revive and strengthen the neglected trades councils, working for every trade union branch and district committee to affiliate to its appropriate trades council and to transform these bodies into local centres for co-ordinating the workers' struggles. (In October 1922, largely in consequence of these efforts, a national conference of trades councils was convened by the Birmingham Trades Council, with Alex Gossip in the chair).[179]

At the same time, a new and more honest approach was made to the Labour Party for affiliation (November 1921). The issue of violence was frankly faced.

> Under normal circumstances the Labour Party acted within the law; the Communist Party declared itself prepared to do the same. However, should extraordinary circumstances arise, the Communist Party would be compelled to consider other means, in much the same way as the Labour Party had, in 1920, in forming Councils of Action ...[180]

Within the party leadership there was a deep resistance, however, to the entire united front conception, and the policy conference held in March 1922 agreed to embrace it only on the basis of T. A. Jackson's notorious formulation about 'taking the Labour leaders by the hand in order later to take them by the throat'. With all its weaknesses, however, this conference was a landmark in the party's history in that it signalized the 'abandonment of the tradition of claiming the allegiance of the workers as a right'.[181] The British

---

[178] See article by R. P. Arnot in *Labour Monthly*, October 1921.

[179] On this period as a whole, see the survey of the first four years of the CPGB in *Communist Review*, August 1924. From the party's proposals during the engineering lock-out developed the programme of the Metal Workers' Minority Movement — increase of wages of £1 on all existing rates; 44-hour working week; two weeks' holiday with pay; amalgamation of all the unions in the industry into one; formation of workshop committees representing all grades.

[180] Summary of the correspondence in S. R. Graubard, *British Labour and the Russian Revolution* (1956), p. 149.

[181] *The Communist*, April 1, 1922.

Communists were trying to put into effect, even though with misgivings and backslidings, the advice that Lenin was offering about the same time to the Communists of Italy: not to 'lose patience' in exposing the social-democratic leaders 'in a practical way', 'not to yield to the very easy and very dangerous decision to say "minus a" whenever Serrati says "a".'[182] In the same period, Trotsky wrote to the Congress of the French Communist Party:

> To put forward the programme of the social revolution and oppose it 'intransigently' to the Dissidents and the syndico-reformists, while refusing to enter into any negotiations with them until they recognize our programme — this is a very simple policy which requires neither resourcefulness nor energy, neither flexibility nor initiative. It is not a communist policy. We communists seek for methods and avenues of bringing politically, practically and in action the still unconscious masses to the point where they begin posing the revolutionary issues themselves.[183]

In August 1922, as an earnest of the sincerity of its approach to Labour, the CPGB withdrew all the candidates it had been intending to stand against Labour candidates in the impending General Election. (This did not affect Communist members of the Labour Party who had been adopted as Labour candidates, or Communists standing where there was no Labour candidate in the field). The new Communist attitude was frankly explained.

> The Communist Party cannot oppose the Labour Party in so far as it is the party of the workers any more than it can oppose the trade unions as such; but it can, as it does with the trade unions, fight the reactionary junta and seek to transform the Labour Party into an instrument of revolutionary progress. The faith of the workers in the present leaders of the Labour Party must be tried and outlived by experience. This experience the Communists will assist them to obtain by their *action*.[184]

Steadily increasing support began to accrue to the demand for Communist Party affiliation to the Labour Party, among the trades councils, notably in London and Glasgow, and in certain unions, especially the Miners' Federation.

---

[182] V. I. Lenin, 'Notes of a Publicist', *Selected Works* (12-vol. ed.), Vol. 10, p. 313. See also the advice against 'stewing in one's own juice', *ibid.* p. 304.

[183] Trotsky, *op. cit.*, Vol. 2 (1974), p. 174.

[184] *Communist Party Policy* and *The Communist Party, the Labour Party and the United Front* (both CPGB, 1922).

The Turn to Mass Work

The party conference of March 1922, besides accepting the Comintern's united front policy, had set up a commission to reorganize the party in accordance with the principles of party structure laid down by the Third Congress of the Comintern. The two questions were closely linked, for if the party was to strike roots in the masses it must cease to be organized primarily as a propaganda society. Broadly speaking, the same section of the membership that was indifferent, or worse, to the united front was perfectly satisfied with the old federal structure, the old large, debating-society branches and the old concentration on street-corner meetings, though it was already plain that a party so organized could never get into a position to lead a British workers' revolution. The Reorganization Commission reported to a party Congress held in October 1922 which accepted its report, and in the ensuing six months this report was put into effect. A certain amount of financial looseness had flourished under the old order, and the elimination of this led to the departure of certain 'leading comrades', while others turned away from a party which was being transformed into a *working* party in a new sense. By and large the effects of the reorganization were salutary, and it is a pity that the Commission's report has become a rare document and the story of its work so little known among Communist Party members.

At the same time, the centralization of power in the party, the break-up of branches into small groups and the emphasis upon work involved potentially a serious danger — that the party might be transformed into a mere executive mechanism, submissive in the hands of an uncontrolled leadership. Lenin showed himself aware that the resolution of the Third Comintern Congress on organization might do harm as well as good, and sounded a warning note in relation to its application, in his speech of November 13, 1922,[185] but his call for caution in this matter was overlooked by some, and perhaps deliberately ignored by others, when illness withdrew him shortly afterwards from regular political activity. In 1924 a significant exchange of views took place in the pages of the *Communist Review* regarding the negative aspects of the reorganization. J. T. Murphy drew attention to the submergence of members in organizational work

[185] Lenin, *op. cit.*, pp. 332-3: See the discussion of this speech in A. Rosmer, *Moscou sous Lénine* (1953).

and the lack of education and discussion in the party. 'Already the party lead is accepted too formally, and the voice of political criticism too seldom raised within our ranks'. Pollitt, replying, jeered at concern with thinking and discussion on the part of the membership — carrying out the line was the thing for them. T. A. Jackson, answering Pollitt, supported Murphy's criticisms and asked : 'Is an ignorant membership necessary to the working of the plan of organization adopted at Battersea?' Was it to be accepted that the leading committee's task was to 'understand' while 'our job is only to carry out all instructions at the double, and stand to attention until the next order comes'? 'The meaning of "instructions" . . .is lost because the reason for their adoption at the point of incubation is rarely given . . .Little or no discussion is possible, except on the pettiest of petty details.'[186]

At the beginning of 1923, however, the negative potentialities of reorganization in a political setting in which the views of Lenin and Trotsky counted for less and less, and the consequences of bureaucratic degeneration in Soviet Russia spread throughout the international communist movement, were still hidden in the future. The immediate effects were positive. The weekly, *The Communist*, an essentially propagandist paper, was transformed into the *Workers' Weekly*, a real newspaper of the day-to-day struggle, giving timely and detailed leads on the living issues arising in the working-class world. The transformation of the party's structure helped to bring about a marked strengthening of its influence through the movement, both on the industrial and on the political side. Successful anti-war campaigns were conducted at the time of the Chanak crisis and on the occasion of the Curzon ultimatum. A Left wing appeared and became prominent in the Labour Party, its growth expressed in the defeat of Clynes as party leader and the emergence of the Clydeside group of MPs around John Wheatley, who maintained friendly relations with the Communist Party.[187] Above all, militant rank-and-file movements began

[186] *Communist Review*, January, February and April 1924. See also Report of Sixth Congress of CPGB (May 1924) and articles by E. Cant and C. M. Roebuck in *Communist Review* of March and June 1923. Cant, at this time party organizer for London, warned against a tendency for members to become robots, and observed that 'the comrade who said he was too busy selling the *Workers' Weekly* to read it himself is not a myth'. Significantly, the same negative consequences of reorganization that were noticed in Britain were also noticed in the French party: see chapter XI, 'La Bolchévisation du parti', in G. Walter, *Histoire du Parti Communiste français* (1948).

[187] On personal relations between Clyde Group MPs and communist leaders, see W. Gallacher, *The Rolling of the Thunder* (1947). For the role of communist journalists on the *Daily Herald* in 1923, see Hamilton Fyfe, *My Seven Selves* (1935).

to arise in union after union, with programmes of specific demands directed against the employers and definite proposals for democratizing and strengthening the unions themselves.[188] Of great importance in this connection was the conference on British Communist affairs held in Moscow in July 1923 and attended by most of the leaders of the CPGB. From this conference sprang the Industrial Committee of the Communist Party and the moves which led to the drawing together of the various rank-and-file movements into the National Minority Movement, the 'trade union opposition' which became a major factor in the British working-class movement in 1924-25. This was the last occasion on which the Comintern intervened in British communist affairs to good purpose.

The election held at the end of 1923 which brought the Labour Party into office for the first time saw the CPGB at its highest point since foundation. Though the Party had only about 4,000 members, the *Workers' Weekly* sold 50,000 copies — more than any other Labour or socialist weekly — and communists received 66,500 votes in the election. Ties with the working class and its organizations were now substantial and increasing. The situation towards which Lenin had pointed four years before had at last come about, with the reformists obliged to show their true mettle as the ruling party. Trotsky said: 'The result of the MacDonald regime, however it may end from the formal standpoint, will be a deepening of criticism and self-criticism in the ranks of the working class. For Britain the epoch of the formation of the Communist Party is only now really opening.'[189] One of the key questions of British history between the wars is: why did the experience of the first Labour Government not lead to a great

[188] The spring of 1923 saw the first big mass actions in industry since 1920 — among dockers, vehicle builders, jute workers, builders, boilermakers, agricultural labourers — and the first check to the decline in trade union membership. At the Labour Party Conference of 1923 the leadership was forced to withdraw the so-called 'Edinburgh clause' adopted the previous year, recommending trade unions not to elect communists as their delegates. It was understood that a number of unions would have withdrawn their delegations altogether if the credentials of the communists among them had been refused.

[189] Trotsky, *Through What Stage Are We Passing?* (June 21, 1924) Vol. p. 203. Cf. the resolution of the executive committee of the Comintern, February 6, 1924: 'If, as is expected, the Labour Government betrays the interests of the proletariat, it will thus offer the best object lesson to the proletariat, enabling it to free itself from the illusions of capitalist democracy, and will thereby accelerate the revolutionizing of the working class.' Radek wrote, in the *Communist International*, No. 3 (new series): 'For the first time in history the British communists have been given the opportunity of transforming themselves into a mass party . . .'

strengthening of the position of the Communist Party in Britain and so within a short period to that British revolution which down to 1926 was widely considered, among capitalists and workers alike, a perfectly definite possibility? Why, when at the beginning of 1924 the CPGB's prospects of integrating itself organically in the British working-class movement, and becoming the leading force within it, were so promising, had so little advance been made two years later that such a disaster as the betrayal of the General Strike could occur?

The German Events of 1923: Comintern Reaction

When, at the Fourth World Congress of the Comintern in 1922, Trotsky had spoken of the prospect in the near future of a Labour government in Britain opening a 'Kerensky' period here, this forecast had been linked with that of a victorious revolution in Germany.[190] In July-October 1923 a revolutionary situation had arisen in Germany in connection with the invasion of the Ruhr — and the Communist Party, held back by the new Zinoviev-Stalin leadership in Moscow, had 'missed the bus'. The developments in Germany had attracted enormous attention, in Britain as elsewhere, the CPGB carrying on a campaign against intervention, should the revolution succeed, under the slogan: 'Hands off Workers' Germany!' The disappointment felt at the revolution's failure was proportionate. On the basis of the defeat of the German workers, German and international capital proceeded to 'stabilize' the situation in Germany (Dawes Plan), and revolutionary moods and strivings received a setback everywhere. Frank recognition of what had happened was the urgent need of the day, with adaptation of policies to the new conjuncture. This was recognized and urged by Trotsky in a number of speeches and articles in early 1924.[191] A very different state of mind prevailed, however, in the leadership of the Soviet Communist Party and of the Comintern.

---

[190] Trotsky, *The First Five Years*, Vol. 2, pp. 211, 301.

[191] E.g., *On the Roads of the European Revolution*, April 11, 1924. 'We are living in the interval between the first and the second revolutionary blow. How long this interval will last we don't know.' (In this speech Trotsky forecast that the effect of the Dawes Plan would be to improve the position of German capitalism at the price of intensified economic difficulties for Britain — as actually occurred in 1925.) See also his introduction to *The First Five Years*. For a comprehensive survey of the 1924-25 and 1925-27 phases in Comintern policy, see his *The Third International after Lenin* and *The Permanent Revolution*.

These bureaucrats were unwilling for prestige reasons to acknowledge that they had brought about a defeat, and were already too much out of touch with the realities of the working-class movement to understand the consequences which this defeat had produced. From this un-Marxist reaction of the Soviet leadership to the defeat of the German revolution, and their vindictive onslaught on Trotsky for trying to correct them in this matter, all the disintegration and corruption which now developed in the international communist movement had their beginning.

In his article on 'The Lessons of the German Events'[192] Zinoviev affirmed that 'as before, the tactics of the German Communist Party and of the entire Communist International must rest on the assumption that the proletarian revolution in Germany is a question of the near future', and *Pravda* of April 20, 1924, treated the defeat of the German workers as 'only an episode — the fundamental estimation remains as before'.[193] The Fifth Congress of the Comintern presented the world with a spectacle of political unrealism and fantasy which profoundly discredited the cause of communism and helped to check the advance of the Communist Parties in a number of countries, including Britain. 'At this Congress argument no longer has weight. Whoever talks the most radical language carries the day.'[194] Not only was the objectivity and genuine self-criticism characteristic of the first four Congresses replaced by wishful thinking and empty boasting, but the former freedom of debate was encroached upon by a threatening attitude on the part of the leadership towards critics and the organized howling-down of the latter. The British communists had to endure some ignorant hectoring by the German 'Lefts' now basking in Moscow's favour, who were unable to distinguish between the problem of the Labour Government and that of the Labour Party. (As E. H. Brown, one of the CPGB spokesmen, ventured to remark, Lenin had spent some considerable time and effort curing British Communists of the ideas which Ruth Fischer was now trying to foist upon them.) The entire approach to British affairs by the new leadership was remote from reality. Zinoviev spoke of the power of the British bourgeoisie having been so badly shaken that the Labour Party would be in office 'for many years to come', maintaining the so-called

192 *Communist International,* No. 2 (new series).

193 Cf. J. V. Stalin, letter to Demyan Byedny, July 1924 (*Works,* Vol. 6, pp. 288), and review of the international situation, September 1924 (*ibid.,* pp. 292 ff).

194 'Ypsilon', *Pattern for World Revolution* (Chicago and New York, n.d. [1947]), o. 95.

'Kerensky perspective' of 1922. (Trotsky pointed out in his speech of July 18, *Europe and America,* that the defeat of the German revolution had radically changed the situation, and 'in all probability MacDonald will this time cede place to the Tories, in accordance with all the rules of parliamentary procedure'.)

It was in 1924 that the enemies of Communism could accuse the world Communist movement, for the first time with adequate grounds, of adopting a political standpoint which was not justified by the actual facts but arose from the sordid requirements of the internal politics of the Soviet bureaucracy.[195] In 1924, too, they could point unanswerably to the phenomenon of dismissal and appointment of Communist Party leaderships in accordance with their readiness or otherwise to adapt themselves to the latest 'line' from Moscow. The first instance of this occurred with the Polish Communist Party — always something of a problem for Stalin, until in 1938 he dissolved it altogether and had its principal leaders executed. In December 1923 the Poles had written to the Soviet Communist Party expressing alarm at the prospect that Trotsky might be ousted from the leadership of the Comintern. The Fifth Congress of the Comintern was called upon to pass a resolution condemning those chiefly responsible for this letter, and Stalin, in his speech on the Communist Party of Poland, virtually declared war on any and every Party leadership that showed sympathy with the Opposition.[196] In Germany and a number of other countries sweeping changes were carried through so as to eliminate all who doubted whether the right faction was winning in Russia or questioned the wisdom of its interpretation of the political situation in the capitalist world.

All this was not lost upon the leadership of the British Communist Party: at the party Congress in May, Gallacher duly declared that 'the German workers . . .are even now preparing for the mighty struggle that will end the power of their own bourgeoisie', and at the Comintern Congress the British delegation was one of a group which submitted a resolution denouncing the opposition in the Russian party.[197]

---

[195] The communist putsch in Estonia in December did 'untold harm to . . .the idea of proletarian revolution all over the world' (C. L. R. James, *World Revolution, 1917-36* [1937]). Even greater scandal was caused by the bomb outrage in Sofia Cathedral in April 1925, which may be taken as concluding this phase of Comintern policy.

[196] Stalin, *op. cit.,* pp. 276 ff.

[197] Zinoviev 'prepared' the constituent parties for the Comintern Congress by sending representatives to them to explain the views of the dominant faction on the key issues. According to the account of a meeting of the central committee of the CPGB in *Workers'*

Nevertheless, these were merely advance warning symptoms of a disease which did not show itself in strength until the following year. The effects of the 1924-25 Leftist phase in the Comintern and the first stage of the anti-Trotsky struggle were only indirect and muted so far as Britain was concerned, and the main line of development all through 1924 and on into the early months of 1925 was a continuation of the upward trend begun in 1923.[198]

The Party and the Minority Movement

In August 1924 the first annual conference of the National Minority Movement was held, with 200,000 workers represented. The conference called for the setting up of factory committees, as a stage towards industrial unionism and an instrument of workers' control, and for further work to develop the trades councils as local centres of militant leadership. Of particular importance, however, was the resolution calling for a strengthening of the powers of the TUC General Council in order to enable this body to lead the entire mass of trade unionists in a common struggle such as a General Strike. The resolution warned:

It must not be imagined that the increase of the powers of the General

---

Weekly, June 6, 1924, 'a report was presented by the representative of the Comintern on two of the principal questions arising before the Congress — the question of the German retreat and the controversy in the Russian Communist Party'.

[198] Significant in relation to developments in a later period is the controversy which took place between R. Palme Dutt and J. T. Murphy in the *Communist International*, 1924-25. Following the fall of the MacDonald Government, Dutt rushed into print to proclaim the 'decomposition' of the Labour Party, its transformation into an 'obstacle' to the workers' struggle, and the rise of the Communist Party to 'replace' it. Murphy showed the baselessness of Dutt's views, referring to him as one who 'sees the Labour movement from the newspapers, as one reading from afar, and impatiently dismisses the Labour Party as finished'. Dutt reaffirmed his view that the strengthening of the Communist Party and of the Labour Party were mutually incompatible aims, and referred to the resolutions of the Fifth Comintern Congress for backing. Murphy rejoined that it was not the task of the CPGB 'to split the Labour Party, although a split may be forced upon the Labour Party by the reactionaries, but certainly not by us': and commented shrewdly on the 'non-historical approach to the question and the Leftist kink which repeatedly manifests itself in Comrade Dutt's outbursts' (*Communist International*, Nos. 8, 9, 11, 12 [new series]). The Comintern's swing to the Right in 1925 deprived Dutt's special flair of any immediate bearing upon policy. In 1928-29, however, when the needs of the faction fight inside the CPSU, together with the disastrous failure of the Right zig-zag of 1925-27 dictated a sharp swing to the Left in the parties of the Comintern, and some of the British communist leaders were dragging their feet, then Dutt came into his own, as the high priest of the 'fight against social-fascism'. (See 'The Communist Party and the Labour Left, 1925-29'.)

> Council will have the tendency to make it less reactionary. On the contrary, the tendency will be for it to become even more so. When the employing class realise that the General Council is really the head of the Trade Union movement, much more capitalist 'influence' will be brought to bear on it ...The reactionaries desire a General Council which will check and dissipate all advances by the workers. We of the minority movement desire a General Council which will bring into being a bold and audacious General Staff of the Trade Union movement. We can guard against the General Council becoming a machine of the capitalists, and can really evolve from the General Council a Workers' General Staff only by, in the first place and fundamentally, developing a revolutionary class consciousness amongst the Trade Union membership, and in the second place, by so altering the constitution of the General Council as to ensure that those elected thereon have the closest contact with the workers.

The call for increased powers for the General Council had been an element in Communist policy since 1922, and from the beginning the necessity of associating such an increase of power with an increase of control from below had been stressed. Thus, Pollitt had written in the *Labour Monthly* of November 1923 that a 'real General Council must be established, with power to direct the whole movement, and not only with power, but under responsibility to Congress to use that power and direct the movement on the lines laid down each year by Congress'. J. R. Campbell, too, as editor of the NMM paper *The Worker*, had warned in an article in the *Communist Review* of May 1924 that the slogan of 'More Power to the General Council' might be taken up by elements who wished to see the General Council not co-ordinating struggles but stifling forward movements; the only answer to this danger was to strengthen the militant spirit and control from below. The communist fraction at Trades Union Congresses worked steadily in this direction; e.g., it was they who secured that the General Council's annual report should be issued to delegates seven days prior to Congress, instead of, as previously, when they took their seats.[199]

The successes achieved by the National Minority Movement in connection with the strike wave of 1924, which was on a bigger scale than that of 1923, stimulated a reaction on the part of the trade union bureaucracy. This took two forms. The bureaucracy as a whole, hitherto lukewarm, compared with the "politicians", on the question of excluding communists from the Labour Party, quite suddenly

[199] H. Pollitt, *Communist Review*, October 1923.

became galvanised into support for MacDonald on this issue — hence the decision of the 1924 Conference of the Labour Party attempting to close the door on individual membership by Communists.[200] Part of the bureaucracy, however, while in no way linking up with the Minority Movement, began to adapt themselves to the increasingly Left mood of the workers by striking Left-wing attitudes, more particularly on international questions such as relations with the USSR. The initial response of the Communists was to welcome this latter development as a reflection of the more militant mood among the workers, while guarding against the attribution of too much practical significance to it. Thus, Campbell, in the *Communist Review* of September 1924: 'It would be a suicidal policy, however, for the Communist Party and the Minority Movement to place too much reliance on what we have called the official Left wing.' The transformation of the trade union movement was still the main thing: 'The formation of workshop committees will provide a necessary means of counteracting the bureaucracy.' And Dutt, in the *Labour Monthly* of October 1924: 'A Left wing in the working class movement must be based upon the class struggle, or it becomes only a manoeuvre to confuse the workers.' The editorial in the *Communist Review* of November 1924 was far from starry-eyed about the new 'Lefts':

> On the trade union field we find the Left wing in the main representative of the smaller unions, e.g., Purcell, Bromley, Hicks. In previous years such unions played a very small part. But the increased activity of the masses has made it possible for them to gain prominence and ultimately position [in the General Council] by expressing 'Left' sentiments on a number of popular subjects, e.g., Soviet Russia . . .

---

[200] G. D. H. Cole, *A History of the Labour Party from* 1914 (1948), pp. 146-7. See also *Communist Review*, July 1924, on the extraordinary outburst of feeling against the communists on the part of trade union leaders in connection with the railway strike of that period. The standing of the communists in the working-class movement at this time was still such (shown, e.g., in the tremendous protest against the arrest of J. R. Campbell, which indirectly brought about MacDonald's resignation; the endorsement and election of Saklatvala as a Labour candidate in Battersea; and the increase in the circulation of the *Workers' Weekly* to 100,000 during the election campaign) that the attempt to exclude them from the Labour Party remained largely inoperative until after the 1925 Conference, and even then met with the organized and determined resistance through the formation of the National Left-Wing Movement, described in 'The Communist Party and the Labour Left, 1925-29'. It was only after the collapse of the General Strike that the exclusion policy could be put through on a grand scale; and by their policy change of 1928-29 the communists bolted on their own side the door that had been shut in their faces, voluntarily renouncing the prospect of getting the exclusion decision reversed.

The Party and the TUC 'Lefts'

On the initiative of the newly emergent Lefts among the top leadership of the trade unions, the Trades Union Congress of 1924 decided to send a delegation to the USSR. The delegation visited Russia in November-December 1924 and issued its report in February 1925. A paean of praise for the Stalinist regime, this report was written by the delegation's expert advisers Harold Grenfell, A. R. McDonell and George Young, and the Labour Research Department's *Monthly Circular* for March 1925 remarked of it that 'the Report is in no sense to be taken as a work of critical Marxism, or even as something written from the normal trade union outlook. But just for this reason it is likely to have a special appeal to middle-class readers'. Another important aspect of the report can best be illustrated by means of an excerpt from the article 'Stalin: Slanders and Truth', by C. Allen, in the *Communist Review* of January 1950:

> The trade union delegation that visited Russia in November 1924 recognized the bourgeois character of Trotsky. 'Trotsky, who only joined the party just in time to take a prominent part in the October Revolution, represents liberal nonconformity (in other words, capitalism — C.A.) as against die-hard communism.' (*Russia*, Official Report of the British Trades Union Delegation, London, 1925, p. 15).

The group of British trade union leaders who issued this report — Purcell, Hicks, Bromley, Swales — about the same time began to make speeches in favour of unity between the trade unions of the USSR and of Britain as a step towards international trade union unity.[201] Very rapidly thereafter the entire work of the British Communist Party came to be redirected so as to concentrate on support for this group of trade union leaders in their work for Anglo-Russian unity, any demands and activities which might antagonize them being abandoned or played down. (As outlined in 'British Communist History', this change of orientation did not bring about Anglo-

---

[201] More than somewhat belatedly, in his introduction to Lozovsky's *British and Russian Workers*, published in the latter part of 1926, Pollitt reproached the Russian trade union leader for underestimating the significance of mass pressure led by the National Minority Movement as the decisive factor in this development. The NMM held a successful conference on international trade union unity in January 1925; the delegation to Russia 'had kept absolutely silent on the whole question of unity' from its departure from Russia in December till after this conference.

Russian unity or any other good thing — it led through the betrayal of the General Strike to the Arcos Raid.)

The keynote for the new period was sounded in the editorial in the *Communist Review* of March 1925: 'The immediate task before the whole trade union movement in this country is the realization of the Anglo-Russian Trade Union Committee.' Lozovsky, leader of the Red International of Labour Unions, wrote, in *The World's Trade Union Movement* (English edition, April 1925) that 'the plan of the Right wing is falling through. The British representatives, and particularly Purcell, have already gone far beyond the line marked out for them by the Right-wing leaders of the Amsterdam International', and, while noting that the Trades Union Congress had rejected the communist-sponsored 'unambiguous' resolution on international trade union unity, had 'made up for that' by endorsing Purcell's proposal that the General Council try to bring the various trends together: this was, comparatively speaking, a step forward. The speeches of Tomsky, leader of the Soviet trade unions, which were published in English,[202] radiated confidence in Purcell and Co. R. P. Dutt's Notes of the Month in the *Labour Monthly* of May 1925 were devoted to the question of the working-class movement's attitude in the sphere of foreign relations, especially Anglo-Russian relations, and throughout the succeeding twelve months that journal was dominated by the question of Anglo-Russian trade union unity and allied matters.

The implications of this switch of attention quickly showed themselves. In the article by P. Braun on 'Problems of the Labour Movement', in the *Labour Monthly* for June, international trade union unity and the need for increased powers for the General Council were put in the forefront, factory committees being mentioned almost as an afterthought — and they were to be set up 'with the backing of the General Council'. At the second annual conference of the National Minority Movement, in August, stress was laid on the granting of full powers to the General Council, with only a brief and vague reference to 'obligation . . . to use that power to fight more effectively the battles of the workers', contrasting with the careful indication of the need to develop the control from below, lest the General Council use any increase in its powers to betray the workers, which had been a feature of the previous year's decisions. Dutt's Notes of the Month in the

[202] M. Tomsky, *Getting Together* (Speeches, 1924-25), published by the Labour Research Department, with an introduction by R. P. Arnot, 1925.

Labour Monthly for September left nothing to chance, stressing the need for increased powers for the General Council without even a formal warning or qualification. The helpless trailing behind Purcell and Co. to which the Communist Party was now reduced found pitiful expression in Dutt's Notes of the Month in the *Labour Monthly* for November, where he tried to explain away the fact that Purcell and Co., those great Left-wingers, the darlings of the Kremlin, had not lifted a finger to prevent the exclusion of the Communists from the Labour Party when this was reaffirmed at the Liverpool conference in 1925. They had 'failed even to attempt to put up a fight'; the trouble was that they lacked 'self-confidence, and 'to overcome this weakness' was 'an essential task for the future'. Wagging his finger, Dutt told these future betrayers of the General Strike that they had ...'acted very foolishly'. At the enlarged plenum of the Comintern executive in February 1926, George Hardy could cheerfully answer foreign comrades who wondered whether the campaign for 'All Power to the General Council', unlinked with a struggle for democratizing the unions, and with factory committees still 'music of the future', might not prove misconceived, by saying: 'Should they use that power wrongly, it only means that we have got another additional task before us of forcing them in the right direction, which direction they must ultimately take.'[203]

This political misorientation was the reason why, in spite of Red Friday and all that followed, the fiasco of the General Strike could nevertheless occur. It is heart-rending to observe how strongly the tide was running in favour of the Communist Party in the latter part of 1925 and in the opening months of 1926, when one knows what was to come. The arrest of some of the communist leaders in October 1925 evoked a wave of protest and indignation that dwarfed the reaction to the 'Campbell case' of the previous year. In spite of the anti-communist decision just passed at Liverpool, the Miners' Federation headed the list of protesting organizations. While Wally Hannington

---

[203] *Orders from Moscow?* (CPGB, 1926). After the terrible damage had been done, Dutt by implication criticized the glossing over in 1925-26 of the issue of structural reform of the trade unions which had been put in the forefront in 1922-24. In his Notes of the Month in the *Labour Monthly* for September 1926, he looked back at the Scarborough TUC of a year before, to exclaim upon 'the monstrously unrepresentative character of the existing trade union machinery. Had there existed a real Congress directly elected by the whole organized working-class movement, and had that Congress been able in its turn to elect by free vote a real leadership for the coming struggles and expressing its outlook, the history of the next twelve months would have been different.'

was in jail he was elected to the executive committee of the London Trades Council. Every weekend great marches to Wandsworth prison took place, to cheer up the 'class-war prisoners' with revolutionary songs. The *Annual Register* for 1925 records how the widespread agitation for the release of the Twelve culminated 'in a great demonstration at the Queen's Hall, London, at which some Labour MPs ostentatiously used language which they held to be seditious in order to provoke the Home Secretary to have them arrested'. A petition for the release of the prisoners secured 300,000 signatures. Among those who stood bail for the Twelve during their trial were Lady Warwick and G.B. Shaw. MacDonald was provoked by all this to write to *The Times* asking, 'What good is it our fighting Bolshevism if it is to be manufactured by the Government?'[204]

The leaders of the CPGB both underestimated the workers and overestimated the 'Left' trade union leaders. 'Not one of us as we emerged from Wandsworth [three weeks before the strike began — B.P.] thought there would be such an event' as the General Strike, writes J. T. Murphy, who was one of the Twelve, in his autobiography.[205] And, on the impact of the sell-out by Purcell and his associates, the editorial in the *Communist Review* of August 1926 declared: 'This treachery, unexpected and fatal, was greater than the certain and expected treason of Thomas.' Throughout the international communist movement the calling off of the strike came as 'a surprise and a shock'.[206]

The Comintern Leadership and the CPGB

Why did the Comintern leadership adopt, in the early months of 1925, the policy of unlimited confidence in the Purcell group and subordination of the British Communist Party to the convenience of this group? The 'imminent revolutionary developments' prospect of 1924 failed to justify itself. Already at the Fifth Congress of the Comintern Zinoviev hinted that perhaps the British Communist Party was not, after all, going to become a tremendous force in the immediate future, and if the Russians wanted to see big things happen

[204] On this episode, see E. H. Brown, 'The Persecution of the CPGB', in *Communist International*, No. 18 (new series).
[205] J. T. Murphy, *New Horizons* (1941), p. 220
[206] *Communist International*, January 30, 1927, article on the world-wide solidarity campaign.

forthwith in Britain they had better seek out other instruments.[207] Before 1924 was out, Trotsky warned against the kind of manoeuvre to which the bankruptcy of the current ultra-Left policy could easily lead: 'Opportunism expresses itself not only in moods of gradualism but also in political impatience: it frequently seeks to reap where it has not sown, to realize successes which do not correspond to its influence.'[208] He himself saw the way forward in Britain as lying through a steady growtn in the influence of the CPGB: 'Slowly (much more slowly than we should wish) but irresistibly, British Communism is undermining MacDonald's conservative strongholds.'[209]

By the end of 1924, signs of a new trend in Stalin's views on the international working-class movement became apparent, following upon his declaration of the possibility of building socialism in isolated Russia. In December, in his preface to *On the Road to October,* he wrote of Trotsky's being infatuated with the necessity for a revolution in the Western countries and underestimating the effectiveness of the 'moral support' already being given by the workers of Western Europe to Soviet Russia.[210] Here already is the germ of the Anglo-Russian Committee and the policy based upon it, the scrapping of the CPGB as an independent revolutionary force. In January 1925, while emphasizing that the international proletariat was showing itself 'tardy in making a revolution', he spoke of what he called the 'incipient split between the General Council of the TUC and the Labour Party' as a sign that 'something revolutionary . . .is developing in Britain'.[211] (Here the apparent contradiction is resolved if one interprets 'revolutionary' in the latter quotation as meaning for Stalin 'favourable to the defence of the Soviet Union conceived as something quite distinct from the revolution'.) Interviewed by a German Communist in February 1925, Stalin spoke of a measure of stabilization having been achieved by German capitalism and placed a question-mark over the immediate possibility of revolution in Germany.[212] Allying himself with Bukharin, Stalin was now moving against the super-Leftist Zinoviev, that specialist in cheap pseudo-revolutionary optimism. In *Pravda* of March 22, 1925 he declared flatly that capital

---

[207] Passage quoted in my article above. R. W. Postgate drew attention in *Plebs* for March 1925 to the significance of this passage when Zinoviev's speech was reprinted by the CPGB under the title *Towards TU Unity!*

[208] Trotsky, Introduction to *The First Five Years,* Vol. I.

[209] Trotsky, *Prospects and Tasks in the East* (1924).

[210] Stalin, *op. cit.*, pp. 374 ff.

[211] *Ibid.* Vol. 7, pp. 11 ff. 21, 26.

[212] *Ibid.*, pp. 34 ff.

had 'extricated itself from the quagmire of the post-war crisis', 'the positive trends that are favourable for capitalism' were 'gaining the upper hand' and there was 'a sort of lull'.[213]

A year earlier it had been the rankest 'Trotskyism' to speak of stabilization; now however — just when signs of the break-up of the stabilization of 1924 were beginning to appear in a number of countries, notably Britain and China — Stalin inscribed 'stabilization' on his banner and launched a struggle against all who questioned it. The task of the March-April 1925 plenum of the Comintern executive was to convey this new orientation to the parties and ensure their acceptance of it. The wretched Zinoviev did his best, but produced a speech of extraordinary confusion, trying to conceal the fact that the new line constituted a repudiation of that which he had promulgated at the Fifth Comintern Congress. One of the Czechoslovak delegates, Kreibich, drew attention to the contradictions in Zinoviev's speech and referred him to Stalin's *Pravda* article of March 22 for a correct exposition of the new set-up! So far as Britain was concerned, Lozovsky, in his speech at this plenum, clearly presented all the party's tasks as revolving around the Anglo-Russian Trade Union Unity Committee then just being formed: this was to be the meaning of 'stabilization' for the CPGB. What should have been only a tactical episode, temporary and auxiliary in character, was made to determine the entire strategical line of the British Communists for a long period ahead.[214] 'Stabilization' was to be the basic assumption and framework of Comintern policy thereafter for two and a half years — a period that saw mighty mass upsurges in Britain and China, contradicting 'stabilization', and betrayed by Purcell and Chiang Kai-shek respectively thanks to the policy of the Comintern under Stalin's leadership.[215]

---

213 *Ibid.*, pp. 51 ff.

214 *Bolshevizing the Communist International* (1925). The letter of May 8, 1925, from the Comintern section supervising work in the Co-operative movement to the Co-operative fraction of the CPGB (Document No. 17 in Cmd 2782 of 1926, documents confiscated in a police raid on 16 King Street) listed 'support for the actions of the Anglo-Russian Trade Union Committee' first among the urgent tasks of British Co-operators.

215 That the revolutionary movement was going through 'a period of ebb' was reaffirmed by Stalin at the Fourteenth Congress of the Soviet Communist Party, in December 1925. Not the revolution, but 'the workers' confidence in our State', to be secured by visits from delegations such as the British TUC delegation, was 'the fundamental antidote to imperialism and its interventionist machinations'. (*Works*, Vol. 7, pp. 171, 191). The enlarged plenum of the Comintern executive held in February 1926 once again reaffirmed this estimate (see *Communist Review*, April 1926 and *Labour Monthly*, May 1926).

The Struggle against 'Trotskyism'

The fact that after more than a year of disastrous make-believe the Soviet bureaucracy was forced to recognize stabilization — just as it was coming to an end in two of the principal centres of the capitalist world — did not, of course, mean that those who had faced the facts from the beginning now enjoyed any more friendly treatment — quite the reverse. Following the March-April 1925 plenum of the Comintern executive, a joint session of this body and the central committee of the Soviet Communist Party was held for the purpose of launching a new drive against 'Trotskyism', heralded by a speech from Bukharin, who had now replaced the discredited Zinoviev as the chief spokesman of the Stalin faction. Facilities for reply were increasingly restricted, but Trotsky still managed to voice his criticism of the new official line, even though only indirectly and allusively. His book *Where Is Britain Going?*, written in early 1925, had for its central theme the indispensability of building a strong Communist Party in Britain, which must combine flexibility of tactics and appreciation of the peculiarities of the British Labour movement with the maintenance of political independence and revolutionary principle. Deviations by British Communists, in the early years, in the direction of sectarianism, had been opposed and corrected by the Soviet Communists; now any tendency towards opportunism and tailism should likewise be resisted — certainly not encouraged.

In his last article in the *Communist International*[216] Trotsky urged the British Communists to learn from the experience of the Russian Revolution: 'Ready at any moment to act with the Left wing against all attempts at counter-revolution, the [Bolshevik] party at the same time [in 1917] pursued a ruthless ideological struggle against the parties which, against their will, found themselves "heading the revolution". It was only this that made October possible.' Why had not the Left wing in the TUC General Council played a greater role in the Labour Party? 'The party continues to be led by extreme Right-wingers. This is to be explained by the fact that the party cannot be restricted to various Left sallies, but is bound to have a finished system of politics . . .In order to rally their ranks, the Left-wingers

[216] Problems of the British Labour Movement' in *Collected Writings and Speeches on Britain*, Vol. Two, Part 2, pp. 124-184.

will first of all have to collect their thoughts. The best of them are only capable of doing this under the blows of ruthless criticism based on the everyday experience of the masses.' The divorce between words and deeds, benign gestures towards Russia and indifference or worse to the class struggle in Britain, must be exposed and broken down. On this it depended whether the Communist Party would 'come through the first revolutionary stage at the head of the working masses, as we did in 1905, or . . .let slip the opportunity of the revolutionary situation as the German party did in 1923. This latter danger is extremely real. It may be diminished only by aiding the Left wing to find its proper orientation for action (the *real* Left Wing and not Lansbury or Purcell).'[217]

Replying (in an article written on May 3, 1926, but not published in *International Press Correspondence* until June) to a criticism by Bertrand Russell of his *Where Is Britain Going?* , Trotsky dealt with the idea that the policies of the Communist Parties should be subordinated to the alleged requirements of the defence of the Soviet Union. Though he discussed this question in relation to the rebuke given by Lenin and himself to the German comrades who tried in 1921 to justify their artificial and premature attempt at revolution by the need to protect the Soviet Republic from renewed intervention at the time of Kronstadt, the following words were well understood by informed readers to bear also upon the holding back of the workers' movement, on the pretext of safeguarding Soviet interests, which was characteristic of the epoch in which Trotsky was writing: 'It would be essentially wrong to believe that the proletariat of any country ought to take any steps whatever in the interests of the Soviet State which do not arise from its own interests as a class which is fighting for its complete emancipation.'

The full story of how the leadership of the British Communist Party put itself completely in the hands of the Stalin faction in 1925 will only become known, if ever, on the basis of personal reminiscences. It is possible, however, to trace some of the outlines from the printed records. The *Communist Review* for February 1924 carried an article surveying the discussions in the Soviet Communist Party which gave a

---

[217] The materials constituting this article were written between December 1925 and March 1926, but the *Communist International* did not publish it until after the General Strike. (A resolution of the central committee of the CPGB, protesting against this article and condemning Trotsky's call for the Soviet trade unions to withdraw demonstratively from the Anglo-Russian Committee, was printed in the *Workers' Weekly* for August 13, 1926.)

fair presentation of the views of Trotsky and Preobrazhensky. The *Labour Monthly* of the same date carried a similarly objective and balanced report. Even after the resolution of the Thirteenth Conference of the Soviet Communist Party, condemning the 'factional' activities of Trotsky and classifying 'Trotskyism' as a petty-bourgeois deviation, had been published[218] the *Labour Monthly* featured (July 1924), an article by Trotsky,[219] though, to be sure, it was one that did not relate to the current disputes. As the campaign against 'Trotskyists' got under way in the Comintern, however, and assumed the form of dismissal and expulsion of officials of Communist Parties, King Street appears to have seen the red light. Anti-'Trotskyist' writings began to appear in British Communist publications with increasing frequency, starting with an Alice-in-Wonderland exposition of the issues by Tom Bell in *Workers' Weekly* of December 5, entitled 'The Truth About Trotsky' ('Needless to say, the ideas of Comrade Trotsky found ready support among the bureaucrats...') A resolution denouncing Trotsky was sent to Moscow. This aroused some uneasiness among a section of the membership, and at all-London aggregate in January a motion was put forward regretting the 'hasty' action of the leadership. The mover, A.E. Reade, was so rash as to quote Lenin's 'Testament' to the meeting. A. Rothstein rose to dismiss this document as 'a gross forgery'. R. P. Arnot explained that the Trotsky opposition was an affair of a few students, of no concern to the Russian workers (Cf. similar 'explanations' of the Hungarian rising in 1956!), and the leadership got away with it, only 15 votes being cast against their action in a house of 200-odd. The same issue (January 23, 1925) of the *Workers' Weekly* in which the report of this aggregate appeared carried an article affirming that 'those few comrades in our party who think that our executive committee should not have adopted any decision until it (or even until the whole party membership) had become acquainted with the full text of Trotsky's book [i.e., *Lessons of October* — B.P.], instead of with a summary as was actually the case, only show that they have a terrible deal to learn yet before they become real communists . . .' (cf. Pollitt's reply to critics of hastiness in condemnation of Tito in 1948). A piece by Bukharin attacking Trotsky (described in the editorial comment as 'a brilliant contribution to the theory and practice of Leninism') was

[218] *Communist Review*, April 1924.

[219] On H. G. Wells's interview with Lenin in 1920. Re-published in *Collected Writings and Speeches on Britain*, Volume One, Part 3, pp. 186-193

published in the *Communist Review* for February 1925. British Communists were reminded of the urgent importance of remedying the inadequacy of their exposure of 'Trotskyism' in a letter from the Agitprop Department of the Comintern Executive dated February 24.[220] In March the *Communist Review* reproduced a fresh resolution of the Central Committee of the Soviet Communist Party directed against Trotsky: this showed, commented the editorial board, 'that the Communist Party of Russia still remains a real Bolshevik Party, firm in its decisions, merciless in its discipline and united to the core'.

The Comintern Executive meeting of March-April 1925 gave special attention to the danger of 'Trotskyism' and the need to fight against it. Tom Bell reported that the British Communist Party had 'followed the whole discussion around what is called Trotskyism', and had 'no hesitation' in associating itself with the Soviet party leadership. He added a snarl at 'intellectuals' who admired Trotsky, contrasting them with 'workers' who understood the need for 'discipline', and threw in a jeer at Trotsky's 'paper plans' for industrialization. Following this meeting a regular anti-Trotsky campaign was opened up in the British Communist Press. The *Labour Monthly* of April 1925 contained a review by W. N. Ewer of Trotsky's biography of Lenin. Headed: 'The Twilight of Trotsky', the review described *Lenin* as being 'as pathetic a book as was ever unwisely given to the world', 'the book of a sick man consoling himself by telling himself stories of his own great past'. 'It is not good to look upon a strong man in the day of his sickness and mental weakness.' A similarly hostile review, by Arthur MacManus, appeared in the *Communist Review* for May. It was not so easy to get away with this sort of thing in Britain, however, and no small embarrassment was caused by J. F. Horrabin's pointing out in the May *Plebs* that a section of the book now being rejected as worthless had been published in the *Labour Monthly* ('Trotsky on Wells') as recently as the previous July: 'But that was before the party ukase against Trotsky had gone forth.'[221]

However, the Comintern 'ukase' had to be carried out, and May 1925 also saw the appearance of the book *The Errors of Trotskyism*, in which writings against Trotsky by Stalin, Kuusinen and others were assembled, with an introduction by J. T. Murphy. Virtuously, this

---

220 Document No. 14 in Cmd. 2682 of 1926.

221 Ewer had also reviewed Trotsky's book in the *Daily Herald* — carrying inner-party controversy into the non-party Press! — and there had written of Trotsky as 'a senile colonel gabbling in an armchair'.

British Communist leader (himself to be expelled in 1932) rebutted the charge by supporters of Trotsky that 'the present leaders were and are opposed to party democracy, when such was and is not the case'. The *Communist Review* for June printed a new speech by Bukharin against Trotskyism, and the *Labour Monthly* of the same date a review by R. P. Dutt of Eastman's *Since Lenin Died,* ridiculing the picture there given of a bureaucracy, against whom Lenin had warned, intriguing against good Communists. People who wrote such things were disloyal to the working class.[222] In *Plebs* for August, Gallacher sounded off against Trotsky's 'egotism'.

The knowing grins of anti-communist commentators compelled the adoption of a less obviously pre-fabricated attitude, a little more subtlety. This became particularly urgent when a translation of Trotsky's *Where Is Britain Going?* appeared in America[223] and at once attracted much attention in the Labour movement here (an extract was given in *Plebs* for October 1925). In the *Labour Monthly* for November and December an article entitled 'Towards Capitalism or Socialism?' by L. D. Trotsky was printed. Actually, this was merely the first, introductory section of the work with this title, published some months earlier in Russia, and contained nothing controversial: the critique of Bukharin's policy which constituted the main point of *Towards Capitalism or Socialism?* was in the later sections, which, were omitted without acknowledgement by the *Labour Monthly!*[224] *The Labour Monthly* for April 1926 carried a review by R. P. Dutt of Trotsky's book on Britain — which, while fulsomely praising the author's brilliance, etc., failed completely to relate the book to the current situation and omitted to discuss the very topical criticisms of the party line that were implicit in it.

When the Communist Party at last brought out an edition of its own of *Where Is Britain Going?* it omitted the preface specially written by Trotsky for the American edition in May 1925, which included these

[222] *The Workers' Weekly* of May 8 devoted a whole page to an excoriation of Eastman ('Since Eastman Lies'). According to a letter by Eastman in *Lansbury's Labour Weekly* of August 29, he sent to the *Labour Monthly* a reply to the attacks on his book which had appeared in the communist Press: the editor had accepted this, subject to approval by the party's political bureau, but the latter had refused permission for it to be published.

[223] Under the title *Whither England?*

[224] When the full text of *Towards Capitalism or Socialism?* was published in book form in the following year by Messrs. Methuen, Maurice Dobb gave it a hostile review in *Plebs* of October 1926. Trotsky, he pointed out, led the 'industrialist' wing of the Soviet Communist Party, a wrong-headed lot; his plans for industrializing the USSR were 'the stuff that dreams are made on'.

words: 'The inference to which I am led by my study is that Britain is heading rapidly towards an era of great revolutionary upheavals'; and, though giving the bulk of the introduction written in May 1926 for the second German edition, it omitted the word 'revolutionary' from the phrase 'the revolutionary prediction for the immediate future of British imperialism made in this book' and also an entire paragraph which included these words: 'The most important task for the truly revolutionary participants in the General Strike will be to fight relentlessly against every sign or act of treachery, and ruthlessly to expose reformist illusions.' It was understandable that the CPGB leadership should be shy of Trotsky's views on the immediate prospect in Britain in 1925-26, for about the same time as his book first appeared it had held a Congress which 'gave no countenance to the revolutionary optimism of those who hold that we are on the eve of immediate vast revolutionary struggle. It recognized that capitalism had stabilized itself temporarily' (*Workers Weekly,* June 5, 1925).

The Bureaucratic Degeneration of the CPGB

By the beginning of 1926 the CPGB had acquired the reputation, in spite of its small size, of being a model section of the Comintern, in one very important respect. The resolution of the enlarged plenum of the Comintern Executive held in February praised the 'absence of factional struggles in the British party'.[225] In this respect the CPGB offered a striking contrast to many other constituent parties of the Comintern, and it was to retain and consolidate this characteristic of exceptional readiness to follow the latest Moscow line. Even in 1929, Campbell, Rothstein and the others who at first resisted the 'Third Period' swing to the Left came to heel as soon as they saw that the Comintern meant business. The Murphy and 'Balham Group' affairs in 1932 were teacup-storms by Continental or American standards. (It complements this relative docility of the British Communist Party that in this country 'Trotskyism' developed in the nineteen-thirties mainly outside the ranks of communists and ex-communists, through the ILP). The factors determining this docility were doubtless many, and at present one can only speculate on the basis of insufficient material. Of some importance, probably, was the circumstance that the reorganization of 1923 equipped a small, poor party with a top-

[225] *Orders from Moscow?* See also *Labour Monthly,* May 1926.

heavy hierarchy of full-time officials. In the atmosphere of international bureaucratic centralism as it developed from 1923 onwards these officials evolved a close-knit freemasonry, based on unquestioning loyalty to the Comintern leadership. As it grew more and more apparent that, if only because of the Comintern-imposed policy, the CPGB was *not* going to lead a revolution in Britain, the importance of conformity to the current Moscow line, as against respect for Marxist principle or the facts of the situation in Britain, would acquire increasing weight. There is evidence, moreover, that already by 1925 the financial aid of the Comintern, funnelled through Petrovsky-Bennett, Moscow's representative with the CPGB, was providing essential support for the party 'machine'.[226]

Whatever the details of the mechanism of control, it is plain that the Soviet bureaucracy contrived to secure the connivance of the CPGB officials in transforming what in 1922-24 had been a party full of promise of becoming the Marxist leadership of the British workers, into a servile instrument of their will that they were thenceforth able to use as they fancied, ruining it, in the process, as a Communist Party in the true original sense. As Trotsky wrote in his *Letter on the Work of the British Section* in May 1933, 'the study and critical examination of the policy of the British Communist Party in the last eight or ten years', or 'even the mere selection of the most striking quotations and the presentation of them in chronological order, would lay bare not only the glaring contradictions of the "general line" but also the inner logic of those contradictions, i.e., the violent vacillations of the Centrist bureaucracy [of the Soviet Communist Party] between opportunism and adventurism. Every one of those tactical zigzags pushed communists, sympathisers and potential friends back, to the right, to the left, and finally into the swamp of indifference. We can say, without the least exaggeration, that the British Communist Party has become a political thoroughfare' .... Far too many of those who have passed along that 'political thoroughfare' have set off from it in the direction of indifference or even enmity to Marxism-Leninism and the heritage of the October Revolution and of the first four Congresses of the Comintern. Study of the history of the party which had disappointed them may perhaps help some recent ex-Communists to understand the real causes of its degeneration and enable them to find a better path.

---

[226] Cmd. 2682 of 1926 and Cmd. 3125 of 1928.

The Communist Party and the Labour Left 1925-1929

by Brian Pearce

> We were also guilty of provoking misunderstanding in the early days, and we can frankly recognize many further faults from our side. (R.P. Dutt, at the 24th Congress of the British Communist Party, reported in *World News*, 21st April, 1956.)
>
> 'Orders from Moscow' is one of the oldest slanders in the Labour movement. (John Gollan, in *World News Discussion Supplement* No.1, 26th January, 1957.)

The battle of ideas now in progress in the Communist Party is without any precedent except for that which took place in 1928-29 in connection with what was called the 'New Line'. In so far as the current discussion among Communists, ex-Communists and wide sections of the Labour Left is concerned with problems of unity in the Labour Movement, the issues are similar to those around which the earlier discussions raged. It may be that an examination of the earlier controversy and its setting can help to clarify thinking in the present one; and also that the roots of some present day problems will be discovered to lie in decisions taken in the late nineteen-twenties.

Down to the Liverpool Conference of the Labour Party in 1925, Communists could be individual members of the Labour Party. A resolution adopted at that conference excluded them from such membership, beginning the final drive by the right-wing leaders to ban Communists from any kind of participation in Labour Party affairs. A strong minority in the Labour Party indignantly opposed this drive, and numerous local organizations suspended operation of the Liverpool decision so far as they were concerned. Many Labour men saw the action taken against the Communists as part of a general move to the right and were keen to organize resistance.

In December 1925, following meetings in London and Birmingham, a National Left-Wing Conference was held, under the aegis of prominent personalities such as Tom Mann, Councillor Joe Vaughan (formerly Mayor of Bethnal Green, and member of the London Labour Party Executive), Joseph Southall (ILP), Alex Gossip of the furniture workers, and William Paul, the Communist editor of the *Sunday Worker*, a newspaper of left-wing sympathies, founded earlier in the same year, which claimed a circulation approaching 100,000 (Communist Party membership was then about 5,000). The aim of the Left-Wing Movement was proclaimed to be 'not to supersede the Labour Party, but to "re-mould it nearer to the heart's desire" of the rank and file'. It was reported at the Conference that nearly a hundred divisional and borough Labour Parties had suspended operation of the Liverpool decision. About fifty of these Labour Parties associated themselves with the National Left-Wing Movement, and Left-Wing groups were organized in many others. When Labour Party headquarters began disaffiliating Labour organizations which refused to operate the ban on Communists, this only intensified the conviction of the members affected that something like the National Left-Wing Movement was needed.

The betrayal of the General Strike in May, 1926 gave a further fillip to the new trend, and in September of that year a well-attended conference of the National Left-Wing Movement was held at Poplar, with Joe Vaughan in the chair. The keynote of this meeting was sounded in his call to 'cleanse the Labour Party of the agents of capitalism.' Use of the block vote at the Margate Conference of the Labour Party, held shortly afterwards, disappointed left-wingers' hopes of a reversal of the trend to the right. At this time, however, the Communist-led National Minority Movement in the trade unions commanded the support of nearly a million workers, a quarter of the total trade union membership, and was steadily growing. It was possible to look forward to the winning of both local Labour Parties and trade unions for the left-wing cause of a militant socialist policy in the Labour Party. As Dr. Robert Dunstan, a Communist who enjoyed wide support among Labour Party members in Birmingham, put it, the object of the struggle was to keep to the front those demands which the labour movement had made in the past, such as the capital levy, that the new ex-Liberal elements in the Labour Party leadership were trying to withdraw, and at the same time to advance new demands adapted to the newly-unfolding conditions of the working-class fight.

During 1927 the National Left-Wing assumed increasingly organized form, with a leading committee, chairman and secretary.

The *Sunday Worker* became virtually the organ of the new movement, regularly allotting space to reports of the organizing of Left-Wing groups up and down the country, and to expositions of its programme. A certain amount of trade union support for the movement's aims began to be recorded; in May, for example, the Lancashire and Cheshire Miners' Federation declared for the affiliation of the Communist Party to the Labour Party. In August, the *Communist*, monthly organ of the Communist Party, observed editorially:

> During the past twelve months there has been a very marked growth of the organized left-wing opposition within the British Labour Party. From being a movement mainly confined to London, the left-wing has, in less than a year, developed into a powerful national force, which is causing the right-wing Labour bureaucracy more and more anxiety and alarm.

At this time, it was still Communist policy to work for the transformation of the Labour Party rather than for its destruction. Stalin himself had explained, in May 1927, that, in spite of the actual situation of right-wing dominance at the moment, the Labour Party was correctly regarded as a workers' party if one had in mind:

> . . . the *type* of structure of a workers' party by virtue of which it should in the future, given certain conditions, become a real class party of the workers, standing in opposition to the bourgeois world. (*Works*, IX, 253-254).

When the National Left-Wing Movement held its Second Annual Conference, in September 1927, fifty-four local Labour Parties and many other groups were represented, aggregating, it was claimed, about 150,000 individual members. There were delegates from the London and Southern Counties Divisional Council of the ILP Guild of Youth, and the North London Federation of the ILP. Prominent miners' leaders such as A.J.Cook and S.O.Davies associated themselves with the conference, and Will Crick, Chairman of the Manchester and Salford Trades Council, was elected Chairman. The proceedings of the Conference, embodied in a pamphlet entitled *Towards a Labour Government*, had a wide sale.

Membership of the Communist Party at this time stood at about 7,500. There were large numbers of Labour Party supporters who were becoming disgusted with the policy of their leaders and who were desirous of changing both policy and leaders in the direction of militancy and a socialist programme but who, although friendly to the Communists and in favour of their enjoying equal rights in the Party as individuals, as before 1925, nevertheless did not themselves agree with all of the Communist Party's ideas (especially on the then much-discussed question of 'heavy civil war') and they did not want to join its ranks. The National Left-Wing Movement served as a bridge between the Communist Party and wide leftward-moving sections of the working-class.

To some leading members of the Communist Party it seemed, however, that it was not so much a bridge as a barrier. The leftward-moving masses would find their way into the ranks of the Communist Party, they felt, if the National Left-Wing were not there to intercept them. Morover, the prospect of transforming the Labour Party was no longer a real one, they considered, and only harm was done by keeping the idea of it alive: a thorough-going re-adjustment of Communist policy was needed. R.P.Dutt and Harry Pollitt, who held these views, found themselves in a minority in the Party s leading circles, but during a visit to Moscow in November and December 1927 Pollitt obtained support there, as a result of which the British Communist leadership were obliged to open a fundamental discussion in the columns of the Party press, and, when they attended the Ninth Plenum of the Executive Committee of the Communist International in February, 1928, to take part in a high-level investigation of problems of Communist policy in Britain. (Appendix I)

The majority of the Central Committee (notably Albert Inkpin, then General Secretary, J.R.Campbell, Andrew Rothstein and Arthur Horner) held that the central political fact in the British working class movement still remained that the bulk of the workers continued to have faith in the Labour Party. Lenin's advice given in 1920 had not ceased to be valid; the British Communists must work to push Labour into office and force the right-wingers to expose themselves in practice. In no circumstances must the Communists stand a candidate in an election where this might result in a Tory getting in, for that would discredit them in the eyes of the Labour-minded workers, who saw the defeat of the Tories as all-important.

> The history of the Labour Government (of 1924) in the mind of the average worker (pointed out the 'majority thesis' published in the *Communist Review* of February 1928) will contain not only Court dress and Bengal Ordinances, but also slight concessions to the unemployed, Housing Acts, and a treaty with the USSR, which he is convinced stimulated the capitalists to destroy the Labour Government. The unbridled reaction of the Baldwin Government has by way of contrast strengthened the desire of

> the workers for a Labour Government, and the wide masses of the work-ers, at the moment, are perhaps more anxious than ever before to return a Labour Government to office. We know that *after* the Labour Government, the Labour Party secured a million more working class votes.

The extent to which the efforts of the reactionaries to exclude the Communists had already succeeded should not be exaggerated; Communists could still get on to the controlling bodies of local Labour Parties as trade union delegates. There were twice as many Communists present at the 1927 Trades Union Congress as before, and these combined with a number of non-party Lefts to form a substantial opposition. The May Day demonstration of 1927, under Communist and left-wing leadership, had been, they claimed, the largest and most militant for many years.

> The Party in its policy has hitherto drawn a distinction between the rank and file moving forward in opposition to Capitalism and the leadership engaged in utilizing the Labour Party machine to impose a capitalist policy on the workers. To come out and oppose Labour candidates that have the backing of the local labour movement adds nothing to the independent role of the Party, but will only have for its result the creation of an unnecessary barrier between the Party and the mass of the workers standing behind the Labour Party, whom it is our duty to win for Communism. It is not a tactic calculated to strengthen the Communist Party against the reformists but, on the contrary, a tactic calculated to strengthen the reformist leaders against the Communist Party.

The way forward lay through strengthening the National Left-Wing Movement and work by the Communists within that movement.

The minority (R.P.Dutt, Harry Pollitt, R.P.Arnot and others) argued that the Labour Party had now become something like the Liberal Party of the 1890's, and the Communists must fight it just as the pioneers of the Labour Party fought the Liberals, not hesitating to put up candidates anywhere and everywhere against it. If the workers did not understand now, they would in the near future. As for the National Left-Wing, it served only to foster illusions, and constituted a barrier between the Communist Party and the workers; there must be 'no mediator between the Communist Party and the working class.' The policy of 'support plus criticism' in relation to the Labour Party was nothing but 'a patchwork of confusion, endeavouring to combine mutually inconsistent policies' and incurring the disadvantages of both.

In his Notes of the Month in the *Labour Monthly* of February, 1928, R.P.Dutt affirmed that a 'growing body of workers are looking for new political leadership' and 'are expecting to find that new political leadership expressed at the election.' Since Lenin gave his advice in 1920 'the whole situation and line of development' had changed fundamentally. The self-exposure of the reformist leaders had reached a stage at which 'the revolutionary consciousness of a growing mass-section of the working class has grown strong and ready to advance to a further stage of struggle', having out-grown the Labour Party.

The Executive Committee of the Communist International decided, in the main, in favour of the views upheld by the minority. The Labour Party, it considered, was already well on the way to becoming a unitary Social-Democratic Party like those on the Continent, and this development must be accepted as irreversible. It no longer made any sense to call for a second Labour Government, with no matter what qualification or condition; the Communist Party's slogan should now be: 'For a revolutionary Workers' Government.' Candidates should be put up to fight Labour in as many places as possible. The questions of what was to be done about the Left-Wing Movement, and what the Communist Party should advise workers to do in places where there was a Labour candidate and no Communist candidate, were left without any clear-cut answer at this stage.

There now began a period covering nearly two years during which confusion grew within the Communist Party as to the implications of the 'New Line' laid down by the Ninth Plenum of the Executive Committee of the Communist International. W. Gallacher, writing in the Party organ, the *Workers' Life*, in March, 1928, declared that the Communists could not give 'active support' to Labour candidates other than those who accepted a fighting working-class policy.

> At the same time the Party will not advise the workers to abstain from voting for Labour Party candidates where, for one reason or another, a revolutionary workers' candidate is not in the field.

When a by-election occurred at Linlithgow, first of all a Communist candidate was put up, then he was withdrawn in favour of the Labour candidate, then finally advice was given to the workers to abstain from voting and build up the Communist Party locally so that a Communist candidate could be nominated 'next time'. In the *Labour Monthly*, April, 1928, R.P.Dutt quoted Marx on the need to put up workers' candidates, to fight 'petty-bourgeois democracy,' identifying the Labour Party with the latter.

At the same time, the National Left-Wing Movement continued to develop, and under Communist guidance concentrated on struggle in the localities to replace right-wing Labourites by left-wingers as Parliamentary candidates. The reviving militancy of the working class, after the period of depression following the defeat of the General Strike, expressed itself in a new way in the launching of a manifesto for a socialist policy in the Labour Party by the miners' leader, A. J. Cook, and James Maxton of the ILP, backed by John Wheatley, the most left of the Labour Party's leaders. Gallacher had taken part in the drafting of the manifesto, and the National Left-Wing Movement officially greeted its appearance and pressed Cook and Maxton to go further and put forward a detailed programme along the lines of the Movement's own; which eventually, within a few months, was done.

The circulation of the *Sunday Worker* rose steadily and some 10,000 people turned out for the Left-Wing May Day demonstration of 1928. At the annual conference of the Left Wing Movement in September, 1928, between 75 and 80 local Labour Party Left-Wing groups were represented and the provincial representation in particular was better than it had been in either of the previous conferences.

This promising development collapsed as a result of intensified attacks by the right-wing together with hesitation and something more than that on the part of the Communist Party. In the *Workers' Life* an extremely guarded welcome was given to the Cook-Maxton affair from the first, and this rapidly changed into sharp denunciation of it as 'cant' and 'fooling', bound to 'fizzle out'. Cook and Maxton (and, by implication the National Left-Wing Movement too, and the Communist Party insofar as it still supported this) were on the wrong track altogether, insisted R. P. Dutt in the *Labour Monthly* of May, 1928, ridiculing 'the whole fallacy of the "ginger group" concept in relation to the present formed and hardened Labour Party.' Not only could no good come of such efforts, they represented a positive danger. This was the menace of *centrism;* the workers were increasingly ready to come into the Communist Party and it was all-important not to encourage any organizations or movements that might 'intercept' them. It was not the weakness so much as the potential strength of the left movements of 1928 that alarmed R. P. Dutt and those who thought as he did. (R. P. Arnot, for example, writing in the *Communist International* in the following year, observed that it was only 'the comic-opera futility' of Maxton that saved the day.)

When a pre-Congress discussion was opened in the Communist press in October, 1928, the advocates of a sharp turn to the left in the name of full implementation of the 'New Line' took the bit between their teeth. As Party membership fell and the Party's isolation grew they became increasingly fervent for their ideas. W.Rust complained that the majority of the Party leadership were 'apt to under-estimate our own influence and following' and so to be unduly cautious and over-careful to seek allies and proceed in step with other sections of the labour movement. J.T.Murphy affirmed that:

> . . . we can no longer do a single thing to strengthen the Labour Party — neither affiliate to it nor pay (the political levy) to it, neither work for it nor vote for it.

R.P.Dutt, in the *Labour Monthly* of October, 1928, forecast a process:

> . . . by which the centre of gravity of the parties steadily shifts, and the Labour Party comes to build increasingly on the petty bourgeoisie and a small upper section of the workers for its support, while the Communist Party becomes established as the party of the mass of the industrial workers.

H.Pollitt, in the *The Communist,* December, 1928, wrote:

> We describe the Labour Party as a third capitalist party. If that means anything at all, it is that our strength will grow in the degree that we can weaken the Labour Party.

On the other hand, among contributors to the discussion in the Party press there were some who warned that the workers were only *moving* to the left, and their disappointment with current Labour Party policy did not necessarily mean immediate enthusiasm for the Communist Party and all it stood for.

The municipal election results of November showed an increased vote for Labour along with a fall in the Communist vote; it seemed possible that some former supporters of militant candidates had even transferred their votes to official Labour, out of single-minded determination to 'get the Tories out,' together with perplexity and unhappiness regarding the Communist Party's 'New Line'.

The eve of the Communist Party's Tenth Congress, at Bermondsey, in January, 1929, saw downright denunciation of continued Communist support for the National Left-Wing Movement by R.P.Dutt, both in the *Communist Review* and in his own *Labour*

Monthly. With bitter sarcasm he wrote that the Party leadership were trying to accept the 'New Line' in words while continuing to apply the old one in practice.

> The old line can still go merrily on and find a home in the National Left-Wing . . . If it is argued that it is necessary for the Communist Party to organize this tendency as a bridge to itself, then this becomes in the end equivalent to arguing that it is the task of the Communist Party to organize centrism . . . For our Party to take the responsibility of direct political leadership within this organization and sponsorship of its programme is to frustrate completely the new line, which is based on repudiation of the Labour Party and of the objective of a Labour Government . . . There can be no united front on the basis of a complete political programme, for a complete political programme implies a party . . . Until a comparatively recent period many revolutionary workers still believed in the possibility of a constitutional conquest of the Labour Party and its eventual transformation, as the workers became disillusioned in the reformist leadership, into a revolutionary party by a change of leadership; and at that time any Marxist prediction of the inadequacy of such a perspective, and of the inevitable future disintegration and ultimate liquidation of the Labour Party, and the inescapable necessity of a completely new revolutionary basis, still aroused a sense of shock and outrage. Today, however, the facts are clear to all . . . The Labour Party is . . . a machine of reformism . . . *The decisive fight of the revolutionary workers is and can only be outside that machine and against it* . . . The conception of a socialistic transformation of the Labour Party needs to be denounced . . . With this goes equally the conception of the advance of the workers throught a Labour Government, or a left Labour Government . . . *The path of advance lies through the independent leadership of the revolutionary workers to the working-class conquest of power through a revolutionary Workers' Government.* (My italics B.P.)

Articles to the same effect, by Dutt's associates, R.P.Arnot and W.Rust, appeared in the Moscow *Communist International*.

Spokesmen of the majority on the Central Committee, notably J.R.Campbell, ventured to question Dutt's assumptions, especially the one that great masses of radicalized workers were streaming towards the Communist Party and were only held back from it by the existence of some sort of soft option in the National Left-Wing Movement. 'We must have a Left-Wing Movement,' it was urged, 'in order to unite with the honest rank-and-file of the Labour Party, who are genuinely dissatisfied with some of the Labour policy, but who are not prepared to come right over to the Communist Party.' The

Left-Wing was still growing in many local Labour Parties and should be given every encouragement.

As Party membership fell to 3,000, then to 2,500, the voice of fanatical sectarianism grew proportionately louder in its counsels. At the Tenth Congress a resolution that Party members should leave the National Left-Wing Movement was passed, against the opposition of the Central Committee, by 55 votes to 52, after vigorous speeches for the resolution by J.T.Murphy, Marjorie Pollitt, Idris Cox and others. Shortly afterwards, the National Committee of the movement, on which Communists pre-dominated, decided by a majority vote to dissolve it and advise supporters to join the Communist Party. When this announcement appeared in the *Sunday Worker* the paper was bombarded with letters of protest from readers, who were indignant that the decision should have been taken without any consultation of the membership of the Left-Wing Movement. The circulation of the paper, which had been increasing, turned downwards.

The thoughts of the workers generally were now dominated by the approaching General Election. By-elections showed that a big revival in the Labour Party's fortunes was developing. In this situation, R.P.Dutt proclaimed in the *Labour Monthly* of February, 1929:

> Above all, it is necessary to prepare the workers for the inevitable future fight against the Labour Government, whether coming in the next few months or in the near future, as their enemy, even when it appears to make concessions, and to clear the revolutionary perspective of the period in front.

The Communist Party put up twenty-five candidates in the election in May and advised workers to abstain from voting where no Communists were standing; they should write 'Communist' across their ballot papers. As later leaked out, this decision was not reached without considerable dissension, and in the final voting five Central Committee members were for advising the workers to vote Labour in constituencies where there was no Communist standing. (These were Campbell, Rothstein, Inkpin, G. Aitken and F. Bright. The fact was revealed by W. Tapsell to W. Rust, for the latter to use at the YCL Congress to whip up hostility to the Central Committee members concerned. He was officially reprimanded by King Street for 'factional activity'.) No non-Communist left-wing candidates were endorsed, although preparations had been in train in certain centres, notably in Birmingham, to nominate such candidates. The election manifesto called for 'a Workers' Socialist Republic federated with the USSR'.

The Communist candidates did very badly, getting only 50,000 votes. This was less than a third of the expected figure; and it was pointed out that this vote, in 25 seats, had to be contrasted with the 41,000 votes obtained in 1924 in only six constituencies. There was a particularly striking drop in the Communist vote in old strongholds like Battersea and North Aberdeen.

The Labour Party came in without a majority and was obliged to rely on Liberal support, the right-wing leaders thus possessing a ready-made alibi for betraying the electors' hopes without losing their sympathy. One commentator suggested that they owed this happy situation to the Communist policy of spoiling ballot papers in the constituencies where no Communist stood — there were forty cases of Tory or Liberal majorities of less than 2,000, where a different line taken by the Communist supporters might have made all the difference.

The effect of the General Election on the Central Committee was to confirm the doubts already entertained by the majority about the 'New Line'. The political Bureau was reconstructed in their favour. A gift of £50 was made to the *Sunday Worker,* with a statement that the paper's disappearance would be regarded as a 'disaster' and a hint that the Communist Congress decision regarding dissolution of the National Left-Wing was 'open to reconsideration'.

Very different, however, was the mood prevailing in Moscow at this time. Stalin had recently ousted Bukharin and was waging war on 'the Rights.' Instructions conveyed to the British Communist leaders at a meeting in Berlin immediately following the election included:

> In our general campaign against the Labour Party we should emphasize that *it is a crime equivalent to blacklegging for any worker to belong to the Labour Party*. (My italics B.P.)

The Tenth Plenum of the Ececutive Committee of the Communist International, meeting in Moscow in July, 1929, under the leadership of Molotov and Manuilsky, Stalin's representatives, gave final formulation to the doctrine of 'social-fascism' (adumbrated by Stalin already in 1924), according to which fascism was in process of being introduced in countries like Germany and Great Britain by their respective Social-Democratic Parties, and it addressed a letter to the British Communist Party calling for a still sharper turn to the left, with removal of any leaders who stood in the way of such a turn. (Ulbricht, supporting the Soviet spokesmen at the Plenum, had called for the appointment to leading positions in the British Party of men 'who can be counted on to carry out consistently the line of the Comintern.')

A series of aggregate meetings was held in London, Newcastle and Manchester to discuss the Comintern letter, at which leading local Communists, supporters of the Comintern line, such as Reg Groves, R.W.Robson and Maurice Ferguson, called on the membership to 'fight the Right danger' on the Central Committee and clear the decks for an all-out struggle against the Labour Party and for workers' revolution and a Soviet Britain. The Congress of the Young Communist League also joined in this move, led by W. Rust. King Street's attempts to escape criticism by scare cries of 'fraction work' were ridiculed. The columns of the *Communist International* and *International Press Correspondence* carried articles by the leading critics of the British Party, publicizing the 'revolt of the membership'. On the insistence of the Executive Committee of the Communist International, conveyed by its representative in Britain, D.Petrovsky ('A.J.Bennett'), three members of the Political Bureau were removed from office (Albert Inkpin, Andrew Rothstein and J.R.Wilson) and Inkpin was replaced by Harry Pollitt as General Secretary (August, 1929). A special National Congress was summoned for November, to confirm these changes and draw appropriate conclusions from them, although the previous Congress had taken place so recently as January.

By now the sales of the *Workers' Life* as well as those of the *Sunday Worker* were falling catastrophically. (Already in September, the *Sunday Worker*, then edited by Walter Holmes, was describing the Labour Government as 'social-fascist'.) In spite of the removal of the National Left-Wing 'barrier', Party membership was also declining. (These facts were ascribed by the advocates of the further turn to the Left to the lateness and hesitancy of the old leadership in applying the change of line, not to the line itself.) In the pre-Congress discussion, owing to the powerful backing given by the EC of the Communist International to the Dutt-Pollitt group, full publicity was allowed in the Party press to lengthy, scathing and abusive resolutions passed by district organizations of the Party, and letters, such as one by W.Tapsell, warning the Central Committee that they would not be allowed to get away with a 'mere regrouping of the old gang' ; 'at least over half, if not more', of the leadership must be displaced. The *Sunday Worker* was closed down altogether.

At first the most prominent leaders of the majority on the Central Committee attempted to stem the Leftist tide, but, faced with the fact that their adversaries in the districts were fully informed about proceedings at Central Committee meetings and about the threatening communications sent them by the E.C. of the C.I., they soon had to turn tail and some then endeavoured to join in the denunciation of the 'Right danger' as the only way of saving themselves from dismissal. R.P.Dutt wrote in the *Workers' Life* in November, 1929:

> Certainly we are only concerned with persons as expression of political tendencies, and need to beware of formulating the issues in such a way that the primary question appears to be a question of personalities. But the fight of principles necessarily finds expression as a fight of persons. This is at the very root of the difference of Bolshevik methods from ILP 'gentlemanly' methods.

(In the September *Communist Review* he had demanded that 'the easy-going attitude which is satisfied to 'recognize' mistakes and pass on, without deeper analysis or drawing of lessons for the future, and with the inevitable consequences of repeating these mistakes in new forms, must end.')

Much play was made in the discussion of the fact that Rothstein (seen by some as the arch-embodiment of the Right danger) was an 'intellectual'; though Dutt, undoubtedly the prime mover in the Moscow-backed revolt, was certainly no less an intellectual. (Both are Balliol men.)

The discussion which raged in the pages of *Workers' Life* during October and November of 1929 makes astonishing reading today, so remote from reality and carried away by frenzy do some of the participants seem to have been. There was a letter from Jack Cohen, for example, complaining that the Minority Movement was being allowed to appear as the leader of strike struggles in industry, thus concealing the face of the Party; and one from Emile Burns calling for a sterner policy of splitting the trade unions and forming new, 'Red' ones under Communist leadership.

The Eleventh Congress of the Communist Party, held in Leeds in November-December, 1929, registered the final, total triumph of the 'New Line' in deeds as well as words, with guarantees in the form of changes in the leadership. (These changes were facilitated by the circulation to Party branches of minutes of the Central Committee for a period of twelve months showing how the various members had voted on disputed issues.) Congress in the main shared the spirit of the message which it received from the Presidium of the ECCI, calling for 'a final and decisive break with the opportunist hesitations and vacillations of the past' and speaking of the 'fascization of the Labour Party and its appendage, the sham Lefts' and of 'the fascization of the trade unions.' The only opposition came from the South Wales delegates, led by Arthur Horner.

This Congress opened a period in which, led by Pollitt and Dutt (who emerged as chief theoretician as a result of the 'banishment' of Rothstein to the USSR immediately after the Congress), the Party became completely and utterly isolated from the mainstream of the British Labour movement for several years, functioning as a sort of honorary agency of the Comintern. In August, 1930, the *Communist Review* observed sadly that 'although we have stood on the line of the Comintern . . . yet the membership continues to fall, and the Party is still largely isolated from the masses.' When the Labour Government collapsed in 1931 the Communists were unable to gain a single seat in the resultant election. In essence the Party continued its sectarian line of self-isolation — with special emphasis on denouncing the Left in the Labour movement, such as the ILP, as the 'most dangerous enemies of the working class' until Hitler's victory in 1933 gave a jolt to the entire world Communist movement and in Britain produced a certain thawing in relations with the ILP. A fairly clean break with the outlook of 1929 had to wait, however, until the Seventh World Congress, in 1935, with Dimitrov's speech on the United Front against Fascism.

The story of the Eleventh Congress of the British Communist Party is sometimes told as though the central issue was whether or not a Communist daily newspaper, the *Daily Worker*, should commence publication on January 1, 1930. In fact, as the *Workers' Life* report shows, Harry Pollitt was one of those who argued at the Congress in favour of postponement; the real question at issue was what should be the *policy* to be advocated in the new organ, or rather, what changes of leadership were needed if the policy laid down by the Comintern's Ninth and Tenth Plenums was to be implemented through the *Daily Worker* without reservation or wavering of any kind.

It is also said that among the important issues at the Congress was that of whether or not the Party should be 'solidly based on the factories'. Certainly there was much demagogic talk and writing about factories, factory-workers and the proletarian basis of the Party, for the sake of identifying the Left line with the working class and the

'Right danger' with some intellectuals or other. Nevertheless, the Congress in fact opened a period of several years during which the Communist Party had less of a footing in industry than ever before, and it became predominantly a party of the unemployed — among whom indeed, its best work was done during that period. The Minority Movement in the trade unions (perhaps the most promising achievement of the British Communists in the 1920's) was not long in following the National Left-Wing Movement into dissolution.

APPENDIX I

Extracts from speeches made by British delegates at the Ninth Plenum of the Executive Committee of the Communist International, Moscow, February, 1928.

(This meeting of the Ninth Plenum was the first full dress debate between the advocates of a 'New Line' and the majority of the Central Committee of the British Communist Party. Each group presented Theses to the Plenum. Those of the majority were in the name of the Central Committee while the minority theses were signed by R.P. Dutt and H. Pollitt. At the Ninth Plenum J. R. Campbell and W. Gallacher spoke for the majority of the Central Committee and R.P. Arnot put the case for the minority. Among others who spoke on the Plenum were Bukharin, M.N. Roy and Togliatti. The overwhelming weight of opinion in the Plenum was on the side of the minority and the Resolution summing up the discussions, adopted unanimously, was a defeat for the majority.)

J. R. CAMPBELL

(First Session) . . . Comrades tell us that the situation has changed since 1920, but it has not changed to the extent that the Communist Party is now able on a national scale to put forward its candidates, and to be the national alternative either to the Baldwin Government on the one hand, or the Labour Government on the other. Hundreds of thousands of workers have paid the political levy in anticipation of this contest. Millions of trade unionists are looking forward to this contest as a means of voting out the Government and getting the repeal of the Trade Union Act. We must do the utmost we can during the election to destroy the illusions of the workers with regard to the Labour Party's action on the Trade Union Act; to destroy the illusion of the possibility of the Labour Party carrying out a radically different policy from the Conservative Party. But at the same time we are still faced with the tactical question of what policy we can best adopt to show the workers in actual practice that what the Communists are saying to them is correct. And we believe that the speediest way to show the workers in actual practice that what we are saying is correct, to increase the differentiation of the Labour Movement in our favour, to swing the masses of the workers to the Party and the Left Wing — is to force the Labour Government into office as soon as we possibly can, to vote for the Labour Government in the last analysis as against the open capitalist parties, believing as we do that the further experience of a Labour Government must add further and increasing support to the Communist Party and to the Left Wing. . . .

Then comes the question of putting forward candidates against the Labour Party and under what circumstances we should put forward candidates against the Labour Party. We are told that we are putting the candidates forward — not on political grounds but on empirical grounds, on the grounds that we are choosing the constituency where we are likely to have the greatest possible success. If empiricism consists of facing hard facts, I plead guilty to being an empiricist. Therefore, our line is to proceed to fight either in those constituencies where there is a Liberal-Labour pact and only one Labour man is run for two seats together with one Liberal, or to have a fight in those constituencies which are so overwhelmingly working class that a split vote will not let the open capitalist candidate in, but in the main, to base our fight on the disaffiliated Labour Parties where we have already a local Labour Party struggling with the trade union bureaucracy, and have won over a majority of that local Labour Party from the influence of that bureaucracy. On the other hand, the Comrades believe that we should, while doing this, also put forward three or four candidates against the more prominent Labour leaders in various parts of the country in order to show that we are definitely fighting the Labour leadership, thus sharpening the fight through the country. . . .

R. PAGE ARNOT

(First Session) . . . Now, the first point is that the principle of a sharp turn must be understood by every member of the Party. Otherwise the helmsman of the boat will shift the wheel a few points, but the crew and the passengers and everyone else will not understand that a sharp turn in direction has taken place; whence the need, both here and in Britain, for the fullest Party discussion on this question; which will incidentally be the means of raising the ideological level of the Party, especially as it will be the first full discussion of this kind the Party has had since it was formed seven years ago.

I now come to actual electoral tactics. In order to express the antagonism against the Labour Party in the sharpest way, the principle must be that we put candidates wherever we can. Obviously we want, if possible, to put 600 candidates; but this is physically impossible. Nevertheless, we must somehow try to get the same effect as we would by putting up 600 candidates, the effect that we are standing absolutely opposed to the Labour Party. The one way in which you can get this effect is by striking at the chiefs of the Labour Party. By putting up candidates against the Labour Party chiefs you express the antagonism perfectly, sharply and clearly. No further room is left for doubt. If you select the half-dozen leaders of the Labour Party, you at once make it clear to everyone in Britain that, without any doubt at all, the Communist Party has taken a sharp turn against the reformists — Comrade Campbell, in dealing with that question, was clearly thinking largely in terms of the morning after the election, of how many votes we shall have received, etc., etc. The Communist Party is not going to neglect the question of the number of votes. It is not going to forget the morning after the election; but is going to remember still more the question of the future of the working class and of the Communist Party as leader of the working class — not simply the morning after the election, but the next day, the next year, the next two years. Even supposing the results of the election were not good, it would not be a fundamental argument against the proposal to make quite clear and distinct our antagonism to the Labour Party by opposing MacDonald, Clynes, Thomas, and all the others.

The proposal to oppose MacDonald, Thomas, Clynes, and Snowden and so forth will be welcomed by many workers in Britain, who would be prepared at the same time to continue with the policy of support of the Labour Party elsewhere. This sentimental point of view would simply lead to further confusion. Therefore, in order to make perfectly clear to the working class that the fight of political parties, and the struggle of classes is not a question of individuals whom all dislike or who are particularly reactionary — I would advocate candidates against such men as Lansbury in Poplar and Purcell in the Forest of Dean.

In addition to putting forward candidates wherever we can, in addition to putting forward candidates against the Labour Party chiefs so as to express quite sharply the antagonism, we must also go forward with the proposal to demand new selection conferences in every constituency. At these selection conferences we put forward our candidate. If he is turned down by the weight of official machinery, we are still free to call a workers' conference in that locality and go forward still with a candidate; such a candidate as is not an experienced Parliamentarian but a worker new to the job. If no such worker is selected, if a minor trade union official is selected, nevertheless, for the moment it is possible in such a case as that to put to him the proposal that on certain terms the Communist Party will support him. For example, would he be in favour of the affiliation of the Communist Party? In Parliament would he work together with the Communist fraction? On such terms we could agree to support where a new candidate is chosen.

Where the Party has no influence, where no Communist Party members exist (and there are many such constituencies) there it is our business to put forward in the strongest possible way the Communist Party policy, to carry out the strongest possible propaganda to put forward our point of view and to keep this up until the worker is clear as to the antagonism between ourselves and the Labour Party. In such a case, finally, we should adopt the demonstrative vote and advise workers to spoil the ballot papers by writing across some such slogan as 'To Hell with the Lot!'

One argument put forward in the theses against these proposals is that by such a policy we 'would let the capitalist candidate in.' This argument has to be examined very carefully. The significance of keeping a candidate out, from the point of view of the working class, depends entirely upon what the candidate stands for. Suppose Comrade Pollitt is put up in Derby to fight Thomas, and suppose Pollitt is kept out — this is a crime against the working class. But suppose Thomas is kept out — this is not a crime. J. H. Thomas is of much more value to the capitalists than probably their own capitalist candidate. But in any case this argument of 'letting the capitalist candiate in' is wrong. It was exactly the slogan of the reformists, the Liberal-Labour trade unionists who opposed Keir Hardie thirty-five years ago. When this working class leader, whose ideology was reformist, but whose instincts were revolutionary, proposed to form an independent working class movement against the Gladstone Liberalism, they said, 'You are letting the Tory candidate in.' This is an argument which should not be put forward in our discussion here.

Lastly there is one point I should make clear in which I differ from Comrade (J. T.) Murphy. Comrade Murphy, in his speech in the Central Executive Committee and still to a certain extent in the thesis which he has put forward and which will be part of the materials for this discussion, appears to believe in the building up of the disaffiliated local Labour Parties and of the Left Wing groups into something which even with his modifications at any rate approaches the line of a new federal Labour Party, with the extreme reformists outside of the organisation aad the Communists inside. I think it should be made clear that any such proposal will merely create a barrier between the Communist Party and the workers. It is essential in order to bring out the independent role of the Communist Party, that while we will unite with the workers' organisations locally, there should be no question of any other Party being built up to which their minds should be directed. No intermediary Party, no mediator between the Communist Party and the working class. . . .

W. GALLACHER

(Second Session) . . . Those comrades who are opposed to the Central Committee have been continually using the phrase that the Labour Party is a third bourgeois party. That is a conclusion they draw from the political analysis. One of the C.C. members tried to draw the conclusion that, because the Labour Party was a third bourgeois party, we should drop affiliation. A few others say that the Labour Party is a third bourgeois party, but 'we do not go as far as that.' Arnot says we must make a break and make a clear and straight fight against the Labour Party along the whole front. There is not one of our opponents who is prepared to draw the conclusions from their analysis.

Comrades, if it is a third bourgeois party, and if we have to start fighting it now along the whole front, we should not wait till the election, we should start now. And the first thing to be done is to go to our comrades in the trade unions and say: 'Withdraw from this third bourgeois party.' Instead of the party going forward in the fight for affiliation, we ought to advocate the withdrawal of the trade unions from the third bourgeois party. That would be fighting on the whole front. . . .

So, it is folly to say that the Labour Party is a third bourgeois party. Certainly it is going in that direction and they are trying to take measures now to get a maximum amount of discipline. . . .

(But) if we go along and say that they are simply bourgeois candidates, members of a bourgeois party, then naturally the workers want to know why we apply for affiliation. Comrade Arnot and others say run candidates against MacDonald, Thomas, Lansbury and Purcell to show that you are against the Labour Party. But that's foolish. If you want to prove that you are against the Labour Party as a party and not only against these individuals, as traitors, then you should put candidates against ordinary candidates. . . .

But we are told 'go against MacDonald, Thomas, Purcell, etc., and it doesn't matter whether you get five or ten votes.' We are a Party; we are building up the Party; we are trying to direct the workers in their struggles. But what attracts — weakness or strength? Strength! Weakness would get you a certain kind of sympathy or pity or a sneer but it will not attract. Go where you are strong, go where you have a chance to bring the Party out, to bring the masses behind the Party.

If the Party puts up candidates and as a result of putting them up the Labour leaders should get 20,000 votes and the Party representative gets a thousand votes, you are not demonstrating strength and you are demonstrating weakness.

I say that we as a Party are faced with a situation where candidates are elected or nominated by the organised workers of a constituency, and are put forward against the candidates of the capitalist class; and when it comes to a situation of that kind, it's the business of the Party to support the nominations of the organised workers even while forcing upon the attention of the organised workers that they must accept our programme and must continually fight to force our programme upon their candidates and upon the Labour Party as a whole. . . .

APPENDIX II

Resolution of the Ninth Plenum of the Executive Committee of the Communist International on the British Question.

(The resolution was adopted unanimously and represented a political victory for the minority on the Central Committee of the British CP.)

1. The British bourgeoisie, confronted with acute international competition and chronic depression in the basic industries, will inevitably continue its policy of capitalist rationalisation, greater pressure on the working class, systematic suppression of its most class-conscious section at home and its policy of Colonial oppression, and the throttling of national liberation revolutionary movements, particularly the Labour and peasant movements. In foreign politics preparation for war against the U.S.S.R. will continue to be the main concern of the British bourgeoisie. The resistance of the working class to the policy of the dominant classes, will cause the class struggle in Great Britain to become considerably more acute.

2. The policy of the dominant classes of Great Britain is to strive to bring within the orbit of its influence the principal Labour organisations — the Labour Party and the trade unions, in spite of the determined resistance of the working class. The leaders of these organisations, who betrayed the General Strike and the Miners' Fight and helped to carry through the Trade Union Bill against the resistance of the workers, are endeavouring gradually to convert their organisations into auxiliary apparatuses of the bourgeois State and the employers' organisations.

3. This in its turn brings about a change in the intellectual outlook of these organisations and in their relationship to the political and economic machinery of the bourgeois State. Ideologically the Reformist leaders of the Labour Party and the trade unions are coming out more avowedly and cynically in favour of industrial peace and active collaboration with the capitalists against the revolutionary proletariat. Organisationally, they are endeavouring to convert the formally independent Labour organisations into auxiliary apparatuses of the bourgeoisie by merging their upper strata with the capitalist organisations. From this general orientation follows the whole series of slogans directed along the lines of support of capitalist rationalization, subordination to the anti-Trade Union Law, the tactics of liquidation and betrayal of strikes, substitution of the class struggle of the workers by Government Commissions of Enquiry and bourgeois 'arbitration' courts and other forms of working-class subjugation to the bourgeoisie.

4. This consolidation of the capitalist bourgeoisie and of Reformism is accompanied by the development of the struggle between the Right wing and the revolutionary workers, which is taking the form of a heavy attack by the Labour Party and trade union leaders upon the Left wing of the Labour

Movement, particularly upon the Communist Party, the only revolutionary party of the proletariat. From a federal organisation built up on the basis of the trade unions, the Labour Party is becoming to an increasing degree an ordinary social-democratic party, beginning more and more ruthlessly to expel from its midst even Communists and Left wing workers who represent the trade unions. The leaders of the trade unions in their turn are steadily developing a systematic attack on the Minority Movement and Communist Party workers and are pursuing a policy of victimising Communists and trying to break all connections between the Communists and the proletarian masses.

5. On the other hand, these very circumstances intensify and deepen the discontent among the broad masses of the working class, not only with the general situation in the country, but also with the Reformist policy of the official leaders of the Labour Party and the trade unions. While it would be a mistake to over-estimate the rate at which the masses are swinging to the Left it would be a still greater mistake, however, to ignore the main line of development in the British Labour Movement; the working class continues on the whole to move Leftwards, although this movement is not proceeding in a straight line, but in a zig-zag fashion. The perspective of the Labour Movement in Britain is that of class struggles of increasing acuteness accompanied by an increasingly close alliance between the reformist leaders and the bourgeoisie against revolution.

6. Under such conditions the Communist Party is faced with the imperative necessity to take advantage of the increasing swing to the Left of the masses and to adopt clearer and sharper tactics of opposition to the Labour Party and the trade union leaders in order to arouse the Left wing workers for the struggle against the bureaucracy as a means towards winning the leadership of the working class in the class struggle against capitalism. Only by bringing out more clearly and sharply its own political line which radically differs from the reformist line on all general political questions (wars, relations with the U.S.S.R., China, India, Egypt, etc.) and on the everyday struggle of the working class (against arbitration, against wage reductions, against the lengthening of the working day, against helping the capitalists in the matter of rationalisation, against industrial peace, etc.) will the Communist Party be able to strengthen its influence among the masses, and to organise the latter for the fight against capitalism and its lackeys.

7. Owing to the peculiar form of connection that exists between the trade unions and the Labour Party, the Communist Party, while not affiliated to the Labour Party, and enjoying no rights in that organisation is at the present time compelled frequently to conform to Labour Party discipline (for example: it is compelled to accept the decisions of selection conferences which select Parliamentary candidates in the name of 'organised Labour as a whole'). It is now necessary to begin a strenuous fight against this discipline

which is imposed on the Labour Movement by the Liberal-Labour bureaucracy, which suppresses the will of the workers and hampers the freedom of action of the Communist Party, by inducing local Labour Parties to call new Selection Conferences on the basis of full rights of all workers in the Labour Party, including Communists, and by calling un-official Selection Conferences when the existing local Labour Parties, dominated by the bureaucratic machine, either refuses to do so, or organises the conferences in a purely bureaucratic manner.

8. It is inexpedient as yet to abandon the slogan of affiliation to the Labour Party, as the latter has not yet definitely and completely become transformed into a Social-Democratic Party in organisational structure. The fight for affiliation, however, must be converted into an offensive fight against the treacherous leadership of the Labour Party.

9. An energetic campaign must be organised in the local trade union branches for local control of the expenditure of the political levy, in order that it may be possible to finance any candidates the rank and file of the branch may approve.

10. The general political line must be based on the premise that the Communist Party has to contend not with one camp of enemies, but with two camps: on the one hand, the Tory Party, now at the head of the Government and socially supported by the most important sections of big bourgeoisie and the landlords, and on the other hand, by an alliance of the Liberals, the upper strata of the Labour Party and of the trade unions, supported by a section of the bourgeoisie, the petty-bourgeoisie and the Labour aristocracy. It would be wrong to build our tactics on the basis of struggle against only one (the Tory) camp, though the tactics of the struggle against these enemies will be different in each case.

11. Under no circumstance can the present situation be compared with the situation as it existed in 1918-1920, when Lenin insisted on supporting the Labour Party and pushing it into power. In 1918-1920, a Labour Party Government could have played the part of the Kerensky Government with all its vacillations. Nor can the present situation be compared with that of 1922-23, when the Labour Party had in its programme demands which were sharply resisted by the capitalist class (the capital levy, unemployment, Russia). No comparison can be made with the situation in 1924 when the Government was forced to resign on two objectively revolutionary issues. A Labour Government at the present juncture will be from the very outset an obvious instrument for attacking the workers. The experience of the MacDonald Government, the betrayal of the General Strike and the Miners' Fight, the changed attitude of the Labour Party and the trade union leaders towards the question of war and relations with the U.S.S.R., China, India, and Egypt, their changed attitude on the principal domestic questions (rationalisation, the anti-Trade Union Bill, industrial peace) all this renders it necessary for the British Communist Party to come out more boldly and more

clearly as an independent political party, to change its attitude towards the Labour Party and the Labour Government and consequently to replace the slogan of the Labour Government by the slogan of the Revolutionary Workers' Government.

12. This general change in tactics of the Communist Party determines also the election tactic of the Party. During the elections the Party will act as an independent organisation, with its own platforms, slogans, etc., distinct from and opposed to all other contending forces. The Communist Party will put forward independently the largest possible number of its own candidates. It gives the fullest support to the candidates of disaffiliated Labour Parties and put up against the scab candidates of the official Labour Party. Simultaneously, the campaign for calling of new Selection Conferences by the local Labour Parites, on the basis of equal rights for Communists and Left-wingers, must be intensified. If, in spite of the workers' desire for such conferences, the Labour Party machine refuses to convene them, or does not allow Communists and Left-wing workers to participate in them, the Party must cooperate with the Left-wing workers in organising unofficial selection conferences. In those cases where the bureaucracy imposes its candidates upon the Selection Conferences, it will be the duty of the Communist Party to organise the Left wing elements of these conferences in order to put forward candidates with their help against the official candidates imposed by the bureaucracy. In some districts active support to Labourites, who pledge themselves to vote for the elementary demands of the working class and for accepting the Communist Party into the Labour Party, is admissible.

13. It is absolutely necessary to put up candidates against the leaders of the Labour Party and the General Council. The Central Committee shall immediately proceed to prepare the ground in those constituencies. In view of the fact that considerable sections of the masses still follow the reformist leaders, it is absolutely necessary to propose a united front, both nationally and locally, in order once again to expose the Labour Party, and trade union leaders who prefer unity with the Capitalists to unity with the revolutionary workers.

14. Voting for Labour Party candidates in the remaining districts (see paragraph 12) must be definitely decided upon only after all possible preliminary work has been done in the matter of putting up our own and Left worker candidates.

15. It is necessary to start immediately a broad mass campaign for the creation of a daily paper and the collection of funds necessary for same.

16. Considering the importance of the changes which have taken place in Great Britain and the importance of carrying through the new tactics in a well-organised manner, the Executive Committee of the C.P.G.B. must initiate a widespread discussion upon all problems and questions connected with those tactics.

APPENDIX III

Extracts from main Resolution of the 11th Congress of the Communist Party of Great Britain. Leeds, November 30th — December 3rd, 1929.

(This was an emergency congress – The 10th Congress having been held in the preceding January – and was called to confirm the organisational changes which had already taken place (by which Harry Pollitt became General Secretary) as well as to carry through the far reaching changes in tactics and strategy demanded by the complete acceptance of the 'New Line'. Of the newly elected CC only 12 were members of the old Committee.)

. . . The chief cause of the present critical situation of the Party is a strong opportunist tendency in the majority of the Central Committee, which interpreted the new line as being mainly a changed electoral tactic, and failed to clearly understand it as an entirely new tactical line, a struggle for the independent revolutionary leadership of the masses in all their struggles. Consequently the Party failed to rally the masses behind it because it was unable to present an alternative revolutionary leadership.

The mistakes and shortcomings of the majority of the leadership arising from this opportunist tendency are all the more glaring in view of the growing critical attitude of the membership, which was first revealed after the Ninth Plenum. The Tenth Party Congress showed clearly a new spirit of awakening amongst the membership — expressed in the delegates' criticism of the CC's policy . . .

The chief inner Party task is the struggle against the Right-wing opportunist deviation, which largely takes a concealed form, namely, voting loyally for all Comintern decisions, but carrying out the old line in practice. The old non-Bolshevik traditions must be decisively eradicated . . .

The main political task of the Party is to rally masses of workers around a programme of struggle against the Labour Government and against the so-called 'Lefts' (Maxton, Cook and Co.), binding together all the struggles into the central political fight against the Labour Government. The Party, which aims at winning over the majority of the working class, must come out as the independent leadership of the proletariat in all its struggles, leading and initiating strikes, and must give a clear political character to every fight and show their revolutionary significance. In the fight against the Social-Fascist Government, as a Government of armed attack on the Soviet Union and on the colonial revolt, the Party must mercilessly expose the pseudo-Lefts, the main prop of the MacDonald Government.

This task demands the creation of a national daily paper, for without it there can be no systematic exposure of the Labour Government and of the 'Lefts', nor will it be possible to reach masses of workers in the factories and rally them under the banner of immediate struggle in the pits and factories against the Social-Fascist Labour Government . . .

The Party must persistently expose the Labour Government's imperialist policy and brutal oppression of the colonies, create a united front of the British workers and colonial masses against the common enemy — the imperialist Labour Government, and mobilise the working class for struggle.

The Labour Government is attempting to consolidate the British Empire by winning over the landlord class and the bourgeoisie of the colonies in face of the rising tide of the colonial revolution . . .

The tactic of the united front from below is the most effective means of winning over the Left workers, and, at the same time, exposing the 'Left' reformist leaders, the most dangerous enemies of the workers. When these leaders enter united front movements their role of treachery and sabotage must be made clear to the workers and a struggle should be carried on for their expulsion, and every effort made to win over the Left workers who are under their influence.

The great majority of Left workers are not organised members of the Labour Party and the influencing of these workers in a Leftward direction and their winning for the Party is to be achieved through the formation of united front committees from below under the direct leadership of the Party. The Party, while working to initiate and bring under its influence a genuine proletarian opposition on a district and national scale to the Labour Party, must resolutely oppose the dangerous Right-wing idea that this organisation, and not the united front from below under the leadership of the Communist Party, is the chief means of rallying the masses and fighting the pseudo-Lefts. In no case should we encourage the drafting of a comprehensive programme, which suggests: (i) the possibility of reforming the Labour Party, or (ii) the possibility of carrying out a Left Socialist programme through Parliament . . .

From 'Social-Fascism' to 'People's Front'

by Brian Pearce

Between the beginning of 1933 and the middle of 1936 the international communist movement underwent one of the most startling transformations of policy in all its history. From relegation of virtually all other political trends, and especially the social-democrats of all shades and grades, to the camp of fascism, it moved to a position of seeking a broad alliance inclusive of bourgeois and even extreme right-wing groups. From abstract internationalism it swung over to the criticism of other parties for not being patriotic enough. From insistence on nothing short of a 'Revolutionary Workers' Government' it became the opponent of strikes and revolutions as inimical to the true interests of the working class. The purpose of this article is to trace briefly some of the stages in this evolution with particular reference to Britain, and to point out some of the factors responsible for it. The justification for such a study is that while there are many who appreciate the criminal folly of the Leftist phase of the communist parties, opened in 1928-29, with which my *Reasoner* pamphlet [227] mainly deals, there are as yet comparatively few who have examined critically the succeeding phase, leading through the people's front and collective security campaigns to the world war of 1939 and the Nazi onslaught on the Soviet Union in 1941. The correction of 'Left' errors is grasped but not the commission of a fresh lot of 'Right' errors — and, what is most important, the underlying continuity of the decisive determining factors is not seen.

In view of the attempt sometimes made to show that the change of policy that began in 1933 was not a sudden one but the culmination of a gradual process with roots in earlier years and broadening down from precedent to precedent in traditional British fashion, it may be as well to begin with a quotation from Idris Cox's article in the *Communist Review* of July 1935, looking back over the previous few years:

[227] 'The Communist Party and the Labour Left'.

'The campaign for the united front in Britain', he wrote, 'only commenced in real earnest after Hitler came to power, in March 1933. The manifesto of the Communist International proposing that approaches be made to the Labour Party and trade union organizations came as a surprise to the whole party, including the leadership.' This was understandable, as advocacy of the united front had been for the last three years one of the marks of the Trotskyite beast. Less than a year before, Harry Pollitt had denounced with fury the suggestion that as the capitalist crisis deepened so the gulf between the British Communists and the Independent Labour Party would be narrowed (*Which Way for the Workers?*). Now an appeal for unity had to be addressed to the ILP — and was accepted by them.

Those who hoped that the Comintern had really learnt the lesson of Germany, so that a complete overhaul of communist thought and methods would now follow, were worried by the way the radical change of approach was combined with refusal to admit the disastrous consequences of the old policy. Heckert's report to the Comintern Executive in April presented a prospect of rising waves of struggle in Germany, with revolutionary battles in the offing, and this remained official Comintern theory right through to the Thirteenth Plenum in December, when Pyatnitsky made his notorious statement that 'in spite of the incredible terror, it is easier to work among the German proletariat now'. The ineffable R.F.Andrews (Andrew Rothstein) relayed this pernicious nonsense to British Communists, assuring them that the German workers had 'retained their fighting forces still intact', that the German Communist Party had reorganized itself and was fighting better than ever before, etc.[228]

The concern to play down the consequences of the old policy naturally hindered understanding of the need to go over to a new one. It also rendered perplexing the behaviour of the Soviet Government in this period. If Hitler's victory was so incomplete and his downfall so near, was it really necessary for the Russians to fall over themselves to renew the Soviet-German friendship treaty of 1926, which had been allowed to lapse some years earlier? Here the second concealed factor was operating. What determined international Communist policy from 1933 onward was not only the utter collapse of the German Communist Party, along with all other working class organizations in Germany, but also the extreme weakness of the USSR, caused by the

[228] Articles in *Labour Monthly*, April 1933, and *Communist Review*, May 1933.

economic, social and political crisis resulting from Stalin's 'complete collectivization in five years'. Neither of these factors could be publicly admitted — hence the new round of lies and prevarications which accompanied the change of policy, hindering and ultimately distorting it.

In the initial stages of the new policy there was no question of any bloc with sections of the capitalist class or of substituting 'anti-fascism' for socialism. Some of the Communist leaders would doubtless have been astonished and indignant had they been told in 1933 what they were to say and write in 1936 and after! On the other hand, from the standpoint of 1936 some pretty ghastly Trotskyism was being put out in 1933 by, for example, R.P. Dutt. ('Only the united working-class front can defeat the offensive of fascism. The victory of the united working-class front leads the way forward to the victory of the workers' revolution' — *Labour Monthly*, May 1933. 'The fight against modern imperialist war can only be revolutionary civil war; any other supposed alternative can only mean in practice unity with imperialism' — *Ibid.*, August 1933). The ideas being canvassed in right-wing Labour circles that in view of Hitler's victory in Germany the traditional (and around this time strongly reaffirmed) attitude of British socialists towards war ought to be modified, met with particular scorn. Should a war break out between fascist Germany and fascist Poland, wrote J.R.Campbell (*Labour Monthly*, September 1933), the workers in each of these countries should fight against their own government, and workers elsewhere should oppose participation in the war. To talk of referring such a dispute to the League of Nations would be absurd, as this was dominated by Poland's allies. Communists must expose the attempt being made 'to convince the workers of France and Britain that their heavily-armed imperialist governments, because they have up to this moment preserved parliamentary institutions, are peace-loving and must be supported in any war waged against the countries of dictatorship.' It was all very well to howl at Hitler as a threat to peace, but were not French troops harrying Morocco and British aircraft bombing the North West Frontier tribesmen? (editorial, *Communist Review*, October 1933).[229]

[229] Cf. R. F. Andrews: 'We may justifiably ask, is the Hitler dictatorship any worse than British rule in India?' — *The Truth about Trotsky* (February 1934), defending Soviet continuance of trade relations with Germany after Hitler's victory. (A typical Aunt Sally, incidentally, as Trotsky never called for a Soviet boycott of Germany in this period, pointing out that Stalin had so weakened the USSR that such a measure would probably harm Soviet interests more than Nazi Germany's.)

Of particular interest, in view of the emergence of the 'People's Front' line not so long afterwards and the conflict with other sections of the working class movement to which it gave rise, is Dutt's critique (*Labour Monthly,* October 1933) of those social-democrats who, observing the substantial support won by fascism among the petty bourgeoisie, concluded from this the need to 'learn from fascism, that the workers' movement must adapt itself to the petty bourgeoisie, must drop the narrow working-class basis, broaden its basis, take on a "national" character, etc'. Against such views Dutt maintained that 'it is just the strong independent, fearless leadership and fight of the working class which is able to draw the petty bourgeoisie in its wake'.

At this point it should be mentioned that after the first panic reaction to Hitler's victory, the Comintern had recovered its old aplomb — once Hitler had shown that, for the time being at any rate, he was ready to remain on friendly terms with the USSR. (D.N.Pritt was later to argue, in *Light on Moscow,* 1939, that 1933 was a year of close and growing friendship between Russia and Germany, which the former unselfishly sacrificed in order to make friends with the Western powers. This argument served Pritt's need of the moment, to furnish a 'justification' for the Ribbentrop-Molotov Pact, but proved embarrassing later, when it was necessary to depict 1933 as a year of intensifying menace from Germany towards Russia, in order to provide thereby a 'safe' explanation of Stalin's alleged rise to dictatorial power in that year.) The old nonsense about 'social-fascism' was revived,[230] and nowhere except in Britain was there any substantial progress in actually achieving a united front — while here it was confined to relations with the ILP, and the content of these relations increasingly became reduced to a struggle by King Street against 'Trotskyism' in the ILP. In particular, the anti-Labour Party line at elections continued unchanged. The West London Sub-District Congress denounced as Trotskyist a proposal by Chelsea Communists to 'direct the party back into the situation of critical support' of the Labour Party.[231]

February 1934 saw the opening of a new phase with the attempted fascist *coup d'état* in France. So late as January 24 the Central Committee of the French Communist Party had rejected the idea of offering a

---

230 See, e.g., Whalley's article in *Labour Monthly,* February 1934, and Gallacher's pamphlet, *Pensioners of Capitalism.*

231 *Communist Review,* December 1933, January 1934.

united front to the Socialists, as this would only 'foster illusions' about the latter. At first the Communist leadership in France tried to join in the fascist attack on the Radical Government (somewhat in the spirit of the 'Red-Brown Referendum' in Prussia in 1931),[232] but the spontaneous rallying of Communist and Socialist workers in unity against the fascist bands compelled them to manoeuvre. It was only a matter of manoeuvring however: though the communists officially supported the general strike against fascism, as soon as the immediate danger was past Thorez was once more fulminating against advocates of the united front (April 13, 1934).

Though not immediate as it had been in February, the danger of a fascist victory in France, perhaps leading to a Franco-German alliance, was now, however, always a possibility. The workers had been crushed in Austria and a Bonapartist type of régime installed which might well prove a mere transition to Nazi conquest. What seems to have finally decided Stalin to make a definite turn in the direction in which, since March 1933, only gestures and half-measures had been the rule, was Hitler's 'second *coup d'état*', on June 30, 1934, when the so-called Nazi Left (Roehm and the storm-troop leaders) were massacred. Trotsky had noted signs of Comintern wishful thinking about these people and their prospects as far back as June 1933 (*How Long Can Hitler Stay?*). Serious hope of conflict in the fascist camp had replaced the former denial of conflict between social-democracy and fascism. Ironically recalling a famous pronouncement of Stalin's, Trotsky commented: 'Reformists and fascists are twins; but a disappointed fascist and a fascist who has climbed into power are antipodes.' Nothing would come of this hope, he warned: Hitler would bribe or crush 'the refractory praetorians' and 'to expect an independent revolutionary initiative from this source [was] quite out of the question'. Following the Night of the Long Knives, Stalin appears to have decided that Hitler had come to stay and was growing dangerously powerful, and that it was necessary to proceed through the organization of 'pressure' upon Germany to induce Hitler to come to terms with him. To this Grand Design the tactics of the international communist movement were thenceforth increasingly subordinated.

The immediate effects seemed positive in so far as the task of forming a united front with the social-democrats was now taken up far

---

[232] See, e.g., Jellinek's article in *Labour Monthly*, March 1934.

more seriously than before. Thorez abandoned his April line, made a direct appeal to the French Socialists, and in July signed a pact with them. The Soviet Union's entry into the League of Nations, in September, marked the clearest expression yet of Stalin's departure from the traditional foreign policy of the October Revolution and move towards alignment with one imperialist combination against another. Shortly afterwards, in the last months of 1934, a bewilderingly rapid change came over British Communist policy towards the Labour Party. The right-wing leadership of that party had, during the first half of 1934, moved rapidly away from the anti-war position taken by the Labour Party conference in 1933, and in June had come out with a statement in favour of support for a British capitalist government in the event of war with fascist Germany. This had offered a most respectable pretext for intensified denunciation of the Labour Party by the Communists. Now, however, without any inner-party discussion, on the very eve of the London municipal elections, Communist candidates were suddenly withdrawn from contests with Labour, and in the *Communist Review* for December Pollitt called for reconsideration of the party's approach to the question of 'a third Labour Government'.

Already at this time voices were heard saying that the Communist Party was doing the right thing (belatedly) for the wrong reasons, and that the practical implications of this would be seen in attempts by the communists, in objective alliance with the right-wing Labour leaders, to break down Left Labour opposition to imperialist war. Just because of these warnings, communist publicists redoubled their assurances that this was not so at all. 'R.F. Andrews', in the *Labour Monthly* for November, attacked the view that peace could be ensured by co-operation between governments instead of workers' revolution, and sneered at those who put confidence in the League of Nations ('59 capitalist governments and one Soviet government'). 'The enemy is in our own country, we reply with Karl Liebknecht. . . . If we carry on a revolutionary struggle against imperialist war in Britain, we shall help the heroic German workers themselves to smash the brownshirts.' In his pamphlet (now rare) *The Labour Party and the Menace of War*, published about this time, the same writer insisted that if Germany were to attack Russia and then Britain attacked Germany, the British workers must oppose such a war and fight to overthrow their own government. This would be the best help they could render their Russian comrades. R.P.Dutt, in the *Labour Monthly* of January 1935, similarly warned against any refurbishing of imperialist 'national defence' under the guise of 'defence of democracy against fascism'. 'We need more than ever to warn the workers *never* to become entangled in the lines of imperialist policies, but to judge every question of war and peace solely from the standpoint of the working-class revolution.' Soviet participation in the League no more changed the League's character than Communist participation in Parliament changed the character of Parliament. It was in 'the revolutionary struggle' that there lay 'the final decision of the issues of war and peace'. To support the British Government in conflict with Germany would 'confirm the Nazi propaganda of the vanity of working-class internationalism'.

The month of February 1935 saw the British Communist Party at a high point in its fortunes — the highest since 1926. At the party congress held in that month it was shown that membership had increased considerably and that members were no longer mostly unemployed, but on the contrary mostly held positions in their trade unions. During the second half of 1934 the party had raised its morale and enhanced its prestige by a successful campaign against the Mosley fascists. A detailed programme was adopted by the congress for socialist construction in a Britain ruled by workers' councils, following a revolution (*For Soviet Britain!*), and the congress resolution recognized the working-class united front as the way forward, leading to the defeat of the National Government and the election of a Labour Government, and so the provision of conditions for the advance to workers' power. While it was recognized that broad sections of the petty bourgeoisie should be drawn into anti-fascist struggle behind the leadership of the working class, there were no illusions about any section of the capitalist class or any of the capitalist political groups; in his speech to the congress Pollitt singled out the Churchill trend in the Tory Party as a specially dangerous source of the threat of fascism. February 1935 saw the tremendous demonstrations against cuts in unemployment relief payments which forced the Government to restore these cuts and made *The Times* write of 'the spirit of 1926' being abroad again. In by-elections the Labour vote shot up above the record 1929 level. Trade union membership recorded the first increase since 1930. R.P.Dutt had every justification for writing in the *Labour Monthly* for March: 'The united front is advancing and we need already to be looking forward to the next stages of the fight.' His

March 1935 preface to the second edition of his book *Fascism and Social Revolution* still put forward 'working-class revolution' as the answer to fascism: 'bourgeois democracy breeds fascism', and what is needed is 'revolution before fascism and preventing fascism'.

Like 1926 the year 1935 stands out as a year of 'might-have-been' in the history of the revolutionary workers' movement in Britain. To understand how the Communist Party helped the right-wing Labour leaders to make 1935 end with a resounding election victory for the Tories it is necessary to look overseas again.

In the opening months of the year the French Communists were vigorously campaigning along with Left Socialists against the proposal to increase the military service period to two years. In April, however, a delegation from the Komsomol visited Paris. They held talks with the leadership of the French socialist youth which were later published by Fred Zeller, one of the participants (in *The Road for Revolutionary Socialists*). The Soviet spokesman Chemodanov explained that there was danger of a German attack on the USSR and that if it came French socialists must march against Germany. 'If, in this period, you make your revolution in France, you are traitors.' On May 2 France and the USSR signed a treaty of mutual assistance, and on May 15 Stalin and Laval issued a joint communiqué which read, in part: 'M.Stalin understands and fully approves the national defence policy of France in keeping her armed forces at the level required for security.' Commenting on this declaration, Trotsky wrote:

> The French workers are forced every day to enter into agreements with the capitalists, so long as the latter continue to exist. A workers' state cannot renounce the right which every trade union has. But should a trade union leader, upon signing a collective agreement, announce publicly that *he recognizes and approves* capitalist property, we would call such a leader a traitor. Stalin did not merely conclude a practical agreement, but on top and independent of that, he approved the growth of French militarism. Every class-conscious worker knows that the French army exists primarily to safeguard the property of a handful of exploiters, and to support the rule of bourgeois France over sixty million colonial slaves. Because of the just indignation aroused in the workers' ranks by Stalin's declaration, attempts are being made today . . . to explain that 'in practice' everything remains just as before. But we on our part do not put an iota of trust in them. The voluntary and demonstrative approval of French militarism by Stalin, one must suppose, was not intended to enlighten the French bourgeoisie, who did not at all need any urging and who met it quite ironically. Stalin's declaration could have had only one single aim: weakening the opposition

> of the French proletariat to its own imperialism in order to buy at this price the confidence of the French bourgeoisie in the stability of an alliance with Moscow.

When Lenin made his famous pact with the French military mission in 1918 he issued no declarations of solidarity with imperialist France, which would have disorientated the anti-war movement of the French workers — though Soviet Russia's position then was far more dangerous than in 1935. Now, however, 'for defence of the USSR the bureaucracy places its hopes in its political skill, in Litvinov's diplomacy, and in military alliances with France and Czechoslovakia, but not in the revolutionary proletariat. On the contrary, it fears that the French or Czech workers might, by inopportune action, frighten the new allies. It sets itself the task of putting the brake on the class struggle of the proletariat in "allied" countries.'

The consequences of the Stalin-Laval declaration soon made themselves felt in France. In the previous October, soon after Russia's entry into the League, Thorez had called for a broadening of the Socialist-Communist united front into a 'People's Front' with the Radicals, but the implications of this alliance with a capitalist party only now became fully obvious. Strikes which broke out in the summer of 1935 at the dockyards of Brest and Toulon were opposed by the Communists as the work of 'fascist-Trotskyist provocateurs'. Within a few weeks the British Communists adjusted their line in accordance with developments in France. At a conference called by the *Labour Monthly* in May George Allison was still saying:

> We must be absolutely clear that under no circumstances can we support any kind of war that is waged by British imperialism. Even if circumstances force British imperialism into going into war alongside the Soviet Union, this would not alter the fact that British imperialism was waging a war to defend its Empire . . . We must make it clear that the working class can stage the fight against war, and in the process can actually stage the war against capitalism, which is actually the cause of all wars.

But in the August *Communist Review* J.R.Campbell was already raising the question: 'Can we argue that the proletariat's attitude to a war in which its bourgeoisie (for its own interests) is co-operating with the Soviet Union is the same as the attitude of the proletariat in a country which is attacking the Soviet Union?' — and answering it in the negative.

The Seventh (and last) World Congress of the Communist International, held in July and August 1935, had for its essential task the generalization on the world scale of the development which had taken place in France. 'The congress is important', wrote Trotsky, 'because it marks — after a period of vacillation and fumbling — the final entry of the Comintern into its "Fourth Period"[233] which has for its slogan: "Power to Daladier!", for its banner the Tricolour and for its anthem the Marseillaise, drowning the *Internationale*.' From a means of struggle against capitalism the tactic of the united front had been perverted into a means of coalition with part of the bourgeoisie at the expense of the workers. The *Gleichschaltung* of the various Communist Parties followed rapidly in the weeks succeeding the world congress. Reporting on the congress in the October *Labour Monthly*, Pollitt affirmed that defence of the Soviet Union must mean support of 'everything that the Soviet Union does in its foreign policy'. If war should break out between Germany and Czechoslovakia, the communists must support the Czech ruling class. As regards the Italian attack on Abyssinia which had been in progress since early in the year, 'we must force economic and military sanctions if necessary'. (This was a particularly interesting development, as the Communists had been opposing a campaign for an international trade union boycott of Italy — which would have involved the Soviet trade unions in stopping the flow of Russian oil to the fascists — and the Seventh World Congress had been strangely quiet on the Italo-Abyssinian War. Litvinov's attempts to woo Italy had apparently reached an impasse and there was need for a bit of pressure to be organized from Britain and France).

Pollitt's open call for 'military sanctions if necessary', i.e., for war with Italy, at once split the Left forces in the British working class movement. At the Labour Party conference in October the anti-war element, whose chief spokesman at that time was Cripps, found themselves confronted by a tacit alliance of the Right with those who took their line from the Communist Party. It was amid the confusion and mutual recrimination caused by the Communist change of line that Baldwin held the General Election that gave Britain another spell of Tory Government, sufficient to take her into war and to the brink of disaster. What would have been unthinkable in February — a majority for the Tories — was accomplished in November. While the major

---

[233] The reference is to the 'Third Period' announced by the Sixth World Congress in 1928 (and never explicitly wound up). This was to have been a period of the ending of capitalist stabilization, of a new round of wars and revolutions, with social-democracy fully transformed into social-fascism.

responsibility for making this possible probably rests on the right-wing Labour leaders, some share must certainly be borne by the Communist Party. The masses appear to have reasoned in the usual way: if both sides are advocating Tory policy, that's a sound argument for voting Tory.

In the period of the 1935 General Election the communists completed their return to their pre-1928 relationship with the Labour Party by withdrawing all of their own candidates (except two) and giving active help to Labour candidates, and by applying again for affiliation to the Labour Party. Left socialists who had regretted the self-isolation of the Communist Party after 1928 and worked to bring Communists and Labour together again viewed this development with mixed feelings: in what sense would the admission of this pro-sanctions party strengthen the forces of revolutionary Marxism in the ranks of Labour? The degeneration of the Communist leaders was indeed rapid in the early months of 1936. In the *Labour Monthly* for February we find Gallacher jeering at Cripps for 'the usual "Left" phrases, about war being inevitable under capitalism, that all capitalist States were the same, and until we got socialism we could not get out of war . . . this confused jumble which was all directed towards weakening support for the League of Nations and Collective Peace.'

Stalin's interview with Roy Howard (March 1, 1936) struck a new, even lower, keynote for the period now opening. In this interview Stalin abandoned all pretence of Marxist analysis of the international situation, substituting for class concepts those of 'the friends of peace' and 'the enemies of peace'. And when asked about the Soviet Union's 'plans and intentions for bringing about a world revolution', he replied that 'we never had such plans and intentions' — the idea that they had was 'a tragi-comic misunderstanding'. This categorical repudiation of his own as well as Lenin's declarations regarding the Soviet State's attitude to the revolutionary movement abroad[234] dotted the i's and crossed the t's of the Stalin-Laval communiqué.

---

[234] E.g., in the original (April 1924) version of his *Foundations of Leninism*, Stalin had written that 'the fostering of revolution, the support of revolution, in other countries, is incumbent upon the countries where the revolution has triumphed'. This had merely confirmed Lenin's statement of 1915 that the proletariat of a country where the revolution had won would 'rise against the capitalist world, attracting the oppressed classes of other countries, raising among them revolts against the capitalists, launching, in case of need, armed forces against the exploiting classes and their States.'

Commenting on Stalin's declaration, Trotsky observed that while such a treaty as the Franco-Soviet alliance might well be inevitable, 'there is not the slightest need to call black white and to rebaptize bloody brigands as "friends of peace" '. The French bourgeoisie would not cease to criticize the Soviet Union from their own point of view just because they had signed a treaty with it, and their example ought to be copied. Such great actions of the Soviet people as the aid given to the Chinese revolution in 1924-27 and to the British strikers in 1926 could not be struck out of history by references to 'tragi-comic misunderstandings'. The bourgeoisie would never forget them, though Stalin might succeed in making the world's workers forget them, to the peril of the Soviet Union. But it was full of sinister significance that the Soviet bureaucracy was coming out so openly as the opponent of revolution in the capitalist countries — 'socialism in a single country' was being interpreted to imply 'revolution in a single country'. One might suppose that the Soviet leaders actually *feared* the rise of a mighty revolutionary movement in the capitalist world.

Stalin had included in his Howard interview a formal, vestigial reference to capitalism and imperialism. Even this was omitted from the address given by Ambassador Maisky to the Fabian Society a fortnight or so later.

> The problem of peace in our time (he said) is primarily a problem of creating on the basis of collective security a firm and well-knit 'peace front' including all those powers which, for whatever motive (there is no need to analyse motives at the moment), desire peace and not war. If such a 'front' is really created, if in a short space of time it is transformed into a serious force, capable in case of extremity of talking to the agressor in a language of tanks and machine guns, the peril of a new world war will be postponed for a very considerable period of time, maybe even for a whole generation.

In April, in France, the 'classical' country of the People's Front, Thorez made an election broadcast offering his hand to the fascist *Croix de Feu* on a 'patriotic', anti-German basis — a hint of what was to come later in Britain in relation to the Churchill Tories in whom Pollitt had not so long before seen one of the sources of the fascist danger. In June, when the French workers swept forward in a tremendous wave of stay-in strikes that recalled Italy in 1920, the Communists called them back ('one must know when to end a strike') and settled for some wage increases which were soon cancelled out by the devaluation of the franc. This was the first instance of the people's front policy bringing the Communists into opposition to the workers' revolutionary strivings on a nation-wide scale. (Soon afterward an even starker spectacle of the same order was to be seen in Spain, where in July and the succeeding months the Communists prevented the carrying through of the workers' revolution and in effect ensured the ultimate triumph of Franco.)

Devoting his *Labour Monthly* Notes of the Month of June to the People's Front, Dutt drew attention to the appearance of an English edition of Thorez's book on the subject. Cautiously, he still emphasized that in British conditions transforming the Labour Party was the key to achieving results comparable to those obtained by the People's Front in France, and pointed out that the Liberal Party was 'a party of sections of the big bourgeoisie, not a party of the petty bourgeoisie comparable to the French Radical Party'. (Trotsky had warned only shortly before that it would be fatal to identify the Radical Party with the middle classes, who were increasingly losing faith in it, and for good reason. 'The People's Front, the conspiracy between the labour bureaucracy and the worst political exploiters of the middle classes, is capable only of killing the faith of the masses in the revolutionary road and of driving them into the arms of the fascist counter-revolution.') By the time the *Labour Monthly* for August was being put together, however, greater clarity had been achieved, or perhaps just greater boldness decided on, and William Rust wrote of the need to bring the Liberals into the British People's Front — this, incidentally, in an article regretting that the workers had shown little interest in the People's Front idea and had even expressed concern lest propaganda for it should 'distract attention from the drive for the workers' united front'. The proposal to create a front embracing the Liberals — and it will be remembered that the Communists went so far as to call on the workers to vote Liberal against Labour in the Aylesbury by-election in 1938 — was indeed a strange one to make in British conditions and perhaps did more than anything else to confirm the suspicion in Left Labour circles that cynical motives quite remote from the interests of the working-class movement were at work in determining Communist policy. (Trotsky, writing some years later, gave it as his view that 'the essence of the matter is that the Labour Party's policy is too radical for the Kremlin. An alliance of Communists with Labour might bring in a certain nuance of anti-imperialism, which would hinder the *rapprochement* between Moscow and London. Having the Liberals within the People's Front means a direct and immediate veto by imperialism over the actions of the workers' parties.')[235]

The middle months of 1936 close the period of transition with which this article is concerned, and open that in which the finished and hardened People's Front policy was tested, so leading on inexorably to the next major historical period — that of the war of 1939-45. It is probably not coincidental that mid-1936 saw not only the most open and thorough betrayal yet of the international workers' revolutionary movement but also the beginning of the wave of 'anti-Trotsky' frame-up trials in the Soviet Union. The foreign policy (including Comintern policy) of the Soviet bureaucracy and its home policy have always been closely interrelated.[236]

---

[235] The 1936-39 period was to see the dismantling of communist-directed anti-imperialist organizations and a change in the party line on self-determination for the colonies which brought Communists into sharp conflict with fighters for national independence (French North Africa providing the classic example).

[236] The nationalist propaganda and substitution of the 'people' concept for class concepts which the French, Czechoslovak and to some extent the British communists took up in 1935-36, on the basis of 'anti-fascism', had a curious precedent. In 1931-32 the German Communist Party, in a desperate attempt to compete with the Nazis by some method other than the workers' united front, had gone in for German nationalism and the 'people's revolution'. The Nazis were said to be preparing to sell out to French imperialism — seen as the chief danger to the German workers (cf. R. P. Dutt in *Labour Monthly*, August 1931 and January 1932), and the German communists came forward as the 'true patriots' who would lead a struggle of the whole people to 'break the chains of Versailles'. The communist papers made a tremendous fuss of some officers who came over from the Nazis to the Communist Party on a nationalist basis (see, e.g., the article by one of them, Lieutenant Scheringer, in *Labour Monthly* for May 1931). This only antagonized the genuine Left and internationalist elements among the social-democrats, while not in the long run weakening the Nazis, who could always outbid the communists at this game. One of the nationalist officers 'converted' to communism, Major Ciesecke, is said to have handed over to Hitler a complete list of the personnel of the Communist Party's underground military organization, who were all arrested immediately after the Nazis came to power, so paralysing any resistance that might have been made. Trotsky's contemporary comment on this phase of German communist policy is interesting. 'These wretched revolutionists, in a conflict with any serious enemy, think first of all of how to imitate him, how to repaint themselves in his colours and how to win the masses by means of a smart trick and not by a revolutionary struggle. . .Of course every great revolution is a people's or national revolution in the sense that it unites around the revolutionary class all the virile and creative forces of the nation and reconstructs the nation around a new core. But this is not a slogan, it is a sociological description of the revolution, which requires, moreover, precise and concrete definitions. But as a slogan, it is inane and charlatanish, market-competition with the fascists, paid for at the price of injecting confusion into the minds of the workers.'

The British Stalinists and the Moscow Trials

by Brian Pearce

> Foreigners little realize how vital it was for Stalin in 1936, 1937 and 1938 to be able to declare that the British, American, French, German, Polish, Bulgarian and Chinese communists unanimously supported the liquidation of the 'Trotskyite, fascist mad dogs and wreckers' . . .(W. G. Krivitsky, *I was Stalin's Agent,* 1939, p. 79.)
>
> These apologists for Stalin will one day regret their hasty zeal, for truth, breaking a path through every obstacle, will carry away many reputations. (L. D. Trotsky, *Les Crimes de Staline,* 1937, p. 62.)

Twenty years ago there took place the trial of Bukharin and twenty others, the third and largest of a series of three historic State trials in the Soviet Union. Like the fraction of the iceberg that shows above the water's surface, these trials were the publicly-paraded fraction of a vast mass of repressions carried out in 1936-1938 by Yagoda and Yezhov under the supreme direction of Stalin. It is not the purpose of this article to examine the trials themselves or to discuss their causes and consequences for the Soviet Union and the international working-class movement. Its purpose is merely to recall how the leaders and spokesmen of the Stalinist organization in Britain reacted to the trials and what some of the effects of their reaction were in the British working-class movement, so that lessons may be learned regarding the political character of the organization and the individuals concerned.

The First Trial

The first of the three great 'public' trials took place in August 1936. Immediately upon the publication of the indictment, the *Daily Worker* came out with an editorial (August 17) accepting the guilt of the accused men: 'The revelations . . .will fill all decent citizens with loathing and hatred . . .Crowning infamy of all is the evidence showing how they were linked up with the Nazi Secret Police . . .' This instantaneous and whole-hearted endorsement of whatever Stalin's policemen chose to allege at at any given moment was to prove characteristic of the British Stalinist reaction to each of the successive trials.

The prototype of another statement which was to re-appear regularly throughout this period figured in the *Daily Worker's* editorial of August 22: 'The extent and organization of the plot, with its cold-blooded killings of the leaders of the international working class, has shocked the Labour and socialist movement of the world.' In reality, of course, the effect of the trial was to compromise the Soviet Union in the eyes of many workers and to play into the hands of the most right-wing sections. Accordingly, a third 'keynote' had to be sounded right from the beginning, with the headline in the *Daily Worker* of August 24 to the report that the International Federation of Trade Unions had asked the Soviet authorities to allow a foreign lawyer to defend the accused: 'Citrine Sides with the Traitors'. On the other hand, any expression of approval for the trial by a bourgeois newspaper or other 'source' was to be eagerly seized upon and publicized during these years, and already in this issue we find *The Observer* quoted, in a special 'box', as saying: 'It is futile to think the trial was staged and the charges trumped up.'[237]

---

[237] This was the issue with the editorial headed: 'Shoot the Reptiles!' Commenting on it, the *New Statesman* of August 29 remarked prophetically: 'Those who shoot them today may be themselves shot as reptiles at the next turn of the wheel.' (This was to be the fate of Yagoda, head of the NKVD at the time of the first trial, shot in 1938.) It was presumably by an oversight that the *Daily Worker* never quoted the verses which graced the August 29 issue of the Paris White Guard paper *Vozrozhdenye* following the announcement of the executions after the first trial.

> We thank thee, Stalin!
> Sixteen scoundrels,
> Sixteen butchers of the Fatherland
> Have been gathered to their ancestors!...
> Today the sky looks blue,
> Thou hast repaid us for the sorrows of many years!
>
> But why only sixteen?
> Give us forty,
> Give us hundreds,
> Thousands;
> Make a bridge across the Moscow river,
> A bridge without towers or beams,
> A bridge of Soviet carrion —
> And add thy carcass to the rest!

With the minimum of delay the implications of the trials for current politics began to be drawn, especially with regard to Spain. The *Daily Worker* leader of August 25 affirmed that 'Trotsky . . .whose agents are trying to betray the Spanish Republic by advancing provocative "Left" slogans . . .is the very spearpoint of counter-revolution', and the next day J. R. Campbell had an article comparing Zinoviev to Franco. At the same time, a programme of re-writing the history of the Bolshevik Party and the October Revolution was launched with an article by Ralph Fox in the *Daily Worker* of August 28, entitled 'Trotsky was no Great General', followed by another on September 1, 'He was always a Base Double-Crosser'.[238] A Communist Party pamphlet *The Moscow Trial,* by W. G. Shepherd, carried the retrospective smear campaign further, telling readers that in October 1917 'the organization leadership was not, as is sometimes supposed, in (Trotsky's) hands . . .He was a bad organizer.' The main point of this pamphlet, however, was squarely to identify 'Trotskyists' with police agents.

Shepherd based himself in his defence of the trial upon the declarations of D. N. Pritt, KC ('None can challenge either Mr. Pritt's integrity or his competence to understand the significance of court procedure and the value of evidence'), and indeed the importance of these cannot be exaggerated in assessing how this trial and its successors were 'sold' to the Left in Britain.

Mr. Pritt made two principal contributions to the propaganda for the August 1936 trial. He wrote the preface to the pamphlet *The Moscow Trial,* 1936, a report of the proceedings published by the Anglo-Russian Parliamentary Committee (secretary, W. P. Coates). This report *omitted* from the testimony of Holtzman, one of the accused, his reference to a meeting in a non-existent 'Hotel Bristol' in Copenhagen, a slip in the 'libretto' which had been widely remarked upon. (Compare p. 49 of this pamphlet with p. 100 of the English version of the *Report of Court Proceedings. Case of the Trotskyite-Zinovievite Terrorist Centre,* Moscow 1936.) 'Once again,' wrote Pritt, 'the more faint-hearted socialists are beset with doubt and anxieties,' but 'once again we can feel confident that when the smoke has rolled away from the battle-field of controversy it will be realized that the

---

[238] Fox did not live — he was killed in Spain a few months later — to reflect on the fate of two of the persons whom he named in this article as examples of how there were still plenty of Old Bolsheviks around and loyal to Stalin: 'Bubnov, Stasova and Krestinsky continue to hold important and honourable places in the leadership of the Soviet State.'

charge was true, the confessions correct, and the prosecution fairly conducted . . . But in order that public opinion shall reach this verdict . . . it must be properly informed of the facts; and it is here that this little book will be of such value.' Pritt also wrote a pamphlet of his own, *The Zinoviev Trial,* in which he dealt with the suspicion some sceptics had expressed that the confessions might not be entirely spontaneous — might, indeed, be influenced by torture or intimidation of some sort. The abjectness of the confessions was 'sufficiently explained when one bears in mind the very great differences in form and style that naturally exist between one race and another. . . . In conversations I have held in Soviet prisons with accused persons awaiting trial on substantial charges, I have not infrequently been struck by the readiness with which they have stated to me in the presence of warders that they are guilty and cannot complain if they are punished.' And anyway, after all, accused persons often plead guilty when they see 'the evidence against them is overwhelming'. True, no evidence was actually produced at the trial other than the confessions of the accused; but 'it is no part of the duty of the judicial authorities to publish reports showing exactly how they have conducted preliminary investigations of which the persons who are at once most interested and best informed, viz., the accused, make no complaint.' Actually, 'one can well imagine that the Soviet Government, so far as concerns the point of view of properly informing foreign criticism, would much have preferred that all or most of the accused should have pleaded Not Guilty and contested the case. The full strength of the case would then have been seen and appraised. . . .'

What strikes one most forcibly in re-reading today the literature of the first trial is the complete silence of the British Stalinists about some of the most contradictory and question-begging of its features. Not only the famous Hotel Bristol — the even more famous Café Bristol was not 'discovered' until February 1937 — but many other, less 'technical', points were passed over. Molotov was conspicuously missing from the list of the 'leaders of party and State' whom Zinoviev and Co. were accused of plotting to murder — and from the ceremonial list of these leaders included by Vyshinsky in his closing speech — though he was the nominal head of the Soviet Government at the time. (Alexander Orlov, a former NKVD officer, tells us in his book *The Secret History of Stalin's Crimes,* 1954, p. 81, that the dictator, who wished to frighten Molotov a little, personally struck out his name from the list of 'intended victims of the conspiracy'!)[239] Nor did they refer back later on, when Kossior and Postyshev were put away as 'Ukrainian bourgeois-nationalists', to their presence among the leaders whose deaths had allegedly been demanded by Rudolf Hess, through Trotsky. Nobody questioned the consistency of accusing Trotsky of being a fascist while stating (Smirnov's last plea, *Report of Court Proceedings*, pp. 171-2) that he regarded the Soviet Union as 'a fascist State'. Nobody suggested that it was somewhat premature of N. Lurye to get himself sent into Russia *by the Gestapo* in April 1932 (*ibid*., pp. 102-3); or that Trotsky had shown curious tactlessness in choosing five Jews — Olberg, Berman-Yurin, David and the two Luryes[240] — to collaborate with the Gestapo. That Holtzman testified to meeting Trotsky's son Sedov in Copenhagen whereas Olberg said he had not managed to get there (*ibid.*, pp. 87, 100) excited no surprise. Above all, the complete unconcern of the Prosecutor about these and other contradictions and oddities in the confessions, which he made no attempt to sort out, was matched by a corresponding unconcern among the British Stalinists.[241] Like Vyshinsky, too, they gave no sign of finding it suspicious that the treasonable intrigues of the 'Trotskyites', dating from 1931, had been carried on exclusively with Germany, no role having been played, apparently, by Britain, France, Poland or Italy. (As Trotsky observed, these 'terrorists' might make an attempt on Stalin's life, but never on Litvinov's diplomacy.)

[239] As soon as Molotov had made up his quarrel with Stalin, defendants began confessing to plots against him so far back as 1934 (Muralov, Shestov, Arnold, in the trial of January 1937) of which nothing had been said in the confessions of August 1936. Trotsky commented: 'The conclusions are absolutely clear: the defendants had as little freedom in their choice of "victims" as in all other respects.'

[240] It was Moisei Lurye, incidentally, writing under the pseudonym 'Alexander Emel', who wrote in *Inprecorr* (German edition), November 15, 1932, that 'in Pilsudski's Poland Trotsky enjoys the particular sympathy of the political police'. Cf. J. Klugmann: 'The secret police of the Polish dictatorship were specially educated in Trotskyism....' (*From Trotsky to Tito* [1951], p. 82.)

[241] Contrast the earnest efforts of Christian apologists to reconcile the contradictions and differences between the various Gospels. Anyone approaching the study of the August 1936 trial for the first time is recommended to notice the following points. Ter-Vaganian stated that the terrorist group was formed in autumn 1931 and Zinoviev that it began in summer 1932, while Mrachkovsky made it date from the end of 1932. In November 1932 Kamenev and Zinoviev had been banished to the East and were not allowed back until the middle of 1935 onwards, so could hardly have participated effectively in the plot to kill Kirov (December 1934). Berman-Yurin dated the Seventh Congress of the Comintern in September 1934 (it took place in July-August 1935), and explained that a plot to kill Stalin at a Comintern executive meeting failed because

Jack Cohen, in those days responsible for the political education of Communist students, contributed to the party monthly *Discussion* for September 1936 a piece on 'Heroes of Fascism and Counter-Revolution' in which he asserted that in 1933 Trotsky had issued a call for 'terrorist acts to "remove" the party leaders', in an article in the *Weltbühne* which actually speaks not of terrorism but of a workers' revolution against the bureaucracy. (Neither Cohen nor any of the other Stalinists ever quoted, of course, from Trotsky's numerous writings condemning terrorism as useless and harmful, as 'bureaucratism turned inside-out', such as *The Kirov Assassination* [1935].) Pat Sloan, of the Friends of the Soviet Union (now British-Soviet Friendship Society), wrote in the *New Statesman* of September 5: 'I do not see what was unconvincing in the Moscow trial.'[242] Walter Holmes, in his 'Worker's Notebook' in the *Daily Worker* of September 4, told of a conversation with 'members of the Labour Party' who reassured him: 'What are you worrying about? . . . Everybody in our party has got enough sense to know they ought to be shot.' Reg Bishop, however, admitted in *Inprecorr* of September 5 that Labour was not quite so solidly convinced on this point: 'The Labour *Daily Herald* vies in venom and spite with the *Daily Mail*. . . . It is pathetic to see men like Brailsford and Tom Johnston failing to see through the tricks prepared for them by Trotsky to cover up his tracks.' Douglas Garman, in the *New Statesman* of September 12, demanded: 'If . . . they were innocent, why should they have confessed at all?' (The Editor replied: 'We say that confessions without independent corroborative evidence are not convincing.')[243] Ivor Montagu, in *Left Book News* for

David, the assassin-designate, was unable to get a pass to enter the hall, whereas David said the plot failed because Stalin did not attend the meeting. A number of persons whose alleged testimony was quoted in the indictment or in court (Radin, Schmidt, Karev, Matorin etc.) were never produced either as witnesses or as accused at this or any later trial. Trotsky's appeal (to the central executive committee!) in his *Open Letter* of March 1932 to 'put Stalin out of the way' (*Report of Court Proceedings*, p. 127) was actually an appeal to them to 'at last put into effect the final urgent advice by Lenin, to "remove Stalin",' i.e., a reference to the document known as 'Lenin's Testament', as may be seen from the *Bulletin of the Opposition* in which this *Open Letter* quite openly appeared.

[242] Contrast the sceptical mood of many Soviet citizens reflected in the story which was current in Moscow during the trial: Alexei Tolstoy, upon being arrested and examined, had confessed that he was the author of *Hamlet*. . . .

[243] The example of Galileo, who 'confessed' and repudiated his own discoveries under the mere threat of torture, seems never to have been discussed in Stalinist writing on the trials: nor that of the numerous 'witches' who, during the sixteenth and seventeenth centuries, went to their deaths confessing to having had communication with the Devil;

October, pooh-poohed suggestions that torture, whether physical or moral, or promise of pardon in return for perjury, could have anything to do with the confessions, and gave some historical background in which he quoted Lenin's criticism of Trotsky, Zinoviev and Kamenev, while saying nothing of his criticisms of Stalin. R. Page Arnot in the *Labour Monthly* for October, wrote: 'Trotskyism is now revealed as an ancillary of fascism ...The ILP is in great danger of falling into the hands of Trotskyists and becoming a wing of fascism. Let the members of the ILP look to it.' Pat Sloan, again, in the October number of *Russia Today* specially devoted to the trial, had a new explanation for the confessions: 'These were men who, in their desire for publicity, had never refused an opportunity to speak to a large audience.' From the same inspired pen came an argument, in *Controversy* of December, worthy of the confidence men of South Sea Bubble days: 'The Soviet Government does not intend to broadcast to the whole world all the evidence of activities of Hitler's agents it could broadcast.' (Though well-informed about the secret archives of the Soviet intelligence service, Sloan was, at this stage, a bit shaky on the topography of Denmark's capital: 'Anyway, are we sure there's no Hotel Bristol in Copenhagen? The denial, I believe, comes only from Norway.')

Towards the end of 1936 and beginning of 1937 there were two trials in Germany of real Trotskyites for real subversive activity. In Danzig, Jakubowski and nine others were given severe hard-labour sentences for issuing leaflets declaring that 'the defence of the Soviet Union remains an unconditional duty for the proletariat', and in Hamburg a group of fifteen, which included a Vienna Schutzbund member and a worker who had fought in the 1923 uprising, suffered similarly for similar activity. There were no confessions and there was plenty of material evidence. No report of these cases appeared in the *Daily Worker* or other Stalinist publications. It is curious that Nazi propaganda in this period alleged that in spite of appearances the Fourth International was a secret agency of the Third, operating on the basis of a division of labour. Accounts of a conference (at Breda)

---

nor even that of the Duke of Northumberland who in 1553 confessed to Catholicism even on the very scaffold, in the delusive hope of a pardon from Queen Mary. Krivitsky (*op. cit.* p. 212) remarks that 'the real wonder is that, despite their broken condition and the monstrous forms of pressure exerted by the Ogpu on Stalin's political opponents, so few did confess. For every one of the 54 prisoners who figured in the three "treason trials", at least 100 were shot without being broken down.'

between representatives of the two Internationals were spread by Goebbels, just as Stalin told the world of Trotsky's talks with Hess.[244]

The Second Trial

Already during the period of the first trial, as we have seen, King Street's concern for 'working-class unity' was subordinated to the paramount need to attack anybody and everybody in the Labour movement who expressed doubt regarding the justice of the verdict. This became still clearer when the second trial was launched, in January 1937. The *Daily Worker* of January 25 carried the headline: 'The *Herald* Defends Spies and Assassins', and a leader 'Enemies of the Working Class', which declared: 'It is for the working class of Britain to deal with those who in this country constitute themselves the defenders of the Trotskyites and thereby assist fascism and strike a blow at socialism all over the world.' On January 29 the paper attacked the *New Leader* for 'playing into the hands of the enemy' because it had called for an independent enquiry into the trial such as Pritt and others had organized in connection with the Reichstag Fire trial in 1933. Arnot was the *Daily Worker* reporter at the second trial: he assured readers that the only pressure which had been brought to bear on the prisoners was 'the pressure of facts' (January 27).

The campaign to justify Stalin's purges and to make the utmost political capital out of them was raised to a higher level and put on a more organized basis than hitherto by John Gollan, in his address to the enlarged meeting of the national council of the Young Communist League held on January 30-31. The historical 're-write' adumbrated by Ralph Fox was undertaken more thoroughly and at some length by Gollan. The address was published as a duplicated document under the title *The Development of Trotskyism from Menshevism to Alliance with Fascism and Counter-Revolution*. Gollan showed how Lenin's

---

[244] At the Nuremburg War Crimes Tribunal the Soviet representatives conspicuously refrained from asking Hess about his alleged anti-Soviet negotiations with Trotsky. In March 1946 a number of prominent British people, including H. G. Wells, George Orwell, Julian Symons and Frank Horrabin, signed an appeal to the Tribunal asking that Trotsky's widow be allowed to interrogate Hess in order to clear her husband's name, or that at least the Allied experts examining Gestapo records make a statement showing to what extent they had found confirmation of the story in the Moscow trials. No action was taken on these requests, and to this day no evidence of Nazi-'Trotskyite' negotiations has been published.

chief assistant in building the Red Army was not Trotsky but Stalin, how Trotsky had advocated that industrialization be carried out 'at the expense of the peasant masses' (saved by Stalin), etc. etc. This remarkable assemblage of half-truths and untruths concluded with a list of 'the *real* Bolshevik Old Guard', in which figure the names Rudzutak, Bubnov, Chubar, Kossior and Postyshev, all shot or imprisoned by Stalin shortly afterwards. Harry Pollitt went one better than this in *his* list of 'the real Old Guard' who 'are still at their posts', including the name of . . . Yezhov, whom hardly anybody — probably not Pollitt himself — had even heard of until his sudden elevation in September 1936 to be head of the NKVD following Yagoda's fall! This exploit occurred in a pamphlet called *The Truth About Trotskyism*, published at the end of January. Another gem from the same source is Pollitt's comment on the confessions of the accused: 'The evidence produced in the Moscow trial is not confessions in the ordinary sense but statements signed in the way depositions are signed in any British court . . .'[245] The main point of the pamphlet, made in a contribution by R. P. Dutt, was to show that it was 'essential to destroy the Trotskyist propaganda and influence which is seeking to win a foothold within the Labour movement, since these attempts represent in fact the channel of fascist penetration into the Labour movement'. In addition to the Gollan address and the Pollitt-Dutt pamphlet the *Daily Worker* brought out a special supplement on the trial in its issue of February 1 ('Keep It Always'), in which, after the ritual statement 'everywhere in the British Labour movement the scrupulous fairness of the trial, the overwhelming guilt of the accused, and the justness of the sentences is recognized', readers were urged to send protests to the *Daily Herald* regarding its sceptical attitude thereto. A statement by the central committee of the Communist Party published in this issue emphasized that 'the lead given by the Soviet Union . . .requires to be energetically followed up throughout the whole Labour movement, and above all in Great Britain...'

From this time onward one can say without exaggeration that the fight against 'Trotskyism' became one of the main preoccupations of the Communist Party, diverting the energies and confusing the minds

245 Pollitt also wrote in this pamphlet: 'The bold Trotsky, eh? Wants an international court of inquiry. His tools are left to face it out. Why doesn't he face it with them? Why doesn't he go to Moscow?' Neither here nor anywhere else in Stalinist publications was it ever revealed that Trotsky repeatedly demanded that the Soviet Government bring extradition proceedings against him — which would have necessitated their making a case in a Norwegian or Mexican court.

of its members and disrupting the working-class movement more and more.[246] R. F. Andrews (Andrew Rothstein) now came well to the fore, as might be expected, with a series of articles in the *Daily Worker*. 'The criminals have received their well-merited sentences . . . Millions of people have had their eyes opened to the inner essence of Trotskyism' (February 5); 'Trotsky . . . a malignant, avowed and still dangerous criminal' (February 9); '*Herald* — Shameful Blot on Labour', i.e., for doubting the justice of the verdict (February 15).[247] A mere pamphlet such as Pritt had devoted to the Zinoviev trial was now realized to be inadequate and a whole book, *Soviet Justice and the Trial of Radek* (1937), was published, the work of a fresh legal talent, Dudley Collard, though not without an introduction by Pritt ('The impression gained from Mr. Collard's description will, I think, enable many who were puzzled by the first trial not merely to convince themselves on the genuineness of the second, but also to derive from that a conviction of the genuineness of the first'). This pathetic effort

---

[246] Anti-Trotskyism eventually became for a time the chief activity of J. R. Campbell, as is reflected in Phil Bolsover's article, in the *Daily Worker* of April 2, 1938, 'The Man behind the Answers', describing Campbell at work preparing his 'Answers to Questions' feature: 'And if you see sometimes a grim, but not unhappy, gleam behind those horn-rimmed spectacles that are lifted occasionally to survey the busy room, you'll know it's ten to one that Johnnie Campbell is dealing with some Trotskyist or other. One of his sharper joys is to take an artistic delight in dissecting the sophistries, the half-truths, the complete falsehoods of the breed; laying bare the poverty of their creed for all to see. "Give him a Trotskyist and he'll be happy for hours," someone once said.'

[247] Around this time died Sergo Ordzhonikidze, Commissar for Heavy Industry. Under the headline 'Stalin bears Coffin of "Bolshevism's Fiery Knight",' the *Daily Worker* of February 22 reported the funeral: 'As Stalin stood with his hands sorrowfully crossed, a wave of the people's love and loyalty swept towards him. Beside him stood Zinaida Ordzhonikidze, Sergo's wife. . . .' An article about the dead man which appeared next day was headed: 'Health Shattered by Trotskyist Wrecking.' On August 12 a leader headed 'Foul Lies' denounced the *Herald* for carrying a story that Ordzhonikidze had killed himself and that his brothers had been arrested. ('All Labour men and women [should now] protest against the anti-Soviet line of this most scurrilous rag in the newspaper world.') *Russia Today* for September, under the heading 'Another *Daily Herald* Slander', declared that 'we are able to state definitely there is not a word of truth in this assertion'. In his secret speech of February 25, 1956 (*The Dethronement of Stalin*, 1956, p. 27) Khruschev said: 'Stalin allowed the liquidation of Ordzhonikidze's brother and brought Ordzhonikidze himself to such a state that he was forced to shoot himself.' When Khruschev and Bulganin came to Britain in the warship *Ordzhonikidze*, Walter Holmes published in his Worker's Notebook (*Daily Worker*, April 16, 1956) a note on the man after whom the ship was named: 'Ordzhonikidze died in 1937, when many of his assistants were being arrested on charges of spying, sabotage, etc. There were rumours that he had been driven to suicide . . . It has now been established that Sergo Ordzhonikidze was suspicious of Beria's political position. After the death of Ordzhonikidze, Beria and his fellow-conspirators continued cruelly to revenge themselves on his family. . . .'

contains such propositions as (p.52): 'I have read some statement to the effect that no aeroplanes flew from Germany to Norway in December 1935. It seems hard to believe that this is so...'

Here the reference is to the statement issued by the Oslo airport authorities that no foreign aeroplanes landed there in December 1935, contrary to Pyatakov's confession that he had landed there on his way to visit Trotsky. (Attempts were later made to explain that perhaps Pyatakov's memory was at fault and his aeroplane had actually landed on a frozen fiord; but, alas, this version was incompatible with the accused man's account of his journey by car from the aeroplane to Trotsky's dwelling.) After a display of quite extraordinary gullibility, Collard came to the conclusion (p. 79) that 'the court was more merciful that I would have been!' That was sufficient to ensure his book the maximum boost treatment throughout the Stalinist movement. William Gallacher, reviewing Collard in the *Daily Worker* of March 19, wrote: 'Here one sees the Soviet legal system as it really is, the most advanced, the most humane in the world ...It is a book which once read must make any normal human being resolve that never again under any circumstances will he have truck with Trotsky, his followers or any of his work.' Harking back to one of the mysteries of the first trial, the *Daily Worker* gave a sizeable bit of its valuable space in the issue of February 26 to a plan of the Grand Hotel, Copenhagen, allegedly showing that one could enter a café said to be called the Café Bristol through this hotel — though how Holtzman could have proposed to 'put up' at this café still remained unexplained![248] The egregious Arnot, in an article on 'The Trotskyist Trial' in the *Labour Monthly* for March, quoted Lenin on MacDonald to show how workers' leaders can degenerate (but did not quote Lenin on Stalin!), took a swipe at Emrys Hughes ('a middle-class Philistine') for an article in *Forward* critical of the trials, and opened up with all guns against the *Manchester Guardian*. Principled political criticism of the Liberals was 'out' in this epoch of Popular-Frontery, but here was something more important. *The Guardian* had stated that, in the course of the waves of repression sweeping over the Soviet Union in

[248] The extreme concern shown to shore up Holtzman's evidence is explained by two facts — his was the only statement giving anything like precise details of time and place, and it furnished the basis for all the rest of the story. Concentration on the place where Holtzman allegedly went also served to divert attention from the fact that the person — Sedov — whom he had allegedly met there had been able to prove conclusively, by means of his student's attendance card and other documents, that he was taking an examination in another city at the time!

the wake of the second trial, 'the Polish communists . . .have suffered heavy casualties under the Stalinist persecution'. As is now admitted, almost the entire leadership of the Polish Communist Party was in fact liquidated by the NKVD in this period, and the party itself dissolved. This was the buffoonery that Arnot wrote at the time: 'They have not "suffered heavy casualties"; there is no "Stalinist persecution" . . .At one time the Trotskyists complained that the condemnation of their errors was a sign of anti-Semitism. Now, apparently, the condemnation of their crimes is to be presented as "the assault on the Polish Virgin" . . .'

At this time the Stalinists were putting forth determined efforts to capture the Labour League of Youth, for which they published a paper called *Advance*. The March issue of this journal carried an article, 'We have our Wreckers, Too!' by Ted Willis, later to win fame as author of *The Blue Lamp*, but then the leading Stalinist youth-worker. 'The recent trial and sentences on the Terrorists in Moscow were of particular interest to the members of the League of Youth for an obvious reason. That being the fact that, for the last year we have been blessed (is that the right word?) with a tiny group of people in the League who style themselves Trotskyists . . .Turn them lock, stock and barrel out of the Labour movement!' Fittingly, at the same time as Ted Willis was making his début in this field, John Strachey, then the top Stalinist publicist in this country, was telling readers of *Left News* that he believed that:

> The psychological student of the future will look back on the long-drawn-out incredulity of British public opinion over the Moscow trials of 1936 and 1937 as one of the strangest and most interesting psychological phenomena of the present time. For it will be clear to such a student that there were no rational grounds for disbelief. The fact is that there is no answer to the simple question: 'If these men were innocent, why did they confess?' . . .Before the inexorable, extremely prolonged, though gentle, cross-examination of the Soviet investigators, their last convictions broke down.

Major contributions to the fight against Trotskyism now came thick and fast. Stalin's speech at the February-March plenum of the central committee of the Soviet Communist Party, setting out his thesis that the further the Soviet Union progressed the more intense became the class struggle and the greater was the need for security work, was published in full in the *Daily Worker*. ('Especially in Britain do we require to pay heed to his words regarding the danger of the rotten theory that because the Trotskyists are few we can afford to pay little attention to them . . .This is a report to be carefully read and studied, not once but many times' — March 31). At the second National Congress for Peace and Friendship with the USSR, Pritt soothed the anxieties of those who had doubts about the course of justice under Stalin. 'I do happen to know that, when you are arrested in the USSR... there are very elaborate rules of criminal procedure to see that your case will be proceeded with promptly and to ensure that there shall be no delay in having it put forward' (Congress Report, p. 51). In *Left News* for April, Ivor Montagu reviewed, under the heading 'The Guilty' the official report of the second trial, together with Collard's book. A feature of this article was its misquotation from *The Revolution Betrayed*, designed to show that Trotsky prophesied the defeat of the Soviet Union in war with Nazi Germany. Montagu gives: 'Defeat will be fatal to the leading circles of the USSR and to the social bases of the country.' Trotsky actually wrote 'would', not 'will', and made plain in the following paragraph that he considered the defeat of Germany more probable:

> Notwithstanding all its contradictions, the Soviet regime in the matter of stability still has immense advantages over the regimes of its probable enemies. The very possibility of a rule by the Nazis over the German people was created by the unbearable tenseness of social antagonisms in Germany. These antagonisms have not been removed and not even weakened, but only suppressed by the lid of fascism. A war will bring them to the surface. Hitler has far less chances than had Wilhelm II of carrying a war to victory. Only a timely revolution, by saving Germany from war, could save her from a new defeat. (*The Revolution Betrayed*, chapter viii, section 5).

Montagu also referred to Trotsky as 'perhaps the star contributor to the Hearst Press on Soviet affairs'. In fact, Trotsky always refused even to receive a representative of the Hearst Press, and anything they published over his name was 'lifted', often with distortions, from other papers. (Lenin had had occasion in July 1917 to remark regarding a similar slander by the Menshevik Montagus of those days: 'They have stooped to such a ridiculous thing as blaming the *Pravda* for the fact that its dispatches to the socialist papers of Sweden and other countries . . .have been reprinted by the German papers, often garbled! . . .As if the reprinting or the vicious distortions can be blamed on the authors!'.)

In *Challenge* of May 27 Gollan asserted 'the absolute necessity . . .of once and for all ridding the youth movement of all Trotskyist elements as a pre-condition for unity', thus subordinating the urgent need for workers' unity to the requirements of the NKVD.

Between the Second and Third Trials

The case of the Generals — a sort of intermezzo between the second and third trials — gave the British Stalinists fresh occasion to display their 'loyalty' and quarrel with other sections of the working-class movement on its account. This was a secret trial, without confessions, but no matter: the first announcement of the case was greeted by the *Daily Worker* with a leader stating that 'thanks to the unrelaxing vigilance of the Soviet intelligence service, a further shattering blow has been given to the criminal war-making elements who seek to undermine and destroy the Socialist Fatherland of the international working class' (June 12). On June 14 the paper announced: 'Red Army Traitors Executed'. The leading article affirmed, as usual, that 'the workers of Britain will rejoice', but nevertheless Pollitt, in a special statement published in the same issue, had to rebuke the *Herald* for getting 'so hot and bothered' about this trial. In a statement congratulating the Soviet Government on the executions, published in the *Daily Worker* of June 16, the central committee welcomed, on behalf of the British workers, 'the wiping out of the bureaucratic degenerates associated with fascism . . .'. Arnot proclaimed (*Daily Worker*, June 18) his conviction of the reliability of the official account of the crimes of Tukhachevsky, Gamarnik, Eidemann and the others: 'That it is a true story no reasonable man can doubt.' Montagu added his stone next day ('A Blow at Fascism') and called for heightened vigilance against 'such agents in the working class movement elsewhere and working to the same end'. Pat Sloan's *Russia Today* (July) hastened to identify itself with the executioners: 'No true friend of the Soviet Union . . .can feel other than a sense of satisfaction that the activities of spies, diversionists and wreckers in the Soviet Army have been given an abrupt quietus . . .All talk about the personal struggle of the "dictator" Stalin is rubbish.' Dutt pitched into Brailsford for his doubt ('On Which Side?', *Daily Worker,* June 21)[249] and Jack

[249] Returning to the attack on June 8, Dutt wrote with characteristic scorn of 'liberal intellectual waverers who are incapable of facing the hard realities of the fight against fascism'.

Gaster denounced the 'slanders' of the *Herald* at a Hyde Park meeting (*Daily Worker*, June 22).

About the middle of 1937 it began to be known in the West that a truly gigantic, unprecedentedly sweeping wave of arrests was engulfing many who hitherto had been regarded as secure and loyal pillars of the Stalin regime. This put the British Stalinists in a quandary. When Mezhlauk, for instance, was appointed to succeed Ordzhonikidze as Commissar for Heavy Industry, he was headlined in the *Daily Worker* of February 27 as an 'Old Soldier of the Revolution'. When he was arrested a few months later they could thus hardly dispose of him in the traditional way as 'never an Old Bolshevik'. So they ignored the arrest, and dealt similarly with the many similar cases that now poured out of the tape-machines. A photograph of Marshal Yegorov appeared in the *Daily Worker* of July 14; when he was arrested shortly afterwards, nothing was said. A photograph of Marshal Bluecher was published in the issue of February 25, actually *after* his arrest! (At the same time, the wretched *Daily Herald* came in for another pasting in the *Daily Worker* of October 8 for having published a report of the murder by NKVD agents in Switzerland of Ignace Reiss, an NKVD man who had tried to break with Stalin.)

Perhaps the most revealing instance of the methods of the British Stalinists in dealing with the arrests which they knew about but dared not admit to their dupes is provided by the case of the Lost Editor. When the Soviet official *History of the Civil War*, Vol. I, was first announced as a forthcoming publication, in the *Daily Worker* of March 11, the list of editors, headed by Stalin and Gorky, included the names of Gamarnik and Bubnov. General Gamarnik having allegedly committed suicide as an exposed accomplice of Tukhachevsky ('Entangled with Enemies of USSR, Took Own Life' *Daily Worker*, June 2), his name had of course disappeared from the advertisement of the book published in *Russia Today* of November 1937. But though Bubnov had been arrested as an enemy of the people in time for his name to be removed from the title-page of the book before it reached the shops, it was still to be seen on the fly-leaf! When Rothstein reviewed this work in *Russia Today* of February 1938 he cannily listed the editors as 'Joseph Stalin, Maxim Gorky and others'. The arrest of Bubnov was a particularly hard blow for the British Stalinists, since they had made special use of his name as that of an Old Bolshevik still in favour. Perhaps resentment at his inconsiderateness in getting arrested was the reason why the *Daily Worker* did not report his return to Moscow in 1956, as an old man, after nearly twenty years in prison.[250]

Particularly worthy of being rescued from oblivion, among the achievements of 'working-class journalism' in this period, is an article in the *Daily Worker* of August 20 by Ben Francis, the paper's Moscow correspondent, in praise of the wonderful work being done by Zakovsky, in charge of security in Leningrad. Around this time, as Khrushchev described in his famous 'secret speech' (*Manchester Guardian* pamphlet version, *The Dethronement of Stalin* (1956), p. 15), Zakovsky was having prisoners brought before him after torture in order to offer them their lives in return for their agreement to make a false confession ('You, yourself', said Zakovsky, 'will not need to invent anything. The NKVD will prepare for you a ready outline . . . You will have to study it carefully and remember well all questions and answers which the court might ask').

An example of this contempt into which the trials were bringing both the Soviet authorities and the British Stalinists is provided by the article by 'Y.Y.' (Robert Lynd) in the *New Statesman* of June 26. On the ascription of all shortcomings in Soviet industry to Soviet sabotage, he wrote that, apparently, 'wherever there is a screw loose in Russia it was Trotsky who loosened it', and he summed up the King Street theory of the trials thus: 'Stalin can do no wrong. He will give these men a fair trial, but, as a matter of fact, they would not be put on their trial at all unless it were certain that they were guilty. Therefore, even without knowing the evidence, we know that they are guilty.'[251] Desperate in their concern to keep the other point of view from their

[250] Even nearer the bone than the Bubnov case was that of Rose Cohen, a British Communist Party member since 1921, one-time office-manager of the Labour Research Department and member of the Party's colonial bureau, wife of Petrovsky-Bennett, the Comintern's nuncio in Britain. While working in Moscow on the staff of *Moscow Daily News* she was arrested as a spy and never heard of again. An earlier (and unluckier) Edith Bone, her case was never mentioned in the Stalinist press. For details, see *Fight* and *Militant* (London) of June 1938 and subsequently.

[251] William Rust was perhaps the most honest of the British Stalinists in the matter of admitting that there was nothing whatever to go on beyond the confessions. In his review, in the *Daily Worker* of March 1, 1937, of the verbatim report of the second trial, he wrote: 'Of the treason and the actual negotiations with the fascist governments there is, of course, no documentary proof. . . .' Desperate for 'documentary proof' of some sort, the *Daily Worker* of November 10 published a block showing, side by side, the symbol used by a 'Trotskyist' publishing firm in Antwerp — a lighting-flash across a globe — and the Mosleyite 'Flash-in-the-pan'. The caption supplied read: 'Similarity with a significance.' (During the second world war the five-pointed star was used as an emblem in various ways by the Soviet, American, Indian and Japanese armies.)

dupes, the Stalinist editors of *Left Review* refused to publish an advertisement of *The Case of Leon Trotsky,* being the report of the examination of Trotsky, regarding the statements affecting him made in the trials, carried out by the Commission of Inquiry headed by John Dewey. This was revealed in a letter in the *New Statesman* of November 6 from the publisher, Mr. Frederick Warburg. Replying for *Left Review* in the next issue of the *New Statesman,* Randall Swingler explained that 'there is a line at which criticism ends and destructive attacks begin, and we regret that this line separates us both from Dr. Goebbels and from Leon Trotsky.'[252] This spot of publicity compelled the publication of a review of the book in the *Daily Worker* of November 17, in which J. R. Campbell claimed that it gave 'added confirmation to the Moscow trials, which showed Trotsky as a political degenerate, an ally of fascism, a vile maniacal enemy of socialism and peace'. A letter from Charles van Gelderen pointing out some glaring inaccuracies in Campbell's article was refused publication in the *Daily Worker;* it appeared, however, in the (London) *Militant* for December.

The political consequences of all this pernicious nonsense were well summed up in an article by H. J. Laski in the New York *Nation* for November 20:

> There is no doubt the mass executions in the Soviet Union in the last two years have greatly injured the prestige of Russia with the rank and file of the Labour Party. They do not understand them, and they feel that those who accept them without discussion are not satisfactory allies. I do not comment on this view; I merely record it. In my judgment, the executions undoubtedly cost the supporters of the United Front something like half a million votes in the Bournemouth Conference.

The year 1938, which opened with the final disappearance of the slogan: 'Workers of all lands, unite!' from the masthead of the *Daily Worker,* was to see even further feats of genuine sabotage of workers' unity by the Stalinists under the banner of anti-Trotskyism. Communist speakers refused to appear on the same platform with ILP

---

[252] J. R. Campbell defended in the *Daily Worker* of April 11, 1938, that paper's refusal of advertisements for 'Trotskyite' publications: 'It would be senseless for the *Daily Worker* to give a free advertisement to opposition political tendencies.' With this may be compared Walter Holmes's 'Worker's Notebook' of November 27, 1936, in which he reproduced a letter from Mr. Warburg telling how the *Observer* had refused an advertisement of John Langdon-Davies's book *Behind the Spanish Barricades,* and commented: 'We agree with Messrs. Secker and Warburg about the grave character of this censorship of advertisements.'

speakers at 'Aid Spain' meetings. All remnants of shame and caution were cast aside in this truly maniacal campaign. Thus, in *Discussion* of January, Pat Sloan wrote: 'Masses and leaders are united; the people adore "our Stalin". Stalin respects the masses as no other political leader of today respects the masses ...' In *Controversy* of the same month the same propagandist declared himself unfamiliar with and unready to accept as genuine Stalin's statement of November 6, 1918, on Trotsky's role in the October Revolution (Stalin, *The October Revolution*, published in the Marxist-Leninist Library by Lawrence and Wishart in 1936, p. 30), which had been mentioned by a contributor, and proceeded to withdraw from the battle on the grounds that 'it is impossible to continue a controversy with someone as unscrupulous ...Trotskyism ...is incompatible with historical truth'.[253] Dutt, in the *Daily Worker* of January 21, quoted some remarks of Lenin's about Bukharin (also, incidentally, Dzerzhinsky and other 'Left Communists' who died in the odour of Stalinist sanctity) as though they referred to Trotsky. R. Osborn (Reuben Osbert, the psychiatrist) brought out a book, *The Psychology of Reaction* (1938), in which he tried to identify fascism and 'Trotskyism' psychologically ('A knowledge of the psychology of fascist leaders is at the same time a knowledge of the psychology of the Trotskyists') and this was reviewed enthusiastically by John Strachey in *Left News* for February. (Strachey offered as his own view that 'Trotskyists' were recruited mainly from 'insufficiently sensitive', 'inhuman' types.)

The Third Trial

Now came the third and last of the great 'public' trials — the Trial of the Twenty-One, bigger and more fantastic than any of the foregoing, with Bukharin, Rykov, Rakovsky and Krestinsky in the leading roles. The British Stalinists (who had made extensive use of the writings of Bukharin and Rykov in the anti-Trotskyist campaign of 1925-28, presenting them as great Marxist thinkers and statesmen)

[253] Sloan came back to the pages of *Controversy* in the March issue to denounce Stalin's words as 'an unscrupulous mis-quotation by Trotsky', to defend the Communist Party's refusal to allow republication of John Reed's *Ten Days That Shook The World* ('It is a little naive, I think, to ask communists to popularise an inaccurate account of the internal affairs in Bolshevik leadership in 1917'), and to declare regarding the victims of the trials: 'It is a good thing they have been shot. Further, if there were more of them, then more of them should have been shot.'

did not flinch.[254] The *Daily Worker* leader of March 2 declared: 'Soviet justice will prove itself once again as the unsleeping sword on behalf of the working class and the peoples of the world against their enemies.' Eden having been replaced by Halifax, British agents now found their place in the legend alongside the German ones, and R. Page Arnot, in his dispatches from the Moscow court-room, solemnly explained how Rakovsky had been in British pay since 1924 and Trotsky since 1926. As before — Stalin still retaining confidence in the Franco-Soviet Pact — it appeared that none of the accused had had any contact with France, even in the years when French imperialism was heading the anti-Soviet forces in the world. Even so far back, it seemed, the cunning 'Trotskyists' had foreseen what the pattern of diplomacy would be at the time of their trial.

Furthermore, Trotsky had been a *German* spy since 1921; though why he should wish to link up with an impoverished and defeated State such as Germany was then, or why, indeed, being at the height of his authority in Russia at that time, he should have troubled to make such connections at all, was never explained. The British Stalinists knew their place better than even as much as to comment on these oddities. (Arnot confined his observations to such safe remarks as: 'Vyshinsky...is always a credit to his calling.')[255] As before,

[254] J. R. Campbell, closely associated in his time with the Bukharin-Rykov trend, wrote firmly in the *Daily Worker* of March 17, after the executions: 'It is enemies of socialism and peace who have perished. We should not mourn.' Lawrence and Wishart brought out a book about the trial — *The Plot Against the Soviet Union and World Peace* – by B. N. Ponomarev, in which this Soviet authority made it plain that one of the chief criteria for people's political reliability was 'their attitude towards ...the struggle against Trotskyism' (p. 186). (Ponomarev is a member of the central committee of the Soviet Communist Party, working with Suslov in the department concerned with relations with other Communist Parties, and in this capacity recently received, e.g., a delegation from the Australian Communist Party, according to 'Pravda' of January 5, 1958.)

[255] One really might have expected some comment on the statement made through Rakovsky that Trotsky had put the British imperialists up to the Arcos raid in 1927, arranging through 'a certain Meller or Mueller ...the discovery of specially fabricated provocative documents' (*Daily Worker,* March 7). After all, the line of the Communist Party had always been that the Arcos raid had produced nothing to justify the charges made against the Soviet agencies in this country. No mention of Rakovsky's statement at his trial is made in the detailed account of the Arcos Raid in the *History of Anglo-Soviet Relations* by W. P. and Zelda Coates published by Lawrence and Wishart in 1944. Yet in their book *From Tsardom to the Stalin Constitution* (1938) Mr. and Mrs. Coates had declared their belief in the genuineness of the confessions ...In his dispatch printed in the *Daily Worker* of March 9, Arnot quoted without comment an alleged statement by Trotsky in 1918: 'Stalin — Lenin's closest assistant — must be destroyed'. It would indeed have been hard for Arnot to comment acceptably, for in 1923 he had written for

however, certain ill-conditioned elements in the Labour movement gave trouble. The *Daily Worker* had to devote a leading article on March 7 to — 'Brailsford Again'. ('They did not confess of their own accord. They held out to the last until they realized the Soviet authorities had complete proof of all their crimes, and then admitted only what could not be denied.') The central committee of the party published in the *Daily Worker* of March 8 its routine, required declaration kicking the accused ('Every weak, corrupt or ambitious traitor to Socialism'), denouncing 'the fascist agent Trotsky' and expressing 'full confidence' in Yezhov, 'our Bolshevik comrade'. William Wainwright, in *Challenge* of March 10, really went to town on the trial: 'This is more than a trial. It is a fight between the forces of war and the forces of peace.' After the ritual bit of historical untruth (Trotsky 'was not one of the leaders of the rising. Stalin was'), Wainwright went on to allege that the accused wanted to let the fascists into Russia. 'Just as Franco did in Spain . . .Let us be glad that this has taken place, that these men will be sentenced . . .Let us in our youth organizations clean out those . . .who support those whose crime is against the people'.

The *Daily Worker* leader of March 11, dealing with the ILP's appeal to Moscow not to execute the convicted men, was entitled: 'Degenerates Appeal for Degenerates'. In *Inprecorr* of March 12, Reg Bishop welcomed the publication in certain bourgeois papers of articles accepting the genuineness of the trial,[256] while at the same time deploring that at the most recent meeting of the Parliamentary Labour Party a resolution had been moved condemning it. The resolution was defeated, true; 'but it is a deplorable thing that it should even have been mooted in a responsible Labour gathering'. The *New Statesman's* attitude had been unsatisfactory, too; but then, that was 'mainly read by intellectuals'. Albert Inkpin, secretary of the World Committee of Friends of the Soviet Union, had a letter in the

---

the Labour Research Department a short history of *The Russian Revolution,* in which he showed how far Stalin was from being 'Lenin's closest assistant' in 1918, and who in fact occupied that position! Much was made, by Arnot and others, in connection with all three trials, of the alleged fact that some of the accused had at one time or another been Mensheviks, but no mention appeared of Vyshinsky's having been a Menshevik down to 1920.

[256] All through the period 1936-38 Walter Holmes had kept up a running fire in his 'Worker's Notebook' in the *Daily Worker* of quotations from bourgeois papers directed against the 'Trotskyists'. Perhaps his best bag was one from the *Times of Malaya* which he published on August 7, 1937, reporting the formation of a bloc between Monarchists and 'Trotskyists'.

March 12 issue of the offending weekly, telling the editor that 'all fascists and reactionaries' would applaud his doubts about the trial. (Replying, the editor declared that it was rather the picture of nearly all the founders of the Soviet State being spies and wreckers that was likely to give pleasure to the enemies of the USSR. Besides, if the *New Statesman* had ventured to suggest such a thing, not so very long before, the FSU would certainly have jumped on them. 'What Soviet hero dare we praise today? Who is tomorrow's carrion?')

Harry Pollitt himself, in the *Daily Worker* of March 12, told the world that 'the trials in Moscow represent a new triumph in the history of progress', the article being illustrated by a photograph of Stalin with Yezhov, that Old Bolshevik shortly to be dismissed and die in obscurity. Forces from the cultural field also joined in the battle on this occasion. Jack Lindsay put a letter into *Tribune* of March 18 affirming that 'surely the strangest thing about the Moscow trials is the way that critics find them "psychologically" puzzling . . .That is the one thing they are not . . .The cleavage between the men who trusted the powers of the masses, and the men who trusted only their own "cleverness" had to come. And naturally persons with "individualistic" minds can't understand! Naturally they get scared and see themselves in the dock.' So there! Sean O'Casey contributed a lamentable article in the *Daily Worker* of March 25 ('The Sword of the Soviet') containing such statements as: 'The opposition to and envy of Lenin and Stalin by Trotsky was evident before even the Revolution of 1917 began.' (O'Casey cannot but have known how little cause Trotsky had to 'envy' Stalin before 1917 and would have been hard put to show how such envy made itself 'evident'!)

Rather unkindly, in view of the efforts of Messrs. Lindsay and O'Casey, *Russia Today* for April dismissed the victims as 'almost all middle-class intellectuals'. The same issue carried an article by Kath Taylor describing the anger of Russian workers at the revelations of sabotage made in the 'Bukharin' trial. Now they realized, she wrote, why 'they waited hours long in the food queues only to find the food almost unfit to eat when they got it home . . .Now we knew why our wages had been held up, and the reasons for many other things that had made life so hard at the most difficult moments.'[257]

---

[257] Compare eyewitness Fitzroy Maclean's account of the trial in his *Eastern Approaches* (1949). Zelensky, former chairman of Gosplan, 'confessed' to having put powdered glass and nails into the butter and to having destroyed truckloads of eggs. 'At this startling revelation a grunt of rage and horror rose from the audience. Now they

Let us conclude our quotations with one from John Strachey, who wrote in the *Daily Worker*, appropriately enough on April 1, that 'no one who really reads the evidence, either of the former trials or of this one, can doubt that these things happened', and assessed the conviction of the wretched victims as 'the greatest anti-fascist victory which we have yet recorded.'

---

knew what was the matter with the butter, and why there were never any eggs. Deliberate sabotage was somehow a much more satisfactory solution than carelessness or inefficiency. Besides, Zelensky had admitted that he had been in contact with a sinister foreigner, a politician, a member of the British Labour Party, a certain M. A. V. Alexander, who had encouraged him in his fell designs. No wonder that he had put ground glass in the butter. And nails! What a warning, too, to have nothing to do with foreigners, even though they masqueraded as socialists.' Doubtless taking his cue from the inclusion of A. V. Alexander in the *dramatis personae* of the 'Bukharin' trial, Arnot went even further in attacking fellow-socialists in his *Labour Monthly* article of May 1938 than he had ventured to do previously: he now wrote of 'H. N. Brailsford and ILP leaders, whose position as dupes of Trotsky or agents of Trotsky is still to be examined.'

Index